BULLETS
AND
OPIUM

BULLETS
AND
OPIUM

Real-Life Stories of China After the
Tiananmen Square Massacre

Liao Yiwu

Translated by David Cowhig, Jessie Cowhig, and Ross Perlin

**ONE SIGNAL
PUBLISHERS**

ATRIA

New York London Toronto Sydney New Delhi

ONE SIGNAL
PUBLISHERS

ATRIA

An Imprint of Simon & Schuster, Inc.
1230 Avenue of the Americas
New York, NY 10020

Copyright © 2012 by Liao Yiwu

Translated from the Chinese by David and Jessie Cowhig and Ross Perlin

Originally published in 2012 in Germany by Fischer as *Die Kugel und das Opium: Leben und Tad am Platz des Himmlischen Friedens*

First One Signal Publishers /Atria Paperback edition March 2020

ONE SIGNAL PUBLISHERS / ATRIA PAPERBACK and colophon are trademarks of Simon & Schuster, Inc.

For information about special discounts for bulk purchases, please contact Simon & Schuster Special Sales at 1-866-506-1949 or business@simonandschuster.com.

The Simon & Schuster Speakers Bureau can bring authors to your live event. For more information or to book an event, contact the Simon & Schuster Speakers Bureau at 1-866-248-3049 or visit our website at www.simonspeakers.com.

Interior design by Silverglass

Manufactured in the United States of America

7   9   10   8   6

Library of Congress Cataloging-in-Publication Data

Liao, Yiwu, 1958- author. Kugel und das Opium. English Bullets and opium : real-life stories of China after the Tiananmen Square Massacre / Liao Yiwu ; translated by David Cowhig, Jessie Cowhig, and Ross Perlin. First Atria books hardcover edition. New York : Signal Press/Atria, [2019]
312 pages ; 24 cm
DS779.32 .L53713 2019
ISBN: 9781982126643 (hardcover : alk. paper)

ISBN 978-1-9821-2664-3
ISBN 978-1-9821-2665-0 (pbk)
ISBN 978-1-9821-2666-7 (ebook)

CONTENTS

CONTENTS

BULLETS
AND
OPIUM

Introduction

by Ian Johnson

I t's risky to pick turning points in world history, but it's safe to say that the Tiananmen Massacre on the night of June 3–4, 1989, in downtown Beijing, was one of the most important of the past half century. At the time it was recognized as a momentous event—a bloodbath in the center of a world capital usually is—but three decades later its importance has only grown, marking the end of one China and the rise of today's grim superpower.

For on that night, soldiers armed with automatic weapons and tanks smashed through crude barricades, killing hundreds, possibly thousands, of Beijingers trying to stop the troops from breaking up a student protest. The students had occupied the city's gargantuan Tiananmen Square, calling for an end to corruption and official privilege and for a more open, freer society.

The students were flawed—as are most people, especially when they are eighteen or nineteen years old. Most had little idea of what they wanted. And some were arrogant. But they were well-meaning and idealistic, and many Chinese saw in them a hope for a better, more decent society. From across the country, Chinese traveled to Beijing to support them, wired them money, and wrote poems in their honor.

And so, on that fateful night, thousands of ordinary Beijingers ran out onto the streets to confront the troops. On several previous nights the government had also tried to clear the square but sent in unarmed troops. Locals talked them out of their attack and they returned to their barracks.

But this time around, China's rulers decided to teach their subjects a lesson they wouldn't forget. They sent in hardened troops with orders to shoot their way to the center of town. The carnage lasted hours and the city's hospitals overflowed with the dead and dying. The message was clear: *This will not be tolerated. Ever.*

Since then, China's course has been set: economic development, yes; an open society, no. The government has banned, arrested, and jailed people who tried to set up new political parties or even write about the need for change. It has brought the Internet to heel by deploying thousands of censors. And it has pushed its ambitions abroad by funding Western universities and think tanks and drawing up blacklists of people who mention its deeds. These are the bullets it uses to silence opponents.

The opium is the benefits of economic growth—the real prosperity that makes many people inside and outside of China wary of rocking the boat. For many around the world, China has become an alluring model, and its many apologists, including leading Western political leaders, happily eat from its trough.

So today we have a China that is richer than ever, boasting bullet trains and aircraft carriers, but politically stunted and often driven by nationalistic aims—an unhealthy mixture that has rarely turned out well in world history. It is a country for which 1989 did not mean the fall of communism as it did in Europe but rather is synonymous with a failed revolution.

And yet, for all of their importance, these events have never been told with much élan or vigor. We have deadening academic prose, policy-wonk jargon, but little to connect us with the people who made these events happen.

That is why this book is so important. It is not a definitive history of Tiananmen but something more compelling: intimate interviews with people who fought for the revolution, were jailed, and were then released to a country that had suddenly turned away from politics and embraced the deadening pleasures of consumer society and the cheap thrills of nationalism. That's why this book is about more than the events of three decades ago; it is also a portrait of today's unhappy and repressed China.

Our guide is Liao Yiwu, the most remarkable chronicler of real-life China to emerge from his country. He is something like a Chinese Studs Terkel, compiling oral histories of key turning points in his country's history, but he has the maniacal fearlessness of the great Polish war correspondent Ryszard Kapuściński. He is funny, self-deprecating, and brutally honest about his own failures, making him a compassionate, credible narrator for these stories.

Liao came to international attention thanks to a series of remarkable portraits of China's underclass, which he brought to life in numerous profiles and books. His methodology is that of a gumshoe private eye: he walks, listens, and observes. Himself a participant in the protests, he spent four years in jail and then fifteen years interviewing grassroots China. He went to people in remote mountains or under secret-police surveillance. His work often landed him in trouble and often under house arrest. It cost him two marriages and the loss of contact with his first child. But he has remained driven to write the stories that official history books in China try to censor out of existence.

Most of what you hold in your hands wouldn't have come to light if not for Liao's personal courage. Facing daily police harassment and a ban on travel abroad, Liao decided in 2011 to flee China for the West. After careful planning, he packed a backpack full of tapes, notes, and photos. He traveled to the Vietnamese border and found a place to walk across to freedom. He soon flew off to Germany, where he lives today with his new family, and a new existence in Berlin.

Since then he has been mining his notebooks and now has written what I believe to be his most significant work. A predictable oral history of 1989 would include many of the student leaders of this movement, but

Liao focuses instead on more telling and interesting examples. These are the people who couldn't flee abroad or didn't have the fortune of serving a few years and being released in the 1990s as part of deals to reestablish economic ties with Western countries. For the people in this book there were no fellowships at Ivy League schools, no book deals, no rebirth as a religious celebrity—not even the ignominy of boring but comfortable lives in banking or academia.

Instead, these are the stories of the "Tiananmen thugs," the completely inaccurate name given by the government to the citizens who bore the brunt of the military's assault on the square and the transformation of nearby streets into killing fields. We often think of Tiananmen as a student revolt and its repression as falling on these young people, but in fact only the first part of this statement is accurate. The protests were led by students, but the people who defended them were ordinary Beijingers. These were the people who were gunned down, arrested en masse, tortured, jailed, and forced to labor in the country's infamous *laogai* gulag.

Liao gives us so many moving stories: three young men who defaced the iconic portrait of Chairman Mao that looks down on Tiananmen Square; a worker who was so incensed by the massacre that he set fire to an armored personnel carrier; a bus conductor so angry that he threw bricks at soldiers. In these pages we hear about parents of the victims, and of course we get to know our guide and interviewer, Liao Yiwu, a poet who had the quixotic idea of filming a musical in his native Sichuan Province to protest June Fourth.

These are among the hundreds of thousands of mostly nameless people arrested in 1989, a fact that challenges claims that the pro-democracy protests were something that only concerned students, intellectuals, and other elites. Instead, we meet people from all walks of life who joined in the struggle out of sincere patriotism and paid for it in varied ways: destroyed marriages, lost careers, or a lifetime of sexual dysfunction brought on by torture.

Thus, this book does more than keep alive the memory of June Fourth; it helps us rethink those days by focusing on the forgotten people who sacrificed the most. Through them we get a radically new view of Tiananmen, one that increases its importance by showing its broad and terrible scope.

But while these stories are depressing, they are also hopeful. Whenever pundits argue that China has created the perfect dictatorship or that the past is forgotten, think of these people. Many were teenagers when their lives changed. Now it is only three decades later. They are just middle-aged. Many will live another thirty years. Their lives will continue to vex the Communist Party for most of the twenty-first century.

These profiles also show the universality of humans' desire for decency and fairness and the right to shape their future. When it is argued that events in faraway lands or distant eras are not our concern, think of these people. They had little to gain. And yet they acted—an inspiration for all of us in today's uncertain times.

PROLOGUE

"All You Want Is Money! All I Want Is Revolution!"

During the predawn hours of June 4, 1989, on government orders, 200,000 troops surrounded Beijing, China's capital, and then marched to its heart. The government's tanks and armored vehicles cleared the way, crushing the barricades, firing into the crowd, mowing human beings down like weeds. Sanctioned at the very top, the massacre they committed in and around Tiananmen Square—against overwhelmingly nonviolent protesters from all walks of life—shocked the world.

Millions of ordinary, idealistic Chinese people had been protesting for democracy for weeks, in dozens of cities across China, including Chengdu, my home at the time and the capital of Sichuan, my native province. In an instant the protesters were scattered like flocks of frightened birds. Arrest orders flew out across the land. Several hundred thousand people fled abroad as political refugees. Meanwhile, untold tens and tens of thousands—mostly working-class people with little connection to the democracy movement leadership—were thrown in jail and became political prisoners.

Over three decades later, the regime that committed the massacre is still in power. To this day there has been no reliable estimate of the number of people killed that day. The official government figure for those "accidentally injured" is 300 or less. Surveys conducted at the time by the Red Cross Society of China and by student movement organizations at 100 Beijing-area hospitals suggested that approximately 3,000 people had been killed. Recently declassified documents from the US and UK governments suggest that the number may have been over 10,000, with many more injured.

How can we find them, the lost ones? The wife-and-husband team of Ding Zilin and Jiang Peikun, after their son was killed near the square, made contact with over 200 family members of June Fourth victims and started the Tiananmen Mothers movement. Over the past decades they have only been able to collect a list of 202 people from all those killed. (See Appendix Two.) Sun Liyong, who fled to Australia, scraped together with great difficulty a list of several hundred people who were imprisoned after June Fourth.

Years have passed. The butchers are winning. Cycles of shameless moral breakdown and misery followed the crackdown: they created and are still creating our past, present, and future. The tyrants seemed to have killed at first with trembling hands. Later, as they killed more people and their blood debt increased, killing became easier and they felt free to do as they pleased.

China's economy grew at a frenetic pace. Every wave of killings seemed to bring forth tremendous economic growth. One fashionable theory held that economic development would bring political reform and that in turn would force the tyrants to move toward democracy. That was why Western economic sanctions against China after June Fourth soon faded away, with more and more countries lining up to make business deals with the butchers. They did this even as the killers kept jailing and murdering, even as new blood spilled over the old bloodstains. New tyrannies replaced the old. To survive and make a miserable living amid such bloodstained tyranny, people learned to live without moral scruples.

After Tiananmen, as everyone else feigned amnesia and raced to make money, waves of brutal crackdowns struck the families of murdered and imprisoned protesters, people practicing alternate kinds of qigong, Falun Gong practitioners, members of the China Democracy Party, people who petitioned higher levels of government to redress their grievances against local officials, peasants deprived of their land, laid-off workers, human rights lawyers, members of underground churches, political dissidents, the families of the Sichuan earthquake victims, people who signed Charter 08, proponents of the Jasmine Revolution online, and those struggling in Tibet, Inner Mongolia, and Xinjiang. Meanwhile, the "June Fourth rioters" were finally quietly released from prison, one by one, without anyone noticing.

The Chinese people have become slaves waiting and willing to be plundered and trampled. And the Party said to Westerners: *Come on over, build factories, set up businesses, construct tall buildings, and design computer networks. As long as you don't talk about human rights or pick political scabs, you can do whatever you want. In your own country there are all those laws to obey and public opinion to worry about. You aren't free to do as you like. You should come here and work with us. Come to our country and get dirty with us. Please go ahead and mess up our rivers, skies, food, and underground water resources to your heart's desire. Come use our cheap labor. Make our people work day and night. Reduce them to nothing more than machines on the assembly line. By the time most people in China come down with different kinds of cancers in their bodies, minds, and characters because of all the pollution, you will have made even more money in this, the world's biggest junkyard, where there will always be more business opportunities than anywhere else.*

In the name of free trade, many Western companies conspired with the butchers. They created a junkyard. Their profits-first "garbage system of values" became ever more influential. The Chinese people all knew that the butchers had the money and had their escape routes ready—that they would, in the end, abandon their scarred and battered motherland. They would all emigrate to the West to enjoy that pure land and its sunlight, its liberty, equality, fraternity. They might even join a church there and ask that same Jesus, who was nailed to a cross in ancient times by tyrants, to atone for their crimes. And once the Chinese people realize that the corrupt officials and businesspeople, the shameless exemplars of "winner takes all," are not going to face justice and get their just deserts in the West, they will imitate them. Soon every corner of the world will be full of Chinese swindlers who have abandoned their homeland—a swarm of locusts who will blot out the earth and the sky, bringing disaster with them wherever they go.

The children born in 1989 have already grown to adulthood. According to the yin-yang transmigration ideas of Chinese Buddhism, they should be the reincarnations of the June Fourth dead, though with absolutely no memory of their previous lives. On the other hand, those tens and tens of thousands of street fighters against tyranny who were thrown into prison in 1989 seem like handfuls of sand tossed into the vast swirling ocean of people.

———

Everything's fucked-up. The woman you used to know has changed; she's completely focused on getting ahead. Then there's the question of taking care of our daughter and the fact that I have nothing more to say to my friends. My wife complains that she's thirty-something years old and still doesn't have a place she can call home. She says I have to find a way of making money to support our daughter. She despises our past, which is brave of her. My flute playing drives her crazy, so I don't play. Somewhere deep inside I still love her, but I can't love her in the way she needs. Sometimes when I'm sitting alone at home, the fights rage on in my head for hours: "You loser." "I'm the husband!" "You're her dad!" "All you want is money! All I want is revolution!"

The letter was dated March 26, 1994, written to my old friend Liu Xia, who would later marry the famous political prisoner Liu Xiaobo. The night before, I sat on my freezing balcony for what seemed like hours. I took out my bamboo flute, but I was so depressed that I couldn't get a sound out of it. I only succeeded in catching a cold.

Soon after, following a violent argument, my wife and I divorced. I moved back to my parents' place on the other side of town, where they took care of me as if I were a child again. Most of the time I had just a few coins in my pocket, not enough even to leave the apartment. My older brother Damao lent me 10,000 yuan, which all went to child support. My daughter is now twenty-one. Of those twenty-one years, we've spent less than two months together.

Before Tiananmen, I was a rebel poet, volatile and impulsive, who loved to pick fights and tell tall tales. I won more than twenty state literary prizes, and I figured that one day I would earn international fame as a writer. But all my poems earned me was a stint in jail. That dreamy poet's look was flayed from my face. In 1990, I was arrested for reciting a poem about the massacre, and I spent nearly four years in prison. Even after I was released, I remained a wanderer, never finding a home in my own country.

The great massacre of June 4, 1989, was a turning point. Before, everyone loved their country; afterward, everyone loved money. People's hearts grew colder. A penniless former labor camp inmate, I could tell people despised me. I felt like my world had been turned upside down overnight. When I got home and saw my wife, my parents, my siblings, and old friends for the first time since jail, they seemed impassive, and there were none of the emotional scenes you read about in books. Born more than half a year after I was jailed, my daughter had turned three. She was scared of my shaved head and began to cry. She hid behind the door and whimpered, spitting at me.

Prisoners, by definition, are all single. Many of my fellow inmates hadn't seen a woman in years or decades. Everyone talked about sex all the time, even the political prisoners with their supposedly lofty ideals. It was our default subject of conversation. The only difference between ordinary criminals and politicals was that when the former steamed up the cell by masturbating in unison, the political prisoners either had to pretend they didn't notice or quietly slip away. I once shared a bunk bed with a man who was in for human trafficking. Whenever the prisoners got a special treat at dinner, he would get himself off that same night. Sometimes he made the whole bed shudder, and I would rap on the iron bed frame in protest. He would yell back up at me without missing a beat: "Don't you know? Use it or lose it!"

I scoffed then, but after my release I realized that I had indeed lost it. That part of the longed-for reunion with my wife was underwhelming; in fact, it was over before it had even really started. She picked herself up, ice-cold, and said, "I didn't really want to, but since you'd just come home, I thought there was no way to avoid it."

The blank look on my face hid my inner turmoil. I quickly got dressed. Life after prison turned out to be a living hell. What was the way out for someone with my combination of insatiable sex drive, sexual dysfunction, and politically suspect past? My former friends would answer the phone the first time I called, but they never answered a second time. Even those who came by especially to invite me to dinner would later vanish.

At the time, my wife was editing a weekly entertainment magazine published by a Chengdu nightclub. She was afraid that my shaved head was too conspicuous, the sign of an inmate, so she bought me a wig and forced me to wear it. I once went to the club to pick her up because it was late and I was worried about her getting home safely. As soon as I entered the club, I ran into the two managers, one fat and the other skinny, both of them drunk, both old friends of mine who used to be poets. Together we had run an underground poetry zine that poked fun at the Party. Of course they were both more idealistic and patriotic than I was during the 1989 student protests, publicly reciting their anticorruption poems on campus. The night of June Fourth found them in Tianfu Square in Chengdu, bringing food and water to the students who were skirmishing with the military police, and ferrying the injured to hospitals.

At the club they recognized me right away. The fat one seized my wig and cried out, "What's this counterrevolutionary doing in disguise?" The thin one yelled, "A girl for the counterrevolutionary!" I broke out in a cold sweat. They both roared with laughter and pulled me into a private room for a drink.

Three hostesses came in and started up the karaoke machine. The fat man produced his wallet and gave them all 100-yuan tips as if he were handing out candy. "Do you still write poems?" asked the skinny man.

"I haven't been able to. I guess I just don't feel like it," I said.

"Well, if you do ever feel like it, try changing your tune and writing poems that sing the praises of nightclubs, Chengdu nightlife, sexy women, and spicy hot pot," he advised. "We can print your poems under a pseudonym in our magazine, the one your wife edits."

I was dumbfounded. "You guys used to be dirt-poor poets who couldn't even afford a decent bottle of booze. Where did you find the money for this place? The rent alone must cost you hundreds of thousands of yuan per year."

"Just take out a loan and you can spend all you want," said the fat man. "There's someone I know at the bank who will take the building and facilities as collateral. Unfortunately, the girls don't count as collateral."

"Being poor hasn't been socialist since Deng Xiaoping touted economic reform on his famous tour of southern China back in 1992," the thin man chimed in. "Protesting for democracy won't get us anywhere. Money will."

———

Life before June Fourth became a distant memory. The months wasted away. I drifted aimlessly, playing the flute in bars and on the street to scrape by while working on an account of my life in prison whenever I could find time. I figured I was the unluckiest man alive. Even my secret-police minder felt sorry for me. One day he paid a visit, announcing he had found a vacant storefront and arranged for me to open a clothing store there. I said I wouldn't know where to buy clothes, let alone how to sell them.

"What do you mean, you don't even know how to do something so simple?" he asked. "I'll take you to the Lotus Pond Market for fake goods, at the North Gate train station. You can stock up there on shirts, pants, and name-brand clothing tags in bulk. Buy a bundle, spray it with water, brush down the clothes, shake out the creases, iron them carefully, and they'll look like the real thing. If you're good at talking up your wares, you can sell a 10-yuan shirt for 50 or 100. You'll be rich in no time!"

"Customers aren't idiots," I shot back.

"No, but you've got to tell yourself they are. Selling is a psychological battle."

"What if someone realizes they're knockoffs?"

"Stick to your guns and insist you'd never sell them a fake. If they really make a fuss and refuse, then give me a call."

"I'm not sure I want to run a business that wouldn't survive without police protection," I said, laughing bitterly.

"If you can pull it off, there's real money to be made," he assured me. "I can get you a rent exemption for the first few years, and once the store really takes off, then you seize the opportunity and open a chain. Aim for ten stores within five years, and fifty stores within ten years. You'll have the leading clothing chain in town. If you take it one step further, hire a few more people and open up your own factory churning out knockoffs of foreign brands and exporting them cheaply; you'll be the boss of a huge multinational company. Before you know it, even the Westerners will be shirtless and pantless without you."

I laughed out loud, but as soon as I shut my mouth, I felt pathetic.

We drank late into the night, getting properly drunk. One moment we were slapping each other on the back, the next moment we'd be eyeing each other warily again. It was nearly dawn when the drinking session ended. "Think about it, Liao," he said in parting.

"It's not for me," I told him. "You can keep your primrose paths. I'll stick to my single-log bridge." That single-log bridge was the prison testimony I was writing in secret.

One year later that same drinking buddy from the secret police came charging into my apartment with a gang of men. "This is a legal operation," he announced. He showed me his police ID and read out the search warrant. They searched the place inch by inch: the bed, the table, the roof, the floor, and all the nooks and crannies that I didn't bother to dust. They opened every drawer and turned all my pockets inside out. Although my old watchdog, Yuzui, protested loudly, they tipped out the contents of his dog bed and inspected that, too. Every written word in the house was confiscated: letters, notes, a missing-dog flyer, and the manuscript of my nearly completed memoir. I signed the list of criminal evidence they had collected. Then I was hustled into a police van and interrogated at a nearby police station until nearly midnight. At that point, the same man who had urged me to take up a career in the clothing industry came to see me before I went home. He shook my hand, patted me on the shoulder, and warned me, "You shouldn't leave your house for a month."

I lost hundreds of thousands of words in the space of one night. I fell asleep cursing myself with every Sichuanese curse word I knew. And then I started rewriting my testimony from scratch. I didn't deserve anyone's sympathy—when we were all barely making a living, no one had time to spare for my ridiculous troubles—but the heavens felt sorry for me and made up for my misfortunes by sending me an angelic girlfriend, Song Yu. She encouraged me and stuck by me during the most wretched time of my life. My problem with premature ejaculation gradually got better, but my mental dysfunction persisted. I was restless and plagued by extreme mood swings. At night, when I performed my music in bars, I was often talkative and subdued by turns. I once smashed a bottle on a drunkard's head in a bar fight that the police had to write up.

In 1995 the secret police were back. Maybe they were bugging my house; they always seemed to know where I'd been and who I'd spoken to. They seemed to have mysteriously penetrated my dreams: I had a recurring dream of escaping, of flapping my arms and suddenly soaring away. Exhausted by flying, I slept in the fetal position, wanting nothing more than to return to my mother's womb, where I would be free from surveillance. When I had nightmares, Song Yu would wake me by shaking me gently and holding me like a mother until another nightmare of a day began.

What had brought the police to my door this time was the "Truth About June Fourth" petition that Liu Xiaobo had sent me by fax. I signed the blurry document without thinking and faxed it back. Two days later I was taken away by the secret police without even realizing why and held in custody for twenty days. Song Yu spent days outside the walls of the jail, trying to find out what was happening to me. When I got home, the first thing she said to me was: "If things go on like this, do we still have a future together?"

There was nothing I could say. The only words that came into my head were from a line of a poem by Dylan Thomas: "On whom a world of ills came down like snow."

I was young and hot-tempered then. Although I made noise about wanting to go abroad, I didn't really want to emigrate, not even for political asylum. I was a natural-born wild dog. I excelled at rolling around in the trash in the alleys, sunning myself, then turning over a few trash cans and looking for stories. I was like a gambling addict in a frenzy. If the Communist Party didn't want me to write something, I just had to go write it. Maybe it started when I was in prison, bunking between two men sentenced to death. They vied at pouring their hearts out to me day and night. One told how he had hacked his wife to death and then had sex with her corpse for a whole hour. The other told me how he reeked after escaping from prison by climbing out of a cesspool. I didn't want to listen—my senses were overloaded—but they wouldn't shut up. "You have to listen," they said. "You're our last audience. How can you not listen to us?" So I listened to their stories again and again. The only way I could get those two condemned bastards out of my mind was to write down their stories. Over the years, I ended up recording and writing the stories of over three hundred people living at the bottom of Chinese society.

By then I was part of it, too. I had fallen into the abyss of the urban underclass, which put me on a level with the city's homeless population. I had no direction in life and no freedom. "If your heart imprisons you, you'll never be free." That was something my bamboo flute master used to say—and where was he now? I started drinking heavily. When I was drunk, I would curse China, the police, the Communist leaders Deng Xiaoping and Li Peng, the intellectual elite, the democracy activists in exile, and all the millions who had taken to the streets in 1989. Why on earth had I decided to recite my poem "Massacre" early on the morning of June Fourth? Was it worth it? It was all very well to be killed for what you believed in, but I had been condemned to eke out a miserable existence indefinitely.

In the fall of 2004, I got divorced for the second time.

Soon after, the secret police came and put me under house arrest after I interviewed two Falun Gong practitioners. My luck was lousy. Since my release from prison a decade earlier, the police tasked with following me had changed seven times. This time what happened was that two shabbily dressed, very worried-looking women knocked on my door. I thought they were beggars and I let them in. Out of habit I got out my notebook and recorded the horrible treatment they had suffered at a mental institution.

A week later I heard heavy pounding on my door. Fortunately, the door was solid and couldn't be opened by punching and kicking. In my desperation, I grabbed my bank card and ID card from the drawer, squeezed myself out the kitchen window, and started climbing up the chimney by grabbing onto two rusty wires. Just as I was reaching for the edge of the concrete, pulling and contracting my body and attempting to hook my right foot on the edge of the roof, my left hand slipped a little. I broke out in a cold sweat. The seventh floor! If I fell, my brains would splatter everywhere like a meat pie.

I took advantage of the heavy fog that night to sneak out of Chengdu and then out of Sichuan altogether. I made my way down to Yunnan to hide out until the situation calmed down. The following year, my work among the June Fourth "thugs" began in earnest.

"You're one of the lucky ones," said Wu Wenjian, the first thug I interviewed, when I started telling him my story.

"Yes," I said. "Compared to those who died."

"And to those who lived," he said.

Wu Wenjian was only nineteen in 1989. Against his parents' wishes, he joined the street protests on the morning of June Fourth, and he was lucky that a bullet only grazed his scalp rather than piercing his heart. He published a speech expressing his outrage; it was called "We Demand the Repayment of This Debt of Blood." It earned him a comparatively short seven-year sentence in prison.

Wu explained how thugs like him were treated after the massacre. For instance, seven of the first eight people convicted of arson—they had been charged with setting army tanks on fire—were promptly executed. The only one spared was Wang Lianxi, a sanitation worker who was found to be severely mentally disabled. As a result, his sentence was commuted on appeal to life in prison. After eighteen years, he was released, shortly before the 2008 Beijing Olympics. Then he was evicted from his apartment, like many other Beijingers, when the city forcibly removed thousands in preparation for the games. Wang Lianxi ended up homeless and was eventually sent to a mental hospital. Those who knew him said Wang had been sleeping on the streets and scavenging in dumpsters for food.

Another man called Lu Zhongqu, who had also committed property damage by setting vehicles on fire, was nearly beaten to death by troops on a rampage. "We saw the soldiers drag him into a tank and take him directly to a detention center," Wu told me. "By then he'd already lost his mind. He was covered from head to toe with bruises. He also had no bowel or bladder control left. He walked around in his own world and spoke to no one. He eventually disappeared, just like Tank Man."

Almost no one I interviewed was willing to speak publicly about sex, but the damage there was deep, too. All over China, many of those arrested after the 1989 protests were teenage boys, virgins, like Wu Wenjian. On their release, they were middle-aged men dealing with erectile dysfunction and premature ejaculation, and their recovery often took months or years.

Wu Wenjian told me his erectile dysfunction lasted at least two years. "I had been studying art, so not long after being released from prison I found a job at an ad agency. I traveled a lot for work, so I was staying in hotels and found myself in places full of sexy women. But I was scared that the police were following me and would catch me in the act if I tried anything.

"My first kiss was a disaster. I managed to crack the skin on her lips. As soon as I put my arms around her, I came, and it was visible. I was nervous and extremely horny, but the hornier I got, the less I could get it up. It went on like that all night. The girl was patient, and she kept stroking me and comforting me, but I was on the verge of tears. I just wanted to slap myself in the face. She left and never came back."

That's what happens when you've been sexually starved for a long time.

Many people were afraid to talk to me at all, like a friend of Wu's named Kun, who had sexual problems that were just a symptom of the wider malaise in his life. Wu tried to talk him into giving me an interview, but he declined: "If my boss finds out, I'll be fired right away."

Kun was a real patriot and had been honorably discharged from the army. The night of June 3, he was at Muxidi Bridge, one of the people directing the crowds of protesters from above to collectively resist the tanks. Someone later betrayed him to the military police, and he was convicted on charges of subversion and given a death sentence that was later commuted to life in prison. His wife left him not long after, taking their child with her. By the time he was released, years later, he was single and living with his eighty-year-old parents.

Kun told me a little of his employment history after getting out: "My first job involved standing outside big department stores, watching their customers' bicycles. It paid next to nothing. Out on the street on snowy days, I stomped my feet so they wouldn't freeze. Then my friends pulled some strings to get me the job I have now, working in a public bathhouse as a janitor. I clean toilets day and night, but at least it's a stable income. Forget nightclubs. Now bathhouses are the new thing. Drinking, kara-oke, mah-jongg, bathing, full-body massages, foot massages, back mas-sages, hand jobs . . . We'll satisfy the full range of the customer's desires.

"In that den of vice, I'm just the janitor who cleans the toilets. When the fat cats and magnates come in with girls hanging off their arms, I stand respectfully to one side and hand them napkins. In the 1989 stu-dent movement, we ordinary people supported the students because we were sick of corruption. We wanted the top Communist officials to dis-close their 'gray income' and private assets. We wanted a fresh start for our country. Government officials are still in league with big business, while ordinary people can barely make ends meet. Society is suffering from a crisis of trust. Those of us who paid the price for supporting Chi-nese democracy are left waiting on the fat cats."

One time Kun was cleaning the toilets at work, when two shirtless businessmen came in. One was a former neighbor of his who had battled the tanks side by side with Kun during the movement. "I got lucky and slipped away into the crowd," the neighbor told Kun after recognizing him. "They had no proof that I'd taken part in the protests, and I denied my involvement strenuously. Eventually I got away with nothing more than making a self-criticism at work."

Responding to the Party's call to go into business, the neighbor went into food processing, making a fortune "selling dead pigs as live ones," as the saying goes. As long as you never breathe a word of 1989 and never reopen those old wounds, he advised Kun, you can keep making money. "You were literally on the top of the world back then!" exclaimed the neighbor, still expounding and shirtless as Kun waited to clean the bathroom. "There's no predicting what will happen to anyone," he added.

———

With the help of Wu Wenjian, his contacts, and my own contacts from prison, I interviewed June Fourth thugs in Beijing and in Sichuan, my native province, from 2005 to 2011, when I finally fled China. With these secret interviews with the unknown survivors of June Fourth, I wanted to document what happened to them during the movement, the torture and imprisonment they endured, and how they are getting by today on the margins of Chinese society. Unable to stop listening and recording, I compiled this book of interviews, calling myself a remembrance worker. Many of those I interviewed were under house arrest or surveillance, including from their own families, and every rendezvous was difficult, requiring careful, secret preparations. For reasons of safety, few in today's China are willing to speak about Tiananmen, let alone in front of a tape recorder using their real names, but these brave men were. I had suffered less, but I was one of them, and I had the help of trusted go-betweens. Nonetheless, harrowing episodes recounted to me in dozens of interviews will never be published because the victims refused to allow me to make them public.

In each of these stories, including my own, a young idealist is swept along by the revolutionary tide of 1989, when the fall of the Soviet Union made it seem as if democracy might finally come to China. After the massacre, each faced the brutalities of the Chinese prison system, including "reeducation through labor." Sexual dysfunction, divorce, estrangement from family, homelessness and joblessness, bitterness and betrayal—this is the world of most former protesters, especially those from working-class and provincial backgrounds.

One former protester is virtually homeless, while another plans to self-immolate, and a third dreams of becoming a Buddhist monk. Another, released from prison, has an apparently successful life in advertising but secretly, obsessively, paints scenes from Tiananmen. Others remain committed to the movement, enduring imprisonment, harassment, house arrest, and endless surveillance again and again for the tiniest crimes, like paying their respects to the tomb of a slain protester or joining a political party.

Today's China was forged at Tiananmen Square, and *Bullets and Opium* is the story of how it happened, in the words of those who were there—the "thugs," to use the name the Party used to slander them. They were not the "protester elite": students at top universities, usually from privileged families, who became the voice of the movement and in many cases fled abroad afterward or got off relatively easily. The thugs were working-class people and peasants who supported the students, bore the brunt of the crackdown, and were treated more brutally in prison because of their lower social status. Many of them were men, for reasons that are deeply rooted in Chinese society, and all those interviewed in this book, partly for reasons of access, are men. Far from the human rights limelight, I found the thugs at hot-pot dives in distant suburbs, scraping by on the streets, dodging house arrest and police surveillance, living with parents and without prospects.

The West knows of only one protester: "Tank Man," the man in the iconic photograph who stood in the street, physically blocking the oncoming column of tanks billowing exhaust like gigantic farting beetles. They kept trying to make their way around him, but he kept getting in their way. "You're steel, and I'm flesh and blood," he seemed to be saying. "Come get me if you dare!" This moment was preserved for posterity because a foreign reporter happened to capture it on video, but there were countless Tank Men whose deeds were not captured on camera.

This book is a record of those countless others, people scarred by history and then worn down by money and power. But my dejected interviewees do not think much of the record. I, too, had my own doubts about testimony being collected to be used in the future.

In 2011, after years of listening, it was a story I finally wanted to escape from. After half a lifetime in the nightmare, I wanted to say farewell to 1989. Had it been worth it? I tucked all the testimonies I had collected into my clothes. I turned off my cell phone and took out the batteries, hoping to evade police tracking. That also allowed me to avoid worried relatives.

The first day I officially went missing, I was in the distant city of Dali, drinking with a pack of disreputable friends. Seated across from me were two beautiful female writers in their twenties who could outdrink and outcurse the men. Pointing at my nose, they shouted, "Stupid cunt!" so I had to flip the table. The gang applauded my guts and figured I would hang around there for a while. I could never tell how many informers were around. But seeing me drinking heavily there night after night, not doing anything serious, they relaxed their surveillance. Then, just like that, I suddenly left and never looked back.

Arriving in another city on a long-distance bus, I chose a small inn at random and hid there for two nights to make sure nobody knew where I was. *Keep moving, keep moving!* I yelled to myself even in my dreams. Before dawn broke, I headed out the door with my bag over my shoulder. It was already dark when I reached a small town on the border. Amid thunder, lightning, and pouring rain, I checked into a hotel and got in touch with the person from the border region who was supposed to help me.

It took him a long time to show up. We whispered to each other for over ten minutes. He said that crossing the border was easy. You could get a boat and just row over to the other side. "The police don't pay attention," he said, "and we regularly 'pay our taxes.'" I said I didn't want to ride in a boat. I wanted to cross over on the bridge.

"That would be a bit difficult," he said, "but we could try."

Ghosts of 1989, brothers who suffered hardships in 1989, mothers and fathers of 1989, those of you in heaven, those of you buried underground, those of you in the rain or blown by the wind—from the shadows of the border, I bow to you. The next night, when I walked out of China into Vietnam's Lao Cai Province, I looked back at my native land as if in a dream and an old line came to me:

The world is a very narrow bridge
Don't be afraid
You can cross it

PART I:

BEIJING

The Performance Artist

On the afternoon of May 23, 1989, at home in Sichuan a thousand miles away, I saw a live broadcast from Beijing showing the "Three Brave Men from Hunan"—Yu Zhijian, Yu Dongyue, and Lu Decheng—who had thrown rotten eggs at the portrait of the dictator Mao Zedong hanging from the Tiananmen gate tower. Officials called them the "Three Thugs from Hunan."

Their protest came just over three months after the China/Avant-Garde Exhibition, the most complete exhibit of Chinese performance art ever shown. Among the exhibits were people shooting at a telephone booth, a living person incubating a chicken egg, mourners dressed in white funeral garments, and people distributing condoms to passersby. The performance artists constantly clashed with the police—getting beat up, dragged away from the scene, and detained. A few exhibits were closed down, too. Among progressive young people, it aroused wild enthusiasm, launching performance art in China and adding to the revolutionary mood in the streets.

The smashing of Mao's portrait by the Three Brave Men from Hunan must have been the most outstanding piece of performance art since the Chinese Communist regime was established in 1949.

A friend asked me if I would be interested in interviewing the ringleader of the Three Brave Men, Yu Zhijian, since Yu Dongyue had lost his mind and Lu Decheng had fled. Yu Zhijian himself was under house arrest for writing a "reactionary article" and publishing it online. Taking every precaution, I traveled to the city of Changsha, and we arranged to meet one night when he would be able to slip away from his captors.

When we finally found each other, Yu looked like an old Shanghai gentleman down on his luck. He was half a head taller than I was, with a head of shiny hair. Before we even had a chance to shake hands, we quickly got into the same cab speeding down ramrod-straight May First Avenue toward the city center, crossing the Xiang River by bridge, and passing Orange Isle in the middle of the river. The car stopped after we went over the bridge. We went behind the Fenglin Hotel and found a divey, rancid teahouse. We had to shout for a long time before two disheveled-looking waitresses came out and allowed us to pay 80 yuan for a private room and a pot of tea. The women had us wait for a moment and then opened a dark curtain, waking up the three other women workers sleeping there and making them put away their makeshift bed. They put out the tea tables and chairs and began boiling some water for tea.

We closed the door so tight that there wasn't even any space for air. We were both ashen-faced from sleeplessness. Yu smoked one cigarette after another, his already small eyes narrowing as he squinted. He joked that all we needed in order to look like bandits were two knives.

Yu Zhijian: I've been under house arrest for a number of months. The police have been watching me in shifts, twenty-four hours a day. But even tigers take naps, so at five a.m. today, before dawn, I took advantage of an opportunity and hurried to the train station. I took the train from Liuyang to Changsha. When I got off, I went in circles for a while. Once I knew I wasn't being followed, I could relax.

You look like you couldn't care in the least. You are an artist.

Thanks for your flattery. But playing hide-and-seek with the police is instinctive in a liberal. It has nothing to do with being an artist.

In 1989, Lu Decheng, Yu Dongyue, and I were all poor and none of us had ever been to Beijing before. How could we ever make revolution? We took out all our wages and counted them up, but it still wasn't enough. The night before we left, I went to visit a classmate who made a living as a self-employed businessman selling electrical appliances. He made a generous contribution to the revolution, lending me 1,000 yuan, which would be worth twenty times as much today.

A train ticket from Changsha to Beijing only cost several dozen yuan. When the driver on the bus from Liuyang to Changsha heard that we were going to Beijing to support democracy, he gave us free bus tickets. When we got to Changsha at dawn, we went straight to May First Avenue and the provincial government buildings to find out what was going on. The Hunan student movement was spreading like wildfire. The intersections were full of students and city people marching. We couldn't help but get very excited. I had long legs, so I ran to the market to buy brushes, ink, and cloth. Yu Dongyue immediately started to dash off a banner. He wrote in giant characters: "Let's March to Beijing," "Down with Deng Xiaoping! Support Zhao Ziyang!" At the bottom of the banners he wrote, "Hunan Petition Team."

We occupied the square in front of the Changsha train station, put up our banners, and took turns speaking. The speeches were about the most popular topics of this movement: fighting corruption, stopping official profiteering, changing the political system, amending the constitution, and opposing the system of one-party dictatorship. Yu Dongyue had one of those scarce high-quality Japanese-made cameras, which he used for interviews as a journalist for the *Liuyang Daily*, so he was in charge of documenting it all in photos. I never thought the photographic masterpieces he so painstakingly made would end up being used against him in court as evidence of his counterrevolutionary propaganda and crimes of incitement.

The crowd in the square by the station was huge. Though I was just an average rural elementary school teacher and it was my very first time doing what the authorities later called "counterrevolutionary incitement" in front of a big crowd, I spoke very well and was very effective. Everybody got excited and started throwing money into our collection box. Some threw in dimes, some 2-yuan bills, and some even the new 10-yuan bill. I was very moved. That was the biggest bill then; they weren't making 100-yuan bills yet. I remember to this day a man stuffing two whole handfuls of bills into our collection box. We stirred things up for just a few hours and the box was full; we had collected over 3,000 yuan. Some Hunan students, forty or fifty people, joined our petition group on the spot. They all wanted to go to Beijing to support the student movement.

Tickets in hand, we poured onto the train, which was crammed with patriots pressing against each other in the crowded passageway. When the conductor who came to check our tickets heard that we were a Hunan petition group going to support the movement in Beijing, he called for the train crew captain, who told us he completely and totally supported us and wanted to put us into the lounge car usually reserved for railway personnel.

The next day we arrived at the station in Beijing. As soon as we got off the train, we attracted a lot of attention when we raised our banner, which was half as long as a railway car. Our group marched together yelling slogans as we walked toward Tiananmen. When I stole a look behind us after a while, I saw that coming up behind us was a crowd of hundreds, mostly students from various places who had just gotten off the train but couldn't find their own groups. Strength in numbers took our enthusiasm to new heights. We shouted slogans like "Return Hu Yaobang to us! Down with Deng Xiaoping! Support Zhao Ziyang! We want freedom, we want democracy, we want human rights, the Chinese people want to stand up." Our yells were louder and came faster and more furious than the drumbeats in country operas, drawing even more of a crowd. About forty or fifty minutes later we saw the famous Tiananmen gate tower, which before we had seen only in newspapers.

We were just about to plunge into the boundless sea of people, when a person who seemed to be a student leader asked us where we were from. We answered in unison: "We are the Hunan Petition Group and we have come to support the student movement." "Very good," he said several times, but added: "Your slogans are somewhat inappropriate and too extreme. People on the square are not just shouting whatever comes to mind."

Over the next two days, the Hunan University students who had come with us gradually dispersed to their own groups and organizations, so the so-called Hunan Petition Team gradually dissolved. All that remained were the three of us: Yu Dongyue, Lu Decheng, and myself, the core members who didn't belong anywhere else, exposing the true nature of our isolation.

We got to Beijing on May 18 and landed in trouble on May 23. We had five or six days of excitement in all. We participated in some student and citizen marches and made some speeches calling for the end of one-party dictatorship and for complete Westernization. We hardly slept those days. At night, when we were simply too tired, we would find an underground passageway or a street corner, put down some plastic sheeting, wrap ourselves in military jackets, and doze off. I remember one morning when I woke up there was a female university student lying on top of me. It was a very romantic scene.

Three things stood out for me. The first was an extra-large banner hung on the Great Hall of the People proclaiming the "Emergency Meeting of the Standing Committee of the National People's Congress." It made people fantasize that the democratic utopia was about to appear before our very eyes.

The second was that many military helicopters were flying over Tiananmen. Sometimes they flew very low, nearly brushing the top of the gate tower. They were always dropping propaganda leaflets addressed to the "hoodwinked masses" and calling on us to surrender. All kinds of plausible but false rumors spread across the square, making people nervous.

The third thing that made a deep impression on me was the speeches of student leaders like Wang Dan, Wu'er Kaixi, and Chai Ling. Nonsense like "Maintain order as strictly as possible on the square." Nonsense such as "City people and workers, return to work as normal." Chai Ling even talked like she was an entertainer, saying things like "Thank you, thank you everyone for your support!" It was as if the university students were God's chosen ones, as if they were the only ones with the right to be true patriots. Other social forces, they apparently thought, were just clueless idiots stirring up trouble. Well, fuck that. If it weren't for everybody's support—if it all depended upon the students—could it have lasted that long? The Communist Party would have long since put an end to them. At the time I was disgusted by what they said. The martial law troops were already in the Beijing suburbs. What good would all the internal strife, bickering, panic, and standoffs within the student leadership do? What use was it pretending to be calm? Were all those fully armed troops vegetarians? What would happen if they started shooting?

How could such a broad-based democracy movement supported by tens of millions of people be handled smoothly by a few little kids? Bloodshed was looming before our eyes and they were still obsessed with all their empty talk. People like us, grassroots, from the provinces, couldn't join the conversation. We tried several times to get past the guards so that we could talk with the student leaders. Every time the students disciplinary patrol saw what a mess I was, they absolutely refused to let us enter the Tiananmen Square command post, much less see the leaders of the Capital Autonomous Federation of University Students. Things weren't going well, so what could we do? We left a written recommendation and tried to persuade the student disciplinary patrol to pass it on at least as a "document for reference."

First, we recommended that the Capital Autonomous Federation of University Students proclaim, in the name of all the Chinese people, that the Chinese Communist government was an illegal government. Second, we called for a general strike of all workers in Beijing and the entire country, as well as a strike by all shopkeepers. Third, there was something about a disciplinary patrol of workers and students; I can't remember it exactly right now. We never heard a word about any of it. Things were chaotic; maybe our suggestions were never passed on at all.

You didn't agree with them and you couldn't work with them. You could have just dusted yourselves off and left.

We couldn't do that. We had come such a long way to Beijing. We had to take responsibility for what was happening. Yu Dongyue was depressed, inconsolable. He suggested that we self-immolate together. We planned many different ways of doing it, like going up on the Jinshui Bridge, dousing ourselves with gasoline, and lighting ourselves up, which would have made quite an impression. But what would we achieve? Should we publish a "Self-Immolation Declaration" beforehand? Who should we send to tell the whole country that we had given our lives for democracy, for freedom, to resist tyranny, and to wake everyone up? The situation was desperate. If we didn't do it properly, people wouldn't understand why we had done it, and the regime might even use our deaths to slander the democracy movement.

There was just no point. I made an alternate proposal to attack the famous portrait of Mao Zedong on the Tiananmen gate tower, symbolically declaring an end to Communist tyranny. Yu Dongyue and Lu Decheng agreed right away. From midnight until dawn on May 22, we discussed our plan. We thought of climbing up onto the tower and taking down Mao's portrait. It didn't look like we would have to climb very far, but when we saw how well guarded it was, the climb up the wall looked harder than climbing up to heaven. The next morning, all red-eyed from lack of sleep and looking like feverish patients, we racked our brains and managed to get a ladder and carry it to the doorway under Mao's portrait. Even with a ladder the height of several men, we still couldn't reach that damn tyrant, already dead for many years, who had stomped all over us while he was alive!

We took turns studying the situation from below, examining the area around the gate. Finally we saw that the nails that held the Mao portrait to the gate were as thick as my arm. That meant that even if we got a high-enough ladder and risked being cut to smithereens, we still might not be able to knock the emperor off his horse.

Didn't anyone notice you?

Nobody paid any attention to anyone else. Very often the center of a movement is like the eye of a hurricane. People are relaxed, marginalized, and isolated. Naturally, people who are at the center of world attention are a different matter.

So that's when you thought of treating the tyrant to some rotten eggs? At that time I was still at home in my Sichuan mountain town of Fuling watching the live television broadcast. So I witnessed your brave act, and I was shocked. I remember the voice of the announcer at the scene, the white-haired Chen Duo of the Central People's Broadcasting Station, trembling with anger.

When we realized we wouldn't be able to take down Old Mao, we had to go to plan C. We went to the department store in Wangfujing and bought twenty eggs. At first we thought we'd just eyeball the distance and throw the eggs right at Mao's portrait. But then we thought about how the color of those eggs wouldn't be dark enough or make a very visible splatter. Fortunately, Yu Dongyue likes painting. He said that it would work if we bought some oil paints, mixed the colors to a dark gray, and filled the eggs with that.

Preparations took a long time, and we were quite serious about it. We bought some calligraphy paper, brushes, black ink, oil paint, paint thinner, and glue, and then rushed to the post office to mail our last words to our families back home. I forget what I wrote. I seem to have quoted a lot of Byron's poems. Lu Decheng put a lot of thought into his. He was full of emotions. He was an only child. I heard later that his parents fainted on the spot when they saw the live broadcast. I still remember some of the things that Yu Dongyue wrote. He had five sworn blood brothers back in Liuyang, so he bent over and wrote letter after letter. Something about how we should learn from Don Quixote's tilting at windmills and the famous line about how "the wind howls across the cold Yi River water; the warriors are gone, never to return." A poet, he wrote lots of stuff like that, with soaring elegance.

I still remember this bit of doggerel he created. "There are a thousand reasons why you walk on this side of the street. There are a thousand and one reasons why you cross the street and walk over to the other side of the street!"

The impulse to cross a line. Of course, you did cross to the other side.

After finishing up our wills, we were hungry. We took those twenty eggs to cook at a small food stand by the north side of the Jinshui Bridge. In a flat wok we spread a thin layer of flour batter, beat in the eggs, and sprinkled some chopped green onion. That day we stuffed ourselves with too many of those thin *jianbing* pancakes that are a specialty of northern China. For a while the bright golden-yellow pancakes smelled great and were tasty. We had never had them before in Hunan. After eating too many of them, we couldn't eat any more. We nearly vomited.

Then we gathered the egg shells and took them to the entrance of Zhongshan Park on the left side of the Tiananmen gate tower. We spread a plastic sheet on the ground and sat down on it to begin making Mao-smashing eggs. We filled the egg shells with oil paint mixed to a dark gray color and then sealed them one by one.

Then we put down a sheet of high-quality art paper, four feet by about two and a half feet, and thought carefully about an appropriate couplet. It had to be the best couplet written since 1949. I suggested a phrase and Yu Dongyue, filled with emotion, wrote it down in one stroke. "Five thousand years of tyranny ends here. No more personality cults starting now." And across the top: "Freedom is mighty."

The arrow was now ready in the quiver. Yu Dongyue got out his camera and took a picture so that the couplet would be "preserved forever." Lu Decheng and I also took advantage of this to have our photo taken at the gate entrance to mark the occasion. Now all those things are sealed in the criminal records of the public security organs.

You didn't give these "revolutionary relics" to some dependable person?

In that sea of people we had no idea who might be reliable. Then we decided on a simple division of labor. I was tall and had the longest arms, so I would block the river of people flowing beneath the gate and announce that the Mao-smashing action had begun. Yu Dongyue and Lu Decheng were responsible for pasting up the couplet and throwing the eggs. So everyone took up their tasks. I started by running to the central gate under the tower and stretching out my arms to block passersby. "Excuse me, excuse me! Please everyone stop for a minute," I yelled a few times. Nobody had the slightest idea what was going on. Fortunately, a few students pushed their way forward to help, and so we were able to stop the stream of people. They thought we were with them, since Lu Decheng and I were just twenty-five or twenty-six and Yu Dongyue was twenty-two, a boy wonder who had graduated from college at eighteen.

The two of them quickly posted the couplets on either side of the central gate—not quite straight, given how nervous they were. Then they rushed back to get into the best position and started throwing the eggs. Originally we thought twenty paint-filled eggs would be enough to ruin that portrait of Mao, but we didn't imagine that those two idiots would be so useless with their egg tossing, all the eggs either overshooting or coming up short, or coming in too slanted, or not thrown hard enough, so that the eggs fell to the ground before reaching their target. I watched helplessly and cursed them. What the hell were they doing? Luckily, they were not totally shameful. Out of the twenty eggs, three hit the portrait. The tyrant's double chin got some pockmarks.

It all happened in just five or six minutes. Smashing the eggs on the portrait took about two or three minutes. It was like a dream. The people in the square didn't react. They were numb, horrified, or blindly applauded—and by the time they woke up, it was already over. Several layers of people suddenly surrounded us and yelled "Criminals!" and someone scolded us accusingly: "What are you doing?" "Where are you from?" "Who told you to do that?"

The disciplinary patrol of the Capital Autonomous Federation of University Students came and pushed back the crowd. I was at the edge then; I could only see the heads of the other two. I could faintly hear some accusatory voices: "You have evil intentions. You want to destroy us all. You want to ruin this patriotic movement." Lu Decheng, who had paints of different colors all over him from the broken eggs, argued hard right back at them. "We are right to punish Mao Zedong. It's legal. We didn't do anything wrong." I also applauded and cheered from a distance: "What you're saying is true!" The students next to me were very stern. They pointed at me and said, "It's none of your business. Shut up!"

"Of course it's my business," I said. "I'm with them!" And by saying that, I was caught, too. I was seized by the students and taken to the headquarters in the square. That's how we finally got to the base of the monument—the very same student movement center we had racked our brains trying to get into but had failed to reach. How we got there, though, wasn't very honorable. The three of us sat there, dejected, with our heads hung low, waiting for what would come next. Off to one side the student leaders were having a discussion. They took a long time. Finally, plainclothes policemen appeared. They went round and round and then entered headquarters asking for us. The student leaders politely refused to hand us over.

At that moment a woman quietly came over and whispered in my ear to say, "The situation doesn't look good for you. You had best look for your chance and sneak away fast." I immediately shook my head, saying, "All three of us will stick together, life or death. I can't just run away all by myself." She pondered for a moment and then said, "I'll give you my telephone number. If you need help, just call me." I promised that I would. I was young then, with a good memory. She said it to me once and I remembered it. I didn't ask who she was, but from the expression on her face I could see that she really did want to help me. Later I forgot both her and her telephone number. I think that now if I saw her again, I wouldn't recognize her.

Ultimately, they handed us over. The standing committee of the Capital Autonomous Federation of University Students at the headquarters had voted, we learned, and decided that we should be taken to Dongcheng District Public Security Bureau's Tiananmen security office. They argued about it for a long time, but in the end we got into a police car in the pouring rain. They handcuffed us. From the time the event occurred at 2:30 in the afternoon until the evening when we were in the hands of the police, I certainly had chances to escape. I don't know about the other two. But why would we want to sneak away? We had long before mentally prepared ourselves to accept the consequences.

We were locked up in the Nanchizi police station for the night. The next morning we were transferred to a holding pen opposite the Beijing Municipality Dongcheng District Detention Center. The whole place was deserted. Besides me, there was only a habitual thief from Beijing in the cell. That guy really had a life of ease. If he didn't have to get up, he would just lie around, smoking and sleeping and then sleeping and smoking. He even asked me to bring him water to drink. I couldn't help it. Loneliness is hard to take. People who were poles apart happened to be thrown together and started chatting casually. I really wanted to continue paying attention to the development of the movement, but now I was isolated. One could say that the Beijing prosecutorial system was half-paralyzed. Even the detention center wardens only rarely appeared. I suppose they were watching and waiting to see which way the scales would tip within the internal Party center power struggle.

For about two weeks on either side of June Fourth there weren't any interrogations or even any questions put to us. Every day, besides eating, drinking, and shitting, we just lay around and slept. My bones ached from sleeping so much. Fortunately, I'm a naturally lazy person, so I learned early on the art of falling into a deep sleep. I didn't worry much about what might happen. If the world is destined to end but in your wishful thinking you hope that it won't, you're just wasting your time.

You had almost reached Zhuangzi's state of mind.

That lasted until midnight on the night of June 3. Suddenly there was gunfire outside the detention center. It sounded like spattering peas in a wok, startling me awake from my dreams. So they were finally shooting, those motherfuckers. This is what they mean when they say political power grows out of the barrel of a gun. This was how the Communists had come to power. How could students and educated people win out over old political hacks capable of murdering without blinking an eye? I didn't get any sleep that night. I paced back and forth inside my cell until dawn. All over my body my muscles twitched uncontrollably. The thief admonished me kindly: the country is in chaos; you won't solve anything by worrying about it.

Early on the morning of June Fourth, the first group came in. They were all hot-blooded young people and university students. Their average age was about twenty. More and more kept coming in through June 5. Our empty detention center overflowed in the blink of an eye. When the cell couldn't fit any more people, they continued to cram people inside. Fortunately, people's bodies are made of flesh and so are flexible.

According to regulations, there should be no more than fourteen or fifteen people in a cell like that, but there were more than thirty people in that cell. There wasn't even enough room to stand. We were formally arrested on June 15. The once-paralyzed prosecutorial system woke up, just like we had, as if from a dream. In an instant it resumed its usual cruel, high-speed operation. Arrest orders flew out. Checkpoints were set up everywhere to arrest people. That Red Terror was like in 2003, when China was hit by SARS [severe acute respiratory syndrome] and you hardly saw anyone on the streets. Ideological disinfection and bodily disinfection are a lot alike.

During the state of emergency, the authorities did not trust the Beijing police. The soldiers who took over the detention center were mostly brainwashed brutes. They were beasts with sharp teeth and claws who knew no laws. They brutalized the detainees. Students and ordinary people alike were nearly beaten to death. When we were arrested and transferred to the detention center, a soldier lifted me up as if he were lifting a live chicken and threw me toward the jeep about three feet away. That wasn't enough to vent his anger. He raised his automatic rifle and smashed its butt against my face. Immediately, fresh blood spewed from my mouth. Liao, do you see the fake tooth in my mouth? That was put in to replace the real tooth that was knocked out.

I was held in the notorious detention center Turtle Mansion, but I wasn't officially considered a thug. Because I wasn't in time to set fires and block military vehicles, I was simply labeled a scoundrel who had violated the Great Leader. We spent five weeks stewing in block seven of Turtle Mansion. On July 10 we were taken to a secret hearing in a Beijing Municipal Intermediate People's Court basement.

Fuck, according to the regular rules, our crime was obvious and we made no defense. The whole thing took less than two hours. The most interesting statement of course was Yu Dongyue's, arguing that we didn't have any political goal. He said it was performance art, the most outstanding piece of performance art of the century. And that people would only understand what it really meant several years later.

I was sentenced to life in prison, and I ended up doing eleven years and six months. Lu Decheng was sentenced to fifteen years; he actually served eight years and eight months. Yu Dongyue was sentenced to twenty years and served sixteen years and nine months. He was the last of us to be released. We didn't appeal: that would have been looking for trouble. We were sent back to Hunan at the end of 1989 to be locked up in Hengyang Prison [Hunan Provincial Prison No. 2].

When I first arrived and still didn't understand how things worked there, I told everybody how many people were killed on June Fourth, how cruel and tyrannical the Communist Party was. I kept talking. I wouldn't work. I was very enthusiastic about discussing with the other political prisoners how things were changing. That got me many warnings from the prison authorities. I didn't pay any attention, so I was declared a prisoner subject to close supervision. I was beaten up five or six times. One time, as two policemen held me, I was beaten with two electric prods. I tried to resist but soon collapsed. After that, fists and steel-toe shoes rained down on me. I rolled all over the floor. My good clothes went missing after that beating. I lay on the ground stark naked. None of my bones were broken. They had a little mercy after all. Hunan prisons are generally barbaric.

Later, I learned to go along. I stopped being so goddamn stubborn. I still insisted that I was a political prisoner and shouldn't have to do reform through labor. Then they assigned a more experienced prisoner to mentor me and establish a so-called teacher-student relationship. Later still, I was transferred to Hunan Provincial Prison No. 3, also called the Yongzhou Prison. Yu Dongyue was transferred to Prison No. 1, where political prisoners were held, widely known to be the most barbaric prison in Hunan Province.

Around 1992 I read in the newspaper about Deng Xiaoping's "Southern Tour" speech. After thinking carefully about it, I decided that China was entering a long, dull, and dark "Brezhnev period," like in the former Soviet Union. My spirits sank with that recognition and I fell into a long period of depression.

In light of that, I needed first of all to survive. So I told the prison authorities that I was a skilled teacher and they transferred me from the metalworking shop to the education department, where I taught classes for the other prisoners.

Of us three, Lu Decheng was the luckiest. He snuck across the border into Thailand, although he was nearly repatriated back to China from there. Yu Dongyue had the worst luck. The day he was released from prison, I asked some good friends from the democracy movement to go meet him. To my great surprise, he was like a block of misshapen wood, completely different from the witty, high-spirited Yu Dongyue that I had known. I said to him over and over, "Dongyue, my old friend, what are you doing? Don't you even recognize me?" He didn't react. When he did react, he suddenly knelt down and grabbed my two legs, yelling out loud, "Don't kill me, don't kill me." I felt a knife run through my heart. June Fourth is too enormous. I'll leave it to the historians and the political scientists to evaluate the whole thing. The problem that I couldn't stop thinking about was only Yu Dongyue. I felt that I had destroyed him. He doesn't know who he is. If you ask him, "Who is Yu Dongyue?" he'll just look at you blankly, with no idea at all.

A while ago, I published a dozen "reactionary" essays online. The Ministry of Public Security's National Security Office gave me thirty-two days of criminal detention for incitement to overthrow the government. After I was released and had a few days to rest, I took a bus to visit Yu Dongyue's family, who live about forty miles from the Liuyang County seat.

He had been out of jail for a while and was calmer. He no longer knelt down when he saw someone, but his eyes were still as blank. You couldn't speak loudly or he would start trembling all over and then kneel down. His family was always trying to help him get his memory back. They were always talking about this or that person from his past and about the names of their next-door neighbors. For a moment it would seem that he had remembered he was Yu Dongyue, but he would soon forget it again, just like the people in Gabriel García Márquez's novel *One Hundred Years of Solitude*, who all lived in their own fabricated worlds. Yu Dongyue had strongly recommended that novel. He had never imagined that he would live in such a world himself.

How do you support yourself now that you are married?

I don't know. We don't have a home of our own, and I don't have any insurance or retirement pension. I'll just have to depend on luck. These days our main source of income is home tutoring. The number of students fluctuates all the time. Our average monthly income is less than 1,000 yuan.

Would you like to go abroad?

What would I do if I went abroad?

You would be free. This is a country of bandits.

But even so, it's the country where I was born and raised. Even if I wanted to leave, I couldn't bear to part from it. Who can take away my inner freedom? At home, there are a few unavoidable small conflicts. But love, family ties, and friendship are the perpetual theme of life. One just has to learn gradually to adjust to changes in society. We're all small people who must resign ourselves to adversity. But compared with other ordinary little people, we have a June Fourth obsession that will never go away, that enables us to confront political fear and feel the impulse to challenge it.

I can't see what future there could still be for this nation and this society. The price we paid, the passion we had for this country—in the end was it just insignificant, even laughable? Our efforts to make people in the future remember may just be wishful thinking. In the end, our very existence may make honorable people, successful people—the ones who manage to make it in any era—feel uncomfortable. So forget it. I'll just have to be content with what I have. Thinking about it too much just gives me a headache.

Do you want to have children?

It would be hard to support them. I'm not thinking about it for the time being.

The Massacre Painter

In the spring of 1989, Wu Wenjian, a nineteen-year-old cook and an aspiring painter who admired Van Gogh and Gauguin, was moved to act after witnessing government troops move into Beijing. For making a speech on June 5 denouncing the bloodshed, he was branded a "violent criminal" and sentenced to seven years in prison.

I first met Wu on a sunny day in 2005 in Beijing's 798 Art District, a thriving colony of studios and art galleries converted from old factories and warehouses. We quickly moved to a nearby restaurant serving northeastern food. I didn't have to do much to get him started. Dressed in a blazing red shirt and apparently in high spirits, Wu talked for several hours nonstop against the cacophony in the restaurant, as though well prepared for what he would say. He barely lifted his chopsticks to touch the food.

"Volumes have been written by and about the 'Tiananmen elite,'" said Wu. "But who is there to speak for the June Fourth 'thugs'? They have no place in history, no voice in society. Nobody has come out to defend them. All their suffering has been in vain." After dinner we moved to a quieter location, where Wu continued to talk until well past midnight. When we finally parted at a street corner, I had photographs of his oil paintings depicting the massacre in my backpack. He has been turning out these nightmarish paintings for years and never yet exhibited one. "They can wait," he said.

———

Let's start from before June Fourth. Your family? Your profession?

Wu Wenjian: I was born into a family of industrial workers—tried-and-true proletarian pedigree by Communist standards. There are two large state-run enterprises in Beijing: one is Capital Steel and the other is [Beijing] Yanshan Petrochemical Corporation, which is part of Sinopec and employs several hundred thousand workers in Fangshan District. Both of my parents worked for Yanshan. My brother and I went to Yanshan company schools.

Going back further, my paternal grandfather secretly joined the Communist Party while attending a technical school in the 1930s. He later attended a military college set up by the Communists during the War of Resistance against the Japanese, and died a hero on the battlefield in 1941. My maternal grandfather also joined the Communist Party in the 1940s. He was arrested once by the Japanese and severely tortured. They burned his back with a branding iron.

My father, his brother, and my mother's two brothers were all also Communist Party members. I was indoctrinated with the traditional revolutionary ideology from early childhood: I was taught to work hard and live simply, to devote my life to the Communist cause and to the liberation of humankind.

Although my family had such a long tradition of supporting the Communist Party, both of my parents earned an honest living as factory workers. I followed in their footsteps. After I graduated from high school, I was assigned to the Yanshan Petrochemical Corporation's general services department to train as a cook. I was young and not at all happy with the assignment, but my father advised me to do whatever the Party asked of me. By 1989, I was nineteen and had worked at the cafeteria for two years.

At that time, I became obsessed with oil painting and started taking lessons from an art teacher. I spent my days studying how to paint.

Even while I was cooking at the cafeteria, my mind was drifting to the works of Van Gogh and Gauguin. I didn't know that the student movement had started. I wasn't at all sensitive to the political climate. A few days after former Party secretary Hu Yaobang died, I took a bus downtown to see an exhibition at the National Art Museum of China. Afterward, as I strolled around downtown, I saw students marching. They were carrying Hu's portrait. I stood watching on the sidewalk for a while and even dropped 1 yuan into a donation bucket.

You were still just an observer. When exactly did you get involved?

I was a nobody, just a sesame seed in a big pot of soup. It would be too presumptuous to say that I was "involved." There still weren't that many people in Tiananmen Square at the time. All the action was centered around the Wangfujing shopping district. And I was this kid dreaming of being a painter, who hated going to work. I got into the habit of running downtown whenever I got a chance. Everything I heard down there was so refreshing.

Ordinary Beijingers like me didn't join the students until May 20, when that idiot Li Peng declared martial law and troops were preparing to march into the city from several directions. On that day, workers at my factory orchestrated a large-scale demonstration to support the students. We first gathered in front of the Beijing train station. All of Chang'an Avenue and Tiananmen Square were packed with people. I stayed with my factory contingent, caught up in the excitement but without any real political motive. Many people were simpleminded like me, just being patriotic and supporting the students.

How many demonstrations did you join?

I would say four. When things heated up in Tiananmen Square, it was thrilling. Sometimes I stayed downtown overnight, sleeping on the grass. After the May 20 demonstration, my coworkers wanted to do more to help the students. They dispatched me to the Tiananmen student command center to seek an assignment. Young hothead that I was, I rushed into it without a second thought. The students had set up six or seven strict checkpoints in Tiananmen Square. I had my work ID with me, and each time the student guards stopped me, I went on and on, explaining why I was there. It took quite some effort to finally pass through the last checkpoint and get a glimpse of the command center, which had been set up in a tent at the base of the Monument to the People's Heroes. Several student leaders were wrapped in shabby grayish coats and looked unshaven and unkempt. I stood there unable to figure out who was who, so I just yelled out: "We are workers from the Yanshan Petrochemical Company. Do you need help? We have a big contingent." The students surrounded me and started sizing me up, then one of them said: "Let us think about it."

I waited there for several minutes and was just about to leave, when someone passed me a piece of paper with a note: "Please go to the northeast corner of Tiananmen Square and help keep order."

With that note, about a hundred of us from Yanshan Petrochemical occupied the northeast corner and kept order there for a whole night. Tiananmen Square was chaotic. Rumors were floating around, speculations about the government's next move, but Beijingers, rather than being intimidated, sprang into action. To use old Chairman Mao's words: The great masses had finally been mobilized.

It was a sea of people. Who could have counted? I was about to collapse from exhaustion, but the nobility of the human spirit around me kept me going. Many people showed up at the square to volunteer. They distributed food and water. An old man in his seventies elbowed his way into the square with the help of his daughter-in-law and handed me two big bags. His daughter-in-law explained: "We wouldn't let Dad come, but he insisted on bringing you food. Nobody could stop him." I was moved to tears. Sadly, that kind of pure humanity is long gone.

So did you stay in Tiananmen Square?

No, we were there for two days and then we went back. Over the next couple of weeks, I only went downtown once. I spent my time painting at home. On the night of June 3, I was painting with my TV on, when suddenly all regular programming stopped. There was an announcement saying something to the effect that people were not allowed on the street and that the government was taking action. I became very anxious. I couldn't sleep at all that night.

First thing the following morning I rushed downtown, prepared to die. I had been brainwashed by the Party since childhood about the army and the people being as close as "fish and water." Not even in my worst nightmare could I have imagined that the soldiers would open fire on people. I couldn't stop myself from going to Tiananmen to see for myself, secretly hoping that none of it was true.

The bus stopped at Tianqiao. I got off and walked to the square. Along the way, pools of blood were everywhere. One of my paintings depicts the scene from that day.

Were you able to enter the square?

No. The troops and tanks were clearing it out. I couldn't get in. I could only see smoke from a distance. But people could get through from the side streets. It was chaos: piles of debris here, sporadic gunfire in the air. When I got near Qianmen, I suddenly saw People's Liberation Army soldiers wielding body-length wooden sticks. I ran over to see what was going on.

You had a death wish?

I'm a pacifist. I may have been only nineteen, but I disliked extremist acts like throwing bricks and smashing bottles. I still clung to the belief that the soldiers wouldn't lose their cool if they weren't provoked. But as I moved closer, someone jumped out from a side street and threw bricks at them from behind my back. I [turned and] quickly waved my hands and yelled: "Stop! Stop! Don't provoke a conflict!"

The guy who threw the bricks ran away. Since I hadn't done anything, I just stood there with the courage of my convictions until a soldier standing opposite me shouted: "He's the one who did it! He's the one yelling!" I instinctively turned around. A sea of green uniforms was moving toward me with sticks raised above their heads. My body went numb and I started running.

Most peasant soldiers have short legs. Hard as they may train, they're no match for my long legs. More importantly, I was running for my life. At one point my legs started weakening and the iron tip of a stick came down on me, scraping my back. My adrenaline shot up, and I bounded forward.

I'm a Beijing native and knew my way around. I turned into a small lane. The soldiers got scared and stopped following me. But I ended up with a big purplish-black bruise on my back, which didn't go away for over two weeks.

How many people were running after you?

I was scared out of my mind. Do you think I was counting? I guess there must have been a few hundred of them. It was like they were chasing after a flock of ducks. I could feel that there were people all around me running away from the soldiers. A young guy only a few steps behind me got hit and fell down. He was immediately covered by a green-clad mass of soldiers raining sticks down on him.

By then I had dashed into a small lane near the old Beijing train station. When I saw the soldiers give up on me, I hid behind a broken wall to watch. [The guy who fell] was less than two hundred feet away. I could see very clearly. Only after the soldiers left him for dead did I dare come out to help him with several people who were hidden inside the train station. I took his head in my arms. He was still breathing, but his smashed head had changed shape.

There was no blood, but his head didn't look like a head anymore. It looked like a head painted by that foreign painter—what's his name? Bacon. I asked him, "Where are you from?" He responded, "Capital Steel." We intercepted a flatbed three-wheeled cart, put him on it, and rushed him to Tongren Hospital. The hospital corridors were packed with wounded people. We handed him over to two nurses who were covered with blood and we left. I was seized by grief and anger. My mind was in turmoil.

How many people were lying wounded or dead in that hospital?

I really don't know. We were not allowed to go in. The nurses were receiving patients at the entrance to the corridor. When I went back to the street, the tears were just streaming down my face. It was getting late.

June 4, 1989—that date has been etched into my mind and into my bones. All night I was preoccupied by big questions like "Where is this country going?" and "What am I going to do?" I found an empty bus near the Qianmen No. 5 bus terminal. Over a dozen distressed people were already inside—students, locals, workers, people both from Beijing and from out of town.

I waited until dawn to catch an early bus and didn't get home until noon. My blood was still boiling. I found a T-shirt and wrote on it with a paintbrush: "Give me democracy. Give me freedom." On the back of it I put the famous quotation by Dr. Sun Yat-sen: "The Revolution has not yet succeeded. Comrades, you must carry on!"

I put the T-shirt on and wandered around the Yanshan Petrochemical complex, telling everyone I ran into about downtown. Before long, a crowd had gathered around me at a crossroads, blocking traffic. A bus couldn't get through and all the passengers got off. The crowd asked me to give a speech, and before I had the chance to agree, they pushed and shoved, then lifted me on top of the bus. But people didn't think that was high enough, so they led me to a nearby scaffolding.

I was a kid, still totally inexperienced: What kind of eloquence could

I summon up? I shouted a bunch of slogans: "Down with Deng Xiaoping! Down with Premier Li Peng! Workers, strike! Businesses, strike! Oppose the government crackdown!" I whirled around like a grindstone, showing people what I had written on my T-shirt. All this later showed up in my indictment.

I assume there were a lot of plainclothes policemen in the crowd.

The crowd was all workers [whose families] had been with the company for two or three generations. We grew up together. Everyone was out of their minds that day—more than a thousand people. After a while they were all shouting slogans on their own. Some people even suggested we drive a bus downtown to fight the army. At that moment my father rushed over. People at the public security bureau had alerted him: "Your second-oldest son is staging a rebellion." He came as fast as he could, seized me as I was coming down from the scaffolding, and yelled: "You bastard!"

I stopped his hand in midair and shouted back like a hero: "Don't hit me!"

A bunch of students from the Second Institute of the Petrochemical Industry happened to be in the crowd. They didn't know my father. When they saw that someone was trying to slap their "hero," they went over to grab my dad and tried to beat him up. I promptly interceded, yelling: "Don't hit him. He's my dad."

After that, events took their course. The passion and excitement died down by that evening. My dad was really strong and wouldn't let go of me for anything. He dragged me all the way home. There was such a gulf between us. My belief in the forever glorious, forever correct, forever great Communist Party, its government and its soldiers, had been turned upside down, but my dad wouldn't agree with me. He was a real macho man. In my memory he had only ever showed vulnerability once, when my mother passed away, but this time he did it again. When we got in the house, he didn't try to beat me. Instead he said: "You went downtown on June 4 without even telling me. Do you know how chaotic it was there? You didn't come back at night. I hardly slept a wink. Each time I heard the wind blowing outside, I woke up and went to check your room. Your mom died young. If anything were to happen to you, it would be all my fault." He stopped and the tears came out.

With my father's rebuke, my whole mood came down. "I don't think I can undo anything," I said. "I'm sure they will arrest me. Why don't I find a place to hide for a little while? A significant movement like this won't be over soon. I suspect that the crackdown could trigger a civil war."

My dad didn't want to hear my analysis. "Don't make trouble again or I'll kill myself," he said. I couldn't argue with him. He still supported the Party, and he was my dad, after all. So I packed up some of my stuff and fled overnight to his native village in Hebei Province. My grandma was still alive then. I stayed with her. I was arrested on June 20, 1989.

That happened pretty quickly. Did your dad's tongue slip? Or did your dad betray you?

I wouldn't call it a slip of the tongue. When police came to our house and asked about my whereabouts, my dad immediately confessed, telling them that I had gone to live in his native village. He even gave them a detailed address.

He trusted the government and the Party. He had a friend who was the deputy chief of the public security bureau in Yanshan. My dad visited him and asked for help. The friend promised: "If you turn your son over to the police, we'll offer him lenient treatment." The deputy chief also contacted the local public security branch near my home, instructing them to take care of me. My dad thought that they would detain me for a few days, teach me a lesson, and then release me.

My dad came to fetch me at my grandma's house. He looked happy. He told me: "Wenjian, let's go home. The situation in Beijing has settled down. Everything is okay now." The two of us chatted, laughed, and walked toward the car. But when the car approached the village entrance, I saw two other cars blocking the road.

So it was a trap?

All the policemen got out of their cars. Someone came up to me and asked: "What's your name?" Before I even finished answering, he barked: "We are here to arrest you."

How many policemen were there to capture you?

Capturing a "violent criminal" who had escaped from Beijing was a great opportunity to showcase their accomplishments, so the entire county police force, over sixty men, was mobilized. They drove me to the Hengshui County Public Security Bureau, where they tied me to a big tree. Then I heard them excitedly phoning Beijing: "Wu Wenjian is now in our hands."

They interrogated me briefly. Before long, police from Beijing arrived. A police director from Hengshui led a group of his men to meet up with his counterparts from Beijng. He even brought a cameraman to record the moment. That director behaved like an actor. He stood at attention, saluted, and then raised his voice solemnly: "I want to congratulate our government on the successful crackdown on this counterrevolutionary riot."

Despite the fact that I was tied to a tree, I laughed so hard that I almost passed out. That director was apparently still living in the Cultural Revolution era. He didn't appreciate my laughing. He came over, pointed his thick fingers at my head, and mumbled through his teeth: "How could you be so arrogant?" He spewed out his words with venom. It was as if I had raped his daughter.

I was handcuffed and taken away. They put me in a detention center for two months. Then the municipal public security bureau officially arrested me, charging me with "counterrevolutionary activities of propaganda and instigation." On September 7, 1989, I was transferred, with a group of people facing similar charges, to the Beijing Municipal Detention Center. I was locked up there for more than six months.

How many people were detained in one cell?

A big one could accommodate a few dozen people, a smaller one seven or eight. The detention center was actually an old prison built by the Soviets in the 1950s. It looked very formidable. Once you walked into a cell, bunk beds were lined up on both sides of the wall. At the detention center, I saw Ye Wenfu, the well-known poet who wrote the famous poem, "General, You Must Not Do This!" During the student movement, Ye publicly resigned from the Communist Party. I sometimes heard him yell at the guards downstairs: "Fuck you."

The three people who had thrown eggs and defaced the Chairman Mao portrait that hangs over Tiananmen Square were also imprisoned there. One of the guys, Yu Zhijian, used to share a cell with me.

During the first wave of the crackdown, nine "violent criminals" from Tiananmen were taken out of the detention center and executed. There was one legendary case. A guy called Zhu Zhongsheng jumped onto a tank when the government troops first entered Tiananmen Square. He tried to pry open the hatch but couldn't, so he jumped off. Later, he was caught on camera. During both his first and second trials, he was sentenced to death. His hands and feet were shackled with heavy metal chains. They locked him up with other death row inmates. He was waiting for a final review, after which he would be on his way to the execution ground. Somehow the final review never came. So he ended up in that death row cell for two years. He was so traumatized that his body deteriorated into a skeleton. The court eventually commuted his death penalty. As you probably know, living in a death row cell was a nightmare. Every couple of weeks there were people being dragged out to be executed. Each time the door opened,

Zhu Zhongsheng would go through the same fear and anxiety. He lived in that fear for two years. While doing hard labor in prison, Zhu slept on a bunk bed above mine. We talked a lot.

I used to be locked up with twenty or so death row inmates. Getting your death penalty commuted was almost unheard of. He really lucked out. In comparison, didn't you feel pretty lucky, too?

I was nineteen years old and got seven years. I was lucky. On the day of my trial, they put me on a prison bus and drove me to the Beijing Municipal Intermediate People's Court. I was led down to the court basement where our trials were supposed to take place. A policeman shoved me into an iron cage. The whole trial process was embarrassing. Since all the rooms on both sides of the basement were fully occupied, the judge started the trial in the hallway. He looked like he needed to take a piss or something. He ran through the procedures fast. I had a court-appointed defense lawyer. He defended me by saying something like "Wu Wenjian was young and ignorant. I ask the court to consider lighter punishment" and so on.

It lasted a little over an hour. After a brief deliberation, the judge announced that my sentencing would be delayed. About a month later they delivered my official indictment. I was shocked to learn that I had gotten seven years. On second thought, it wasn't that bad, since I was only nineteen, and by the time I got out I would be twenty-six. Gradually, I got used to it. After I received my indictment, I filed an appeal. The intention was to buy some time and avoid being sent to do hard labor right away. The second trial was very formal. I didn't ask for a lawyer.

I defended myself: "I simply listened to Zhao Ziyang, who was then the Communist Party secretary. If I didn't listen to our party secretary, who would I follow? You charged me with the crime of overthrowing the government. I was barely nineteen. Was I capable of doing that?"

But there was no point in defending myself. The decision had already been made. Mine wasn't too bad. Many people suffered worse injustices. Have you heard about Zhang Baosheng? He was the youngest June Fourth thug in prison. No dad, no mom. He was only fifteen years old, and he got ten years, as I remember. Charged with the crime of beating up soldiers . . .

On March 9, 1990, I was transferred from the detention center to the Beijing Municipal No. 1 Prison. When I first arrived, I was constantly getting beat up by guards. That seemed to be the rule. Every new arrival would get beat up as an initiation ritual. The government seemed to pay a lot of attention to us. High-level officials kept showing up to inspect things.

Were most of the June Fourth thugs locked up there?

Those who had been sentenced to over ten years were mostly there. Those under ten years were incarcerated in Chadian, near the city of Tianjin.

What was it like in "reform through labor"?

Pretty brutal. We just worked and worked. After arriving at the prison, we went through some brief training and then began to work on export-related jobs, sewing coat linings and buttons for over ten hours a day . . .

The thugs were mostly ordinary Beijingers who had taken action out of anger with the government. They threw bricks or tossed bottles or baskets at the troops. Some had gone to halt a military truck or stood up to deliver an antigovernment speech. Others jumped on a tank. All had a common goal: to stop the troops from entering the city and slaughtering students. Later on, after the students retreated from Tiananmen Square, those guys became the core targets for persecution. But in a world where history is mostly created by the elite, people like us have no place in this historical event.

I met a disabled person who got ten years in jail. I found it strange when he told me about it, so I grabbed the indictment papers from him. He was charged with "slamming his crutches on a tank repeatedly, before staggering away elated." Another person, whose last name was Zhu, found an abandoned military supply truck. He and his friends emptied the vehicle and tossed the food to local people and students. He gave all the food away altruistically. When the truck was empty, he realized that there wasn't anything left for him, so he searched around and dug out a package of roast chicken in the corner of the truck. When he was caught, that piece of chicken became part of the evidence against him. He got thirteen years. When he told me about this, he sighed: "That was an expensive chicken."

We did every kind of work. We conducted inspections on rubber gloves used by sanitation workers and medical professionals. You would put each glove to your mouth and blow into it to check it for leaks. It was exhausting. During that time I also shared a cell with Wu Xuecan, former editor at the *People's Daily*. We worked in pairs. I would sew and his job was to remove the extra threads with scissors. After a year I was so skillful that I could sew buttons with my hands behind my back.

The factory we worked for was called the Beijing Friendship Clothing Factory. We sewed summer clothing in winter and winter clothing in summer. Lint was floating all over the rooms. Sometimes we sweated so much that my underwear was completely soaked. I wanted to smash up the whole goddamn little factory. I went on a hunger strike for four days, and someone advised me: "Are you for real? Just pretend." He then threw a piece of stolen sausage down on my bed.

I was released in 1995. They had reduced my sentence by several months. I hadn't expected that the reunion with my father would take so long. But his trust in the Communist Party remained unchanged. He didn't want to say a single bad word about the government. He still threatened me the same way as before: "If you torment me again, I'm going to kill myself." What could I do? No matter how hopeless his situation is, he is still my dad.

One by one, most of the Tiananmen thugs served out their sentences. As the saying goes, silent and odorless farts don't get people's attention. Nobody cared about us. As time went by, the aspirations and passions we held dear dissipated like passing clouds. We've been thrown into a world without mercy. Most former inmates I know have developed a strong aversion to politics.

To make a living, first I tried my hand at selling clothes at a local market. Since I was a painter, I began designing advertising graphics. It's simple technical work. My mind still lingers over that period. When I was first released, I was constantly painting tanks crushing innocent people, blood flooding Tiananmen Square, the Goddess of Democracy . . . I can't control my dreams and my hands. I'll never sell those paintings, even if the verdict on June Fourth is overturned. My hope is that by then, there will be a museum to showcase the deep disgrace of our nation during that time. I'll donate the paintings to that museum.

Forgive the digression. As far as jobs are concerned, many of my former prison buddies haven't been as fortunate. Most of them were ordinary workers. Times have changed, and they now have problems finding jobs and making a living. One buddy of mine ran a restaurant before 1989 and had a lot of money. When the democracy movement started, he gave away food and drink to students. He ended up in jail for more than ten years.

After his release, he opened a nightclub and helped many of our former inmate friends. He acted like a welfare agency. But when you mention the democracy movement to him, he doesn't even care to talk about his past involvement.

Not long ago I had a phone conversation with a former inmate. He carves seals. We really clicked. I told him that I had done a series of paintings depicting the June Fourth massacre. He interrupted me by saying: "Why are you still messing around with June Fourth? Didn't you have enough in jail?"

I answered: "We haven't avenged our sufferings yet."

"The passion in me is long gone," he said. "Don't touch politics again. It's too brutal and dirty."

He might be right. In the past two decades, the so-called Tiananmen elite both inside and outside China has written hundreds of articles about the movement. I used to read some every year. Not a single piece has been written about us thugs. It is as if we had never existed. The whole world seems to know only about the confrontations in Tiananmen Square between soldiers and students. Anything that happened elsewhere in the city has long been forgotten.

How do we define our group? Officially we're called "thugs." And people like you—historians, writers, journalists, sociologists, or the elite, all of you who have the opportunity to air your views—what will you say about those thugs who formed the core of the Tiananmen movement? The students and scholars delivered some stirring speeches in Tiananmen Square. They talked about fighting for democracy and freedom for the country and for the people. They sounded so idealistic, as if they had been determined to risk everything. They were so impassioned that the residents of Beijing were moved. People like us went to block military trucks so bullets wouldn't hit the elite. Little did we know that the student elite would run faster than rabbits . . . The student leader Chai Ling stood like an innocent angel near the Monument to the People's Heroes. She instigated and urged us into action. Then she ran away to the West and completely dropped out of the democracy movement. Of course, it's her freedom to quit. But don't forget about the fact that regular people joined the student movement because they were inspired by people like her, like Wang Dan, Wu'er Kaixi, Li Lu, and Feng Congde.

In my case, on June Fourth, I heard rumors that Chai Ling, Wang Dan, and Wu'er Kaixi had been killed. I was full of grief and anger. That was what inspired me to go up on that scaffolding. Too many people have paid too high a price. You guys will never be able to pay it back. But in one memoir after another, the writers only focus on what the students did. Right now, most of the former student leaders are doing very well. They're smart and figured it all out.

You probably expected too much of the intellectuals. In fact, Hu Yaobang's death in the spring of 1989 heralded change. Different intellectuals joined the movement out of different motives. Some thought that it would be like a change of dynasty, and they didn't want to be left out. They realized that if they didn't seize the historical moment, they would be deprived of the right to speak in the future.

Those who don't have the right to speak won't have a place in history.

Historically, that's the rule. The only thing that we can do is to dig out the truth and change the history that's written by the elite.

But I can't write. Many of us can't write—and even when we speak, no one listens. Families who lost their children in 1989 are lucky to have Professor Ding Zilin of the Tiananmen Mothers group as their spokesperson. But who is there to speak for the thugs of June Fourth?

The Idealist

Late one winter night, as an angry north wind was blowing through Beijing, Wu Wenjian, now my go-between with other thugs, led me along winding streets for nearly an hour. Bewildered, we were just about to give up when a dark shadow popped up out of a residential building on the opposite side of the street. Wu gestured and called over in a low voice, "Buddy, don't take the overpass." The dark shadow dashed across the road, coming right at us.

The shadow consisted of three men, and they pulled in their necks as we met. There was no need for introductions: everyone knew who was who. Wang Yan, tall and thin, explained that he hadn't been able to come out until his parents were asleep, because his parents watched him closely, afraid he would get into trouble. "Not bad," snickered Wu. "Forty years old and your parents still tell you what to do."

We walked for half an hour until we came to a little unlicensed hotel, where Wu took out his identity card and asked for a standard corner room on the top floor. By the time we were sitting cross-legged on the filthy bedding, it was nearly midnight.

We were all ex-cons, so of course we all smoked. Before long, clouds of smoke filled the whole room. We not only didn't open the windows, we pulled the curtains shut. My stomach was bothering me, but I just clenched my teeth. The tape recorder had been running for quite a while, but the others just blurted out one burst of nonsense after another. Time passed one drop at a time. I don't remember when it was that Wang Yan, the one I was going to interview, finally got around to answering my questions.

We didn't leave the hotel until six in the morning, our faces pale as wax, our heads heavy, and our feet light like a bunch of johns who had indulged too much in sexual pleasures. The markets were starting to come to life, although the curtain of darkness still hung closed over the city. A nearby breakfast shop turned on its light. We went in and had steamed stuffed buns and rice gruel. Wang Yan gobbled up his food. "Eat more slowly," said Wu Wenjian. "Isn't it too hot?" Wang Yan looked up from his bowl and said sadly, "Just think of me as a sleepwalker. I'm exhausted and I want to hurry back home."

———

Wang Yan: My name doesn't matter one bit. People despise poverty but not immorality, as the common saying goes. Everybody thinks people like us are stupid pussies.

During the 1989 student protests, the demonstrators filling the streets were all "stupid pussies."

After the death of Hu Yaobang, everyone rushed out onto the streets. It all happened so fast, there was just no time to think about things clearly. It wasn't at all like the Cultural Revolution, which lasted ten years and started white-hot, then was just kind of hot in the middle and then gradually cooled off. I was a worker, only twenty-four years old. Wasn't I just going along with the patriotic spirit of the times?

I heard that you were in college, taking advanced coursework.

Yes, I looked like the lead in a movie about city life back then: handsome, carefree, honest, and stylish. I was working at the steel mill near Shijingshan and studying law at one of the branch campuses of Beijing Normal University. Our teacher was very enlightened. I learned from him that Western law was three hundred years ahead of China's so-called Chinese socialist law. His ideas were essentially the same as Liu Xiaobo's Olympian view that "China needs to be colonized for three hundred years." My head was filled with ideas like "open maritime civilization" and "closed continental civilization," and the question "where is China going?" from watching Su Xiaokang's movie *River Elegy*, which became famous after China Central Television broadcast it. I was always looking for people to debate with.

You were already very enlightened.

Everybody else was enlightened, but I wasn't. The student protests of 1989 reflected what the people wanted. It was in the natural course of events. Hu Yaobang's character and the trust that he had built up in a few years had come to overshadow Deng Xiaoping. That nasty little shrimp was so envious that he became determined to tear Hu down. When Hu died, Deng quickly reversed course and rushed to proclaim him a "glorious proletarian revolutionary" and shed crocodile tears for him. Everyone from eighty-year-old women down to little eight-year-old kids could see through what Deng was doing. So everyone rose up demanding fairness, democracy, freedom—and that high officials make public all their ill-gotten gains. If they fucking didn't like it, well, they could use high-pressure water hoses on us the way they did during the April Fifth Movement of 1976, couldn't they? During that movement, some people got hurt, some people went to jail, but nobody got killed. But this time several hundred thousand soldiers surrounded Beijing. They opened fire and killed people. Who could take that? Who had ever seen that?

Early on the morning of June 4, I was riding a bright red bicycle and wearing a bright red T-shirt and a pair of green pants on my way to work. At about seven a.m. I passed by the Shijingshan District government office. Unexpectedly, the main road was cut off, blocked by several thousand people. There was an armored vehicle stopped at an angle, with a big stream of people swirling around it like a whirlpool. I saw that I was stuck there, so I just locked up my bicycle on one side of the road and pushed myself deep into the river of people up to the armored vehicle as if I were swimming. I bent over it and noticed that there were metal rings with hooks stuck in the caterpillar treads, as well as an iron club stuck in at an angle, so the vehicle was stuck there, unable to move.

That simple roadblock was quite something.

Chairman Mao said, "The lowly are the most intelligent . . ." Meanwhile, the soldiers were nowhere to be seen. I asked everybody where they were, but nobody knew. Even more peculiar was that nobody knew what had happened there the previous evening. Anyway, people were arriving in wave after wave, and they all felt the same righteous anger toward the same object, punching and kicking it. The vehicle was splattered with dirty smudges. Clubs, rocks, and bricks hit from all sides, leaving marks that looked like a dog had bitten it.

Everyone there was getting angrier and angrier, just as all of Beijing was getting angrier and angrier. They had shot and killed people, but we couldn't do anything about it. We just blew off steam against that useless piece of iron slag stuck there. The crowd's anger was so contagious that I got angry, too, turning into a bull who wanted to make his own run at the thing. I gave the armored car two quick kicks, which really hurt.

Just then someone whispered in my ear, "Let's burn it." I agreed at once. Soon everybody was shouting like thunder: "Burn it! Burn it!" Then someone handed me a lighter and paper. I turned around and said, "How do I burn that shiny, slippery pile of iron slag?" Someone came out of the crowd and tapped it all over until he found the hidden fuel tank. He unscrewed the cover. I stuck the paper into the fuel tank to soak it first, then I lit it and dropped it under the vehicle. "That won't work," someone said, and told me to light another piece of paper and drop it right down into the fuel tank.

The armored car immediately burst into fire, with flames that shot into the sky. The crowd applauded thunderously. It was satisfying! I took advantage of the confusion to find my red bicycle and continued on my way to work.

Were you afraid?

I didn't feel afraid at the time. But as I think back on it now many years later, I wonder just who it was who gave me the lighter and the paper and taught me how to set fire to that armored car.

I don't remember him; it was too long ago. But there were many plainclothes police in the crowd, so it may have been a plainclothesman who taught me how to set fire to the armored car. He might have wanted to provoke a big incident and then take advantage of it by calling it a counterrevolutionary riot. I was lucky, though. Most of the people who were accused of burning vehicles or smashing and looting during June Fourth were shot. Those who weren't shot were sentenced to death with a delay of execution at the very least.

At first Premier Li Peng promised, "We won't be settling old scores later," but after a while the newspapers and TV broadcasts were carrying stories every day about people who had been captured or were being brought to justice. I still went to work as usual. I had never been charged with anything and had never been to jail, so I thought that I was one of the lucky ones. That is, until the morning of July 23, when a notice arrived at the personnel and security office of my work unit, followed by swarms of police. I was arrested on the spot. Burning a military vehicle after the so-called clearing of Tiananmen was seen as a "heinous crime of flagrant defiance." Everyone was sure I would be sentenced to death, and if I had been caught earlier, at the height of the executions, I would definitely have been a dead man.

Things improved a little when I was transferred to the Beijing Municipal No. 7 Detention Center. I was at least able to lie down, and I was never beaten or mistreated by the other convicts. But I remember once a new person came in and was told to strip naked. Everybody was naked, so that was nothing unusual. But this new person was not only stripped naked but had to hold his underpants with his teeth, breathing heavily, dodging between everyone's crotches and mopping the floor as he went. He had to be quick like a rat, since if he didn't, he would get trampled or kicked. Then there was the miserable guy who was forced by the head of the jail to eat the roundworms that came out of his own body while everybody watched. He shat a total of six roundworms. He held the live worms in his fingers and put them in his mouth, crushed them with his teeth, and swallowed them. Then he picked up his soup, had a drink, and smacked his lips. He was not allowed to frown; he was only allowed to wear a smile on his face, as if roundworms and shit were the greatest delicacy on earth.

I can't take any more of this.

I didn't think that I was going to live. The judge announced that my verdict was life imprisonment. I was shocked. Was I going to appeal the sentence? Of course I wasn't going to appeal it. When I was escorted back to prison, the handcuffs and shackles were still on me, but I was in ecstasy.

I was transferred to Beijing Municipal Prison No. 1, like many others. In front is the infamous Turtle Mansion, with two floors, a domed roof, and thick iron bars all the way around. And so my "reform through labor" began. On December 26, 1990, several hundred June Fourth rioters were transferred together to Beijing Municipal Prison No. 2.

Final inspection of latex gloves was the work they assigned us rioters. We trimmed extra material off the edges and then checked the gloves for leaks. Everyone puckered their mouths and puffed into the gloves. With the puffs of air the talcum powder between the gloves would be blown off and into the air into mist-like balls. Soon our faces were completely white. Next our entire bodies would become white, like those hanged ghosts in a Beijing opera. At first we weren't good at it. Everyone had a daily work quota of two boxes, or 2,000 gloves. Then the quota kept going up and up. We had to work night and day. The police, to boost our morale, took the unprecedented step of not locking our cells at night, so the reform-through-labor "battlefront" ran all the way from our beds to the classrooms where we worked.

Why did they do that?

The cells were as narrow as rat holes. With talcum powder flying all over the place, we couldn't even make out the face of the person at the next bed, never mind go to sleep. The classrooms had windows and were spacious, so the air was much better there. In the dead of night, we were like a bunch of obsessed people, puffing air and packing boxes and crates. We were often still working at four or five o'clock in the morning like some kind of perpetual motion machine.

We didn't hear the far-off crowing of roosters. When the wake-up buzzer rang, we shook all over. Our bodies were as soft as noodles, oozing onto the floor and sleeping like the dead. During those days, some people performed amazing feats. They would only sleep two hours and finish sixteen boxes, or 16,000 latex gloves in all. Some people would be so tired that they couldn't get up, or ended up with silicosis for life. Some people just couldn't take it anymore. They would go crazy, stabbing themselves in the chest with steel needles. They wanted to die but couldn't.

What were those latex gloves used for?

The thicker ones were for daily uses such as washing pots and pans and could be purchased in any supermarket. The thinner ones were medical products that were used in hospitals. I heard that our gloves were exported from a Beijing latex products factory through many intermediaries. American companies had ordered the products.

Everybody knew it. One day, another June Fourth "arson rioter" named Shi Xuezhi put many slips of paper, written in English, inside the gloves, saying, "Please, kind person, pass along this message. Save us! Save China! Long live democracy!"

He was found out very quickly and had a very rough time. They threw him into a doghole, twenty square feet in size. After more than three months in there, he couldn't straighten his back at all. This fifty-something-year-old man was stripped naked while the police took turns shocking him with electric prods—under his armpits, on his neck, on his face, his navel, between the legs, on the bottoms of his feet, over and over again. When one prod stopped working, they would use a different one. The smell of burned pubic hair wafted through the air. Shi Xuezhi groaned over and over, his eyeballs looking ready to pop out of his head. He tried to resist, only to be brutalized even harder. He lost control of his bladder; his urine wet the floor all around him. But he never begged for mercy. He never did beg for mercy.

After that, work on the latex gloves screeched to a halt. We started knitting cashmere sweaters. On hot days we would be in there shirtless, threading needles and pulling the thread through, beads of sweat dripping everywhere. Our underpants were soaked through. The fine wool stuck to our skin. And the itch was like a hundred thousand ants hopping up and down on a hot pot. We would often knit for a while and then scratch our crotches for a while, pulling out a handful of pubic hair and mixing it into the wool sweater we were knitting.

Cashmere and pubic hair are both expensive things.

We also did some rock-bottom work, like processing plastic bottles and recycling foreign trash. That was dirty work, and after doing it all day we smelled of plastic bottles or of foreign trash. We folded paper boxes for Hanjing. *Hanjing* means stop snoring. It's a kind of fake medicine. Some of the prisoners tried it, but they still snored as loud as before. The biggest swindle was the paper coffins. Those were the boxes that dead people were put into before they went to the crematorium. Just put a layer of paint on a stiff cardboard box and it looks very realistic.

In prison, working for the crematorium?

That's what "stimulating the economy" means. Every convict is a machine for making money. Think about it. The cost of a paper coffin is very low, but it can be sold to the family of the dead person for many tens of times what it costs to make. For a while we spent a lot of time going in and out of a pile of coffins like we were ghosts ourselves. That was very scary. Some of us joked that if we just lay down in a coffin, all our problems would be solved. I expect that police would search around for a while and still not find us.

With hundreds and thousands of paper coffins around, it would be easy for one or two people to hide in there.

That's why the paper coffin business stopped and we made a 180-degree turn and started processing "pussy hangers."

What?

A gynecological speculum. It's used to look deep into the vagina to check if there are any gynecological illnesses. Don't make a fuss about it. We're both adults.

They were already made. We just had to sand off some of the metal burrs left behind by the machining. Don't underestimate these tiny gadgets. It wasn't easy. It was very demanding work and very tiring on the eyes. There were two June Fourth rioters who became model factory workers. Everyone nicknamed them according to their age, Big Pussy Hanger and Little Pussy Hanger.

Altogether, how long were you in reform through labor?

Not quite sixteen years, but the hardest part came later, when I got out of jail. Superficially I was free, but I still felt like a prisoner inside. I was forty years old. I had to adapt to society and learn some new skills. There was no use for what I had learned in prison. Times had changed too fast. Beijing was now several times the size it had been. Where could I find a place I belonged? My parents had grown old, and it felt awful to still be living with them, getting free room and board. I couldn't sleep at night. Was my whole life a mistake? Maybe I shouldn't have been such a hothead back then? Will the people of June Fourth ever be politically rehabilitated? And what then?

The Arsonists

It was a year later, another winter evening in Beijing, the sky turning the color of dark ink as the streetlights came on, when I saw Wu Wenjian standing with two more "arsonists," Zhang Maosheng and Dong Shengkun. We shook hands warmly and walked the streets before stumbling on a bright red storefront that drew us right in. We rubbed our hands together against the cold, sat down, and ordered food and a 56-proof bottle of Red Star *erguotou* sorghum liquor. Zhang Maosheng went first.

———

Brother, please excuse my directness. You were very young then. Were you really the one who burned that army vehicle on June Fourth?

Zhang Maosheng: Yes. I was sentenced to death with a two-year delay of execution and sent away for forced labor so they could observe my behavior.

What year were you born? What did you do before June Fourth?

I was born on June 23, 1968, so my zodiac animal is the Monkey. Before June Fourth, I was an ordinary worker at a machinery company in the Fengtai District of Beijing. In June 1989, I was not yet twenty-one years old.

My family used to live in Chadian, not far from Tiananmen. Every day after work I liked to take a stroll in my neighborhood. Starting in April, there were many student demonstrations. The demonstrations kept getting bigger, so the students stopped going to classes and the workers stopped going to work. I didn't have anything else to do, so I went out on the streets every day looking for excitement. Back then I was young and not well educated. I had no idea what politics was. I thought that the Party and government were having a hard time, what with so many people demonstrating against them day and night, occupying Tiananmen, making speeches, singing, distributing leaflets, going on hunger strikes and all. Those demonstrators were really messing up the heart of the country, and I thought that wasn't right. But what provoked me to burn that army vehicle was something that happened on the evening of June 3.

That day after dinner I went out as usual and wandered around. Just when I got to Fucheng Road, I saw a big group of Beijingers on the side of the street, discussing something. Curious, I squeezed into the crowd to see what was going on. A heartbroken woman pulling a small cart was crying inconsolably by the side of the road. Inside the cart was the mangled body of a small child. The people surrounding her were all talking and gesturing. They were very angry. From what they said, I gathered that the child, who was only eight years old, had been playing on the grass when the troops came. What does an eight-year-old child know? A soldier's bullet flew by and killed him.

Suddenly I felt my head explode and I started getting very angry. How could anyone do that? Not even an animal would do that. I really wished then that I had a rifle in my hands, so that if I came across some soldiers, I could wipe them out right on the spot! I don't know how much time went by. The crowd dispersed. I don't remember how I got home. I only remember that I felt dizzy, sick at heart, sick in the pit of my stomach, and that I was crying the whole time.

The next day, which would have been the afternoon of June Fourth, I wandered through the streets again. I came to a spot near one of the Peking University hospitals, where I saw many Beijingers carrying injured people on stretchers, running toward the entrance of the hospital, and trailing blood behind them as they ran. At that time there was a Beijing Normal University student standing up high somewhere, making a speech about different places and the numbers of people who had been shot at each one. There were just too many people to rescue. He said the beasts had gone crazy. Some people from the Red Cross had come to help the wounded, but they were shot down, too. How could the rifle barrels of the People's Liberation Army be turned against the people? My grief and my outrage grew as I listened, and I thought of the murdered child I had seen the previous day.

My heart felt like it had been stabbed. I wanted to find a soldier and do the same to him. What do you say, Mr. Liao? Wouldn't any Chinese person with a conscience, in those circumstances, have felt the same way? I wiped away my tears and kept walking ahead. When I got to the Madian Bridge, I came across a convoy of military trucks headed south but blocked by some students. You can see that kind of scene only in the movies these days. An astonishing, chaotic scene, like an invisible powder keg placed right in the middle of the street. The locals were all cursing, and spit was flying all over the sky. At first I kept wiping it off my face, but then I didn't care anymore. People kept jumping up to throw things at the soldiers.

The students, arm in arm, stood in the middle of the street between the crowd of locals and the soldiers. The stalemate continued for a long while. The soldiers got out of their trucks and shouted a few words before starting to shove, pull, and punch. I couldn't stand it anymore! I had repressed my anger for too long and now it surged up in my head. I yelled, "This can't be! This can't be! We can't let these sons of bitches with guns keep on murdering innocents! Compatriots, we have to all fight together to stop them from committing any more crimes!" I rushed over to the truck nearest me. There happened to be a piece of cloth over the fuel tank. I yanked off the cloth and took out a match I had on me, struck the match, lit the cloth, quickly opened the cap on the fuel tank, and stuffed the burning cloth into the tank. A tongue of fire crept along the cloth. Tongues of fire burst out and climbed into the air seconds later. In less than a minute the whole truck was in flames, with fire shooting into the sky.

You were very quick and efficient.

I guess my quick hands and feet made up for my immature head. Then I turned around and went home.

Didn't you hide?

Why should I hide? I was young and didn't think that I had done anything wrong. I didn't even think it was particularly serious. Several days after June 4, we started working again. When I was in Tianjin for work, they came to arrest me.

I think there were seven of them. That day the leader of that work site in Tianjin said, "Please go over there and help me move something." When I got there, I looked around and saw a group of police standing in a circle smoking. They had been waiting for a while. They began by asking, "Do you know why we've come to get you?" I said I knew why. "That's good," they said. "Don't make a scene; just come along with us!" They escorted me back to Beijing to a police station not far from my home, where they interrogated me.

Was it a secret trial?

I suppose so. Anyway, there was no audience and my family wasn't there. I suppose they weren't notified.

Later, when I got the written judgment in jail, I saw that I had been found guilty of counterrevolution and arson and had been condemned to death with a delay of execution. With just one piece of paper, a few people decide a man's fate.

At least you survived. Many others didn't.

Yes, those who survive can hang on for a long while. That mighty man Deng Xiaoping, didn't we survive him? Jiang Zemin hasn't got much longer to go, either. Me, well, I'm not even forty yet. I'll live to see the day when the people of June Fourth are politically rehabilitated.

That will definitely happen one day. You're certainly the most naïve June Fourth rioter I've ever met. What came next must have been a long stretch of reform through labor.

That was hard to take. Before I went to prison, when I was in a work unit, what bothered me the most was having someone order me around all day long. In prison, not only did I have to accept the orders of the people in charge, I also had to accept the beatings. My life was even worse than any animal's. During my whole time in prison, I cried only twice. The first time made a big impression on me. When I first got there, the jailer found an excuse to punish me. He locked me up in solitary, an extremely low and narrow cell. There was nothing but a wooden bed in there, about three feet wide. You needed to bend your head to stand up. Even turning around wasn't easy.

In front of my nose was a window the size of an outstretched palm. The glass was broken and there were some tangled dead vines growing into it. It was cold then, almost Spring Festival time. There was no day and no night in that doghole. I couldn't even smell the outside world. One day in the distance I heard a snatch of a song from the Cultural Revolution–era opera *Taking Tiger Mountain by Strategy*. Something like "We cross the immense forest, climb up through the snowy fields; our courage reaches the starry skies above." Some people must have been practicing for an entertainment program for Spring Festival. I was cold and lonely. I didn't know when I would ever get out of that little cell, or what new punishment might await me after I left it. My parents were in poor health. Would I ever see them again? Would I ever be able to marry a woman and bring her home to them? For all I knew, I might not even be capable of having children. When I thought of all that, my throat tightened and I started to cry.

I was in solitary for more than ten days, but it felt like more than ten years. I left a lot more mature. I seemed to have hit bottom. If I could handle the "little cell," what did the "big cell" have that I couldn't take?

Most of the other prisoners in the big cell were in there because of June Fourth. We were a bunch of pretty similar twenty-somethings, like a little grove of trees just sending out tender young leaves. Everybody talked to relieve the boredom. Everything was great when we were young: going to jail, committing crimes, and smoking opium. We had a good time fooling ourselves. I was a very simple kind of person. If everybody else thought a certain way, then I would think that way, too. But year after year of an endless stream of next winters and next springs, my beard turned yellow and my eyes got blurry. Seventeen years went by. I got out of prison. This year I turned thirty-eight. Those fucking butchers are still there sitting on top of the world. Do we ordinary people dare even say one half of one "No!" to those corrupt or profiteering officials? I'm just angry with myself for being so shameless that at my age I'm still living with my old father and mother. I really am a good-for-nothing.

My father is over eighty. My younger brothers and sisters are married and have children of their own. Making a living isn't easy. We are an ordinary Beijing family. We don't have any special family background or any money. In August 1995 they demolished our old house and resettled my family elsewhere. My residence at the time was prison, and since the government allocates new housing according to the household registration system, I wasn't allocated a place to live. My parents' apartment is 492.8 square feet in area. The room for me is just 97 square feet. Normally, someone my age would be married and have kids by now, and I would be helping my folks live a carefree life. But now they've been supporting me without compensation for nearly twenty years. They're in their declining years now, and I am still a burden. Do you think I can live a carefree life? What can I do? I didn't want it to be this way.

My mother suffers from facial paralysis. She was going to have an operation, but when she heard I was going to be released, she was afraid to have it because the hospital is so expensive. When I had just returned to society, someone got me a part-time job sweeping the streets for 100-plus yuan a month. With the cost of living being as high as it is in Beijing these days, 100 yuan isn't even enough to keep a dog fed, never mind a human being. So I thought it over and decided not to take the job. I spent so long in prison wasting my life, I didn't learn any life skills. A big guy like me, staying home all day, not daring to go out because going out costs money. I don't mind not having money for food or clothes, but with Beijing being so big, doesn't it cost money to ride the bus? If you walk a long way, won't you get thirsty?

I can't keep on going like this. One of my siblings found me a job watching bicycles. I was impatient and went to the work site that same day. They asked about my situation and I was upfront about it. They were dubious and asked, "You really went to jail because of June Fourth? You stayed in there for so long?" They seemed to feel very strongly that it had been wrong to send me to prison. They went and talked among themselves for a while. Finally, they told me that I was young and strong, and they didn't need my services for the time being. "Parking lots don't make much money and the pay is low," they said. "We'll find an older guy who can pass the time here while making a little money. It'll be better for both parties. Why don't you go on home now and we'll notify you when we need you."

Changing the tape, I turned to Dong Shengkun.

"Do you need to do the next one right away?" Wu Wenjian blurted out. "I'm afraid to take a breath."

"Let's take an intermission and have something to eat," I said quickly.

Wu Wenjian sighed. "We rioters, even though we live in this same city of Beijing, get busy with our own daily lives and rarely see one another. Today, thanks to Liao Yiwu, we have gotten together, so we should raise a few extra glasses." With that, we all stood up and clinked glasses of *erguotou*. Wu filled his up again and made a special toast to Zhang Maosheng and Dong Shengkun, saying in a loud voice, "You two have suffered hardships!" To show his respect, Wu went bottoms up first, followed by Zhang Maosheng. Dong Shengkun hesitated. "I still have to ride my bicycle home. My old mother is waiting for me at home."

So that no time would be lost, everyone attacked the food. Finally, Dong Shengkun put down his chopsticks and said, "That's about enough. I hope I am worthy of this meal."

Dong Shengkun: To this day I am still proud of what the people of Beijing did back then. All those people exposed themselves to the heat in the open streets of Beijing during the dog days of summer. To support the students in the heat, many old women brought them mung bean soup every day on their flatbed three-wheeled carts. My family was the same way. Almost every day my mother sent a free box of eggs, cucumbers, and tomatoes. She mumbled as she went, "Mustn't let those kids get sunstroke in this awful hot weather." There was rampant inflation in 1989, but the ordinary person's pay hadn't gone up. I made 80 yuan a month back then and gave 40 yuan of it to the students.

We didn't know anything about politics, much less overthrowing the government. All we thought was that the words and actions of the students in Tiananmen represented the feelings and aspirations of the people. Doesn't everyone want their own country to be healthier? The Communist Party says the same thing, but that's like a cancer patient announcing that cancer is what they wanted all along and calling it perfect health.

I had been in the army for three years. Later I worked making printing plates in a printing plant. You may not believe it, but when I was in the army, we were taught all the positive things: Love the Party, love the country, and love the people. In times of war, Huang Jiguang, who used his body to block the enemy's gun, was our role model. In times of peace, Lei Feng, who always did good deeds, was our role model. But when the guns started firing on June 4, all that was turned upside down. Who could stand it?

On the evening of June 3, I rode my bike to see my parents, who lived near Beijing [Workers'] Stadium. I hadn't been able to go to work for many days, and they were worried about me. The situation had already become very dangerous by then. Soldiers were moving into the center of the city, and civilians were out on the streets to block them. It was chaotic. From my home in Liubukou, I saw someone shot dead for the first time in my life. The badly mangled flesh lying flat on the ground beneath the bridge terrified me. I thought over the situation and realized that I couldn't move any farther toward Tiananmen. The rifle fire was like the spattering of roasting peas in a hot wok. It went on for a while, stopped, then started up again. Bullets don't have eyes.

I hesitated. Just as I was walking past the Cultural Palace of Nationalities on Chang'an Avenue, I could see, far away, a long line of tanks and armored cars rumbling toward me. Behind them was an even longer, endless line of military personnel transporters. The troops were moving very slowly. Their formation and the distance between their vehicles didn't change as they edged forward. Nervous infantrymen with live ammunition were walking along both sides of the convoy to protect it.

I've been a soldier myself, so I knew they weren't playing around. The human body can't stand up to iron. Many Beijingers were watching. People started getting incensed. Someone was shouting, and then people started charging into the middle of the street. Many people were yelling and cursing. I parked my bicycle and told people to stop insulting the soldiers. There was nothing they could do. They didn't want to enter the city, they didn't want to shoot, but they also didn't dare to defy orders.

I'm not brave like Wang Weilin, the Tank Man, but I couldn't let them drive straight in and slaughter indiscriminately the innocent people in the square. So I gathered up my courage and worked together with everyone to block the military vehicles. I even approached one of them, trying to melt the soldiers' resolve. Sitting in the vehicle was a gentle-looking army major. In a loud voice I tried to persuade him and his troops not to turn their rifle barrels against the people, so that future generations wouldn't hate him. He repeatedly sighed and waved his hand at me. What he meant was *Don't be foolish, I understand what is going on better than you do*. When I looked closer at the soldiers, I could see that many of them had red around their eyes, as if they had been crying.

I went for broke, yelling even louder. I had never been so articulate in my life. I said that I had been a soldier, too. We had been comrades in arms, in the same trenches. "If you obey orders and open fire at random, accidents might happen, resulting in death or injury for your very own brothers and sisters. The protesters are standing up for our country in its hour of danger. They're not doing it for themselves. They're doing this for *you*, during a national crisis, out of fear that you'll go down in history as evildoers. Turn around and go back, or drop your weapons and walk away. Don't just shoot because you can't stand to be insulted. The people are yelling insults at you because they feel this intensely. Why do they feel this so intensely? They don't have any personal grudge against you, so why would they be against you? It's because they can't confront Li Peng. They can't meet the arch-criminal. If you take offense and start firing just because of a few words, it will be murder. The life and death of the people depends on your finger on the trigger. Are the divisions among Chinese people so irreconcilable?"

The officer was moved. Initially, soldiers with live ammunition were standing in a circle around the tank, on hair-trigger alert, ready for anything that might happen on the street. But now, after that talk with the officer, he switched out the soldiers standing guard on the outside and replaced them with others who did not have live ammunition.

At that point I turned around and spoke to the crowd that was gathering all around and hurling insults at the soldiers. "Everybody, be reasonable. Control yourselves. Any sudden moves can only make things worse! The soldiers are not to blame. Soldiers have to obey orders. No matter how foolish the orders are, they still have to obey them. If you insult them, there is no guarantee that they won't feel some sudden impulse and start shooting and killing everybody. There is no need for that."

Only after the two opposing sides relaxed did I get on my bicycle and ride away. As soon as I got to my parents' home, they started crying, so deeply worried were they about me. My mother saw specks of blood all over my body. "Those bloodstains are from the blood of other people," I told her, but I was puzzled: How had all that gotten on me? That night we didn't sleep. I don't think anybody in Beijing slept.

During the day on June 4, my mother and father watched me in shifts. They wouldn't let me go out, but I was itching to go out all day. At six p.m. I saw my chance and went. My mother yelled after me, like, a dozen times, but I pretended to be hard of hearing. Never had I imagined that when I looked back, after having pedaled awhile on my bike, that I would see my father following me like a secret agent. "What are you doing following me?" I yelled at him. "I'm not a little kid!" When my father heard this kind of talk from me, he looked embarrassed. He turned around and rode off in the opposite direction.

I kept riding straight ahead. When I reached the Chongwenmen intersection, I could see flames lighting up the sky in the distance. As I got closer, I saw army vehicles on fire. The two in front were already up in flames. It was very hot, so I dodged around them and went behind the third one. The street was full of people blocking the vehicles, all in a state of wild excitement, moving their arms, screaming, and cursing. Standing in the crowd, my anger flared and I shuddered. I needed some way to release my anger. I heard a voice by my ear, "Set the tires of this son of a bitch on fire!"

As if driven by an invisible force, I went to the back seat of the vehicle and found two rags. Someone—I don't know who—had taken the cover off the fuel tank. It was easy. I put the cloth in the fuel tank, let it soak, pulled it out, lit it with the fire that was burning on the ground, and threw it at the wheels.

I was at a loss for what to do. A piece of cloth fell on the ground. Another was sticking to the tire. It burned for a while, then burned down to cinders and then unexpectedly went out. While I was waiting there, the vehicle didn't burn.

When I went home, I didn't take my unsuccessful attempt to burn a military vehicle seriously. I went to work as usual for a few days and then was caught. That was on June 10.

Did you have any accomplices?

No. As for how the truck burned after I left, I really don't know. I did want to burn a military truck. At that moment everybody was in a rage, and the crowd of angry, confused people completely blocked the road. Probably everyone there wanted to set those military vehicles on fire.

On the morning of June 28, my eyes dark from several sleepless nights, I was taken to the Beijing Municipal Intermediate People's Court for the trial in my criminal case. It took about an hour. I didn't say anything. The lawyer's defense was that when the accused burned the military vehicle, society was in chaos, and the crowd, including the defendant, didn't really know what was going on. He hadn't been watching television and so didn't know that Mayor Chen Xitong had proclaimed martial law. He kept on saying the defendant is an army veteran with a good military record and that he hoped that the court, in its sentencing, would consider these mitigating circumstances.

"A death sentence with a stay of execution is not the same as a death sentence," the head judge explained. "If the accused repents and makes a fresh start, and works hard to remake himself, then after two years the sentence can be reduced to life imprisonment. If you align yourself with the government and continue to behave well, life imprisonment can be further reduced to a definite term of imprisonment. You are still young and have a long way to go. You stumbled and fell, but you can pick yourself up again and one day return to society."

On August 30, I was transferred to Beijing Municipal No. 1 Prison. Later on I found out how hard it had been to save my life. My parents had been running all over the city, spending money begging people to use any special connections. Several of the leaders in my work unit had made special visits to the public security bureau to intercede for me, trying hard to convince the government that I was a good person and not someone who would commit a crime with premeditation. You find out who your real friends are over time, when something like this tests them.

And your wife?

She divorced me long ago. We hoped for the first few years that us June Fourth people would be politically rehabilitated after three or maybe five years. Later, by the time my sentence was commuted to life imprisonment, society had changed a great deal as well. People didn't care about their country anymore, only money. She gave up hope and asked for a divorce. Naturally, I understood. It was difficult for a single mother to take care of a child. When I went to prison, my daughter was just three years old. Now she's twenty-one.

I did all kinds of work in prison. I sewed clothes, I made bags, I packed chopsticks. I processed latex gloves that were exported to the United States. I even did farmwork. The old-time armor in Zhang Yimou's film *Curse of the Golden Flower* was all made by us by hand in prison. The prison, like everywhere else, responded to the Party's call to make money.

The work before 1995 was hard, especially processing the latex gloves. We would be blowing air into the gloves day after day and after a while our tongues would go numb, since it was poisonous. For a while we had to knit five sweaters a day. Strong young men doing women's work. There was a lot of poor-quality work that had to be redone. We would start from six in the morning and go until two or three a.m. the following day and still we couldn't finish the work. We would return to our cells to lie down to rest for a little while and then it was time to get up and go to work again.

Did you make any money for working yourself to death?

At the year-end account settlement, we would be given a bonus of 10 yuan or so. The money wasn't important. The most important reward was a reduction in sentence. We would skin ourselves alive—do anything—for our freedom. That I got out after seventeen years, two months, and twenty-one days in prison was the result of my excruciating hard work and the reform-through-labor "work points" that I had accumulated.

On the outside, like Zhang Maosheng, I looked for work many times, but as soon as people heard that I'd been released from reform through labor, they didn't want to hire me.

Human hearts are not what they were in the old days. If one of the people who got out before you would invite you to dinner upon your release, then you weren't doing too badly. The most money I ever got from anyone was 5,000 yuan from my teacher Jiang Qisheng. I hadn't wanted it, because this was money he had earned writing articles, something that he had thrown all his energy into doing, but he insisted: "Take it, take it. I can always write more articles and earn more money. You are in a worse situation than I am. Of all the people involved in June Fourth, you so-called rioters were the ones who have paid the highest price."

That made me cry. Liao, will you blame me for talking about this? How can an able-bodied person accept charity? We were a group that passionately supported the student movement, but after a few years Chinese people forgot all about us. Even the June Fourth elites in China and abroad rarely took our situation seriously or just pretended not to know anything.

A few days ago an old friend came to take me to the bird and flower market. We met a few guys who were taking their birds out for a stroll. One of them made a big fuss as he introduced me, saying, "This is Dong. He was one of the heroes who blocked the military vehicles on June Fourth. He was just released." To our surprise they started to jeer, saying, "Don't play jokes on us. June Fourth was so long ago, the people involved in that were all released ages ago! Then my friend made a great effort to explain, saying, "No, that isn't true. There are still many people in jail." They were astonished, saying, "Oh, then that story about Dong having been in jail is true! Everybody thought that you were trying to kid us!"

Have a drink, Dong. That will make you feel better.

I can't drink. I have to get home. You know, my daughter told me that now there's a popular saying going around on the Internet. "Don't miss out on the most important things in life: the last bus and the last person who loves you." Every night, my mother won't go to sleep until she sees me.

———

Shortly after eleven p.m., we left the restaurant. The north wind howled fiercely as if it were going to peel a layer off the earth. Dong Shengkun put on his quilted jacket and pants and his face mask, leaving only his eyes exposed. He rode away on his bicycle. We tucked in our necks and hurried toward the subway station. On the way we stopped for a moment with Qianmen in the background to take a picture. Before this, both Dong and Zhang had politely refused to have their pictures taken. I understood their situation, so I took a few shots of our empty chairs and a table brimming with picked-over dishes, with a towering bottle of *erguotou* in the foreground, looking toward the sky.

As we stomped our feet and chatted away, Zhang Maosheng mentioned he was in a Christian house church, thinking it would be a good place to meet people. I strongly supported that. "Give it a try. Maybe God will be more dependable than the democracy movement." But Wu Wenjian disagreed: "We should stick together and depend on one another."

I felt a warm feeling running through me, but we are men and can't hold each other's hands and express the closeness we feel. Before going down into the subway station, I patted Zhang Maosheng on the shoulder but didn't say anything.

Wu Wenjian was busy cracking a vulgar joke: "Hey, buddy, does yours still work down there?"

Zhang Maosheng, an honest man, laughed as he replied: "I haven't had a chance to give it a try."

Wu kept at it: "After I got out, mine stayed soft down there for a year or two. If you don't use it for a long while, even if you really want to, it goes soft before going into battle."

"It's that way for everyone who goes to prison for a long while," said Zhang. "Let's go. We could talk about that all night and still not be finished."

The passageway was empty. I couldn't help turning around. Zhang Maosheng was still at the top of the subway entrance, glimmering in the whistling wind. In an instant he was gone. He had gone off by himself, walking home.

The last train rumbled into the station. Wu and I were the only two passengers. Would I ever see Dong or Zhang again in this life?

The Captain

Solid as a stone tower, Liu Yi extended his huge, pincerlike hand and clamped it around mine. Wu Wenjian and I had switched buses several times and contended with the vicious winds of a winter night before we made it to the neighborhood food market where Liu was finishing up his shift.

At six p.m. it was already completely dark. The wind whistled around the ghostly streetlights. Our legs were stiff after just a few steps. Liu said the aboveground restaurants couldn't stand up to the wind and suggested we find an underground one. Soon we were walking straight into a little hole in the ground with an entrance like a mine and dashing down two flights of stairs. Down in those crowded cavities there were people coming and going from a mah-jongg parlor and there were nondescript young women in groups of twos and threes showing off at a karaoke bar. We hesitated just for an instant at the threshold of a restaurant, which looked no larger than a single private room at most other restaurants.

We sat down at a greasy table under a gloomy mineshaft light, just like four peasants from the Northeast having a little spree on payday. We ordered a big pot of bone soup. As soon as the fire beneath the pot was lit, the oil on the soup's surface began to spread. Liu picked up a bone and took a long suck at the marrow. I hurried to get the notebook and recorder out of my bag. "Liao," begged Wu, "can't we eat for ten minutes before we talk about all those heartbreaking things?"

We didn't finish talking until eleven, and there were still many bones left in the pot.

Liu Yi: First of all, I want to state my own personal views. I have opinions about this society, but I don't want to subvert it. Just the opposite. I am a patriot.

My family has been in Beijing for several generations. My father, an old Party member in the Ministry of Railways, went through all the political campaigns. I'm the fifth of six children. Except for my younger sister, all of us children had a rough time. My eldest brother was a businessman and was sent to Yanqing. My second brother, who served in the Ministry of Aerospace Industry, was sent to Baoji. My third and fourth sisters were among the educated youths "sent down" to the countryside, one to the Northeast and the other to Henan. I also spent a year in a work brigade at Daxing, in the Beijing suburbs. Mao alone decided the fate of several hundred million people.

When Mao died in 1976, I was finishing my work among the last group of educated youth who were sent down to the countryside. I came back to the city and went to work in the Ministry of Aerospace Industry. I worked there for a full four years. I got tired of it and tired of being victimized by the state enterprise system, so I decided to get out. I became a businessman working on my own. At first I sold chewing gum. I got up early every day and ran around the Wangfujing and Xidan districts of central Beijing with my backpack. In those days, chewing gum was very popular and easy to sell.

So you were a pioneer of the economic reform policies?

Far from it. In those days everybody thought that individual businessmen were all loafers and bullies or had an exploiter-class family background. Later, society opened up a little and I was able to move from being an itinerant chewing gum salesman to selling fruit at a fixed spot.

I made money and became fairly well-off, so I was able to help support my younger brothers and sisters for a while.

You had been brave and resourceful in the business world, so why did you get involved in politics?

No choice. If you were keeping up with things back in those "good times," that short-lived "thaw" in the eighties, you couldn't avoid getting mixed up in politics.

Wu Wenjian says you were thirty-three years old when you got involved in June Fourth.

I was unsophisticated. I even participated in the April 1989 Muslim street demonstration [despite not being Muslim].

Why?

Because government policies were discriminating against people on the basis of their ethnicity.

And the student protests?

I got into it unexpectedly. After Hu Yaobang's death, I would often walk past the Tiananmen gate tower. That was before the big demonstrations started and many hooligans took advantage of that to stir up trouble. The student demonstrations, the kneeling and the presenting of petitions, the intellectuals supporting them, and the authorities ignoring them—all that came later. Ordinary citizens like us were moved by the actions of the students. They supported the country and the people; they opposed corrupt officials and official profiteering. They were not out for anything for themselves. Even the thieves in the city went on a three-day strike from thievery. People got excited and organized themselves into groups with people they had never met before. They chose some representatives to help keep order in the square. At first it was a group of thirty to fifty people. Later it grew to over 200 people.

Who called it the Tiananmen Square Disciplinary Patrol Team? I heard that you were the captain.

I gave away the entire 2,000-plus yuan that I had saved selling fruit. That's why I was elected the leader. The job also required somebody both bright and passionate. The Disciplinary Patrol Team was actually set up before what became main organizations on the square: the Capital Autonomous Federation of University Students and the Workers' Autonomous Federation. We were also the first ones to put up tents on Tiananmen Square.

Mr. Liao, may I ask *you* a few questions? Who gave that first order? Who fired the first shot? Who burned the first army truck? Weren't the rifles that the crowd destroyed all worthless items about to be discarded, purposely sent there by the government?

I don't know.

That's right. You weren't there, so you wouldn't understand. On the evening of June 4, when two lines of martial law troops drove their tanks from either side into the square, they were going well over 60 miles an hour. Completely insane. At the time, there were still 20,000, 30,000 people or more who hadn't left the square. I left with the last group.

The density of bullets flying was like the screen in a sieve. Many people flattened themselves on the ground and didn't dare get up. Those fuckers! No other invaders shot down ordinary people in the streets with guns and cannons—not the Western powers during the Boxer Rebellion, not the Japanese devils, no one! But those People's Liberation Army soldiers, who claim to serve the people, slaughtered them in broad daylight.

I don't know how many got away. I don't know how many braved the rain of bullets to pull out the wounded. There was nothing wrong with running for your life, so how could there be anything wrong with risking your life to save others? Later, near the Workers' Cultural Palace, the first tank was set on fire. A division commander was inside it.

At 4:45 a.m., all the lights in the square were turned off, as usual. Before dawn, troops in camouflage entered the square. Realizing that the situation was beyond our control, I quickly gathered all the rosters, including the Disciplinary Patrol Team meeting minutes, doused them with gasoline, and set them on fire. That was probably the first flame lit on Tiananmen Square that night.

Many people gathered on the eastern side of the Monument to the People's Heroes hand in hand, singing the national anthem. A voice on the loudspeaker said, "Fellow students! Do not withdraw. We aren't doing anything wrong. Long live the students! Long live the people of Beijing! Down with bureaucracy! Down with corruption!" Later the speaker was shot and the loudspeaker went silent. One unlucky person was injured by a bullet and fell at the base of the Monument to the People's Heroes, where he was losing blood fast. A dense mass of troops started taking down the tents and, as if herding prisoners of war, surrounded us. The area around the monument was in complete disarray.

Finally, with rows of gun barrels aimed at us from both sides, those of us in the Disciplinary Patrol Team finally left the square with tears in our eyes. When we had gotten as far as the eastern side of the Great Hall of the People, a few students suddenly came running toward us from the other side. The soldiers pursuing them shouted, "Halt! Don't run!" No sooner were these words spoken than I heard the sound of a bullet sweeping the ground. Startled, I must have jumped six feet in the air when I heard that bullet. You're shocked? That's how our people's army killed defenseless civilians! The fuckers . . . the bastards . . .

How many people did you see shot down?

Five, including one female student, who covered her stomach as her intestines spilled out. Blood, moaning and screaming. Who would have thought that patriotism could lead to this? Our group withdrew but did not disperse. A dozen or so of us were left.

Where did you hide?

First I went to a friend's home. Nobody dared go outside or use the phone. That friend was very loyal. Ten or more people gathered at his place. We all ate and slept together there, but he didn't complain. On June 7, I noticed that there were suspicious characters wandering around nearby. I immediately led the group to another location, a large farmhouse that belonged to a farmer in Fengtai District, where we stayed for another ten days or so. We didn't have much money among us, so we couldn't go far and we had to go back to our friend's house. So we were found out.

There's nothing to say about it, really. In an instant, my friend's house was completely encircled, caught like in a vise. The police knocked on the door, came in, shouted some orders, and began the roll call. Each time a name was called, a person was handcuffed. When it came to me, they called my name three times. I didn't answer. A local police officer from the precinct station slapped my face and said, "Why aren't you talking now? You're the one we want."

We were sent to the Beijing Municipal No. 7 Detention Center, where fifty-one of us were crammed into a cell designed for about ten. Except for seven or eight ordinary criminals, we were all June Fourth rioters. Forty-seven of us were in leg irons. We were packed so tightly in the cell, there was no way to lie down. We were beaten and interrogated. I spent nearly a year at the No. 7 Detention Center. It was a miracle I didn't become a cripple. Later I was transferred to Paoju Prison [in Dongcheng District, Beijing] and then to Qincheng Prison [in Changping District]. There we ate stewed eggplant every day.

I ate stewed pumpkins for several years in prison. To this day I'm allergic to pumpkin.

I used to be as solid as a bull, but after a half year in prison, I lost over twenty pounds and became just skin and bones. Even worse, there was nowhere in that human-flesh warehouse to wash. We all got scabies. In the middle of the night, the sound of dozens of pairs of hands scratching was like muffled thunder. Did you ever see a scabies bite as big as an egg? The pain was excruciating when the pustule broke and you rubbed it with your fingers. Still, the itching never stopped. I remember when I was at Paoju, we needed to get permission from the group leader to go to the latrine pit. We had to go with another prisoner and the two men would squat down butt to butt. Sometimes, just as we were urinating, we would suddenly be ordered to stand up. If we reacted too slowly, we would be drenched by a hose. That wasn't too bad during the summer, but it was awful in the winter.

I got my indictment about six months after I went to prison. You had to plead guilty. There was no way out. They were going to beat you to death and condemn you one way or another. The crime was organizing a mob for an armed counterrevolutionary rebellion. I was also charged with (1) creating an illegal organization, (2) arson—though I wasn't personally involved in any—and (3) blocking military vehicles. I was sentenced to eight years in prison for this combination of offenses.

I spent time at Beijing Municipal No. 1 Prison and Beijing Municipal No. 2 Prison. Mostly I sewed overcoats, skirts, and shoulder bags. I remember for a while we worked day and night, doing extra shifts to make latex gloves for export to the United States. After a week of doing that, my fingers got bent out of shape. Look, after all these years my fingers still haven't gone back to normal. Naturally, if you had money, you could bribe the guards so that you didn't have to work.

When my prison sentence was finished, my elder brother and younger sister came to take me home from prison. We wept in each other's arms at the main gate of the prison and then the three of us walked in silence toward the bus stop just outside the wall.

By then all the revolutionary ardor had blown away like a cloud of smoke, hadn't it?

While I was on the inside, I thought that people involved in June Fourth would be quickly rehabilitated. But first one and two, then three and four, then five, six, seven, eight years went by and not a word. It was fine with me that nothing happened. We didn't expect to be greeted with fresh flowers or applause. What enraged me, though, was the way we were discriminated against when we returned to society. I remember how, when I got on the bus, the ticket seller gave me a hard shove. "What are you doing?" I asked him. "This is not a place where people like you should be standing," he answered. Anger roared up in me. I couldn't understand what had happened to people's memories in those years. How did ordinary people become a bunch of demons with bared teeth and such snarling faces? Even if I had murdered someone or committed arson and had now been released from reform through labor, he had no right to insult me. Fortunately, my brother and sister calmed me down. I unclenched my fists and said, "Little brother, I just got out of prison today, so it's supposed to be a happy day for me. But I'm not afraid of going back to prison. I caution you not to get yourself all bloodied up because of a trifling insult."

The ticket seller fell silent. The other passengers gave me a look as strange as the freedom I just regained. The bus shook as it made its many twists and turns. *It's been eight years*, I thought to myself. *Didn't the bus routes stay the same? Route 9 goes past Qianmen; we're on Route 10, which should go past Tiananmen and the Chang'an Avenue stop, and then we'll be home.* Suddenly the bus turned without even nearing the edge of Tiananmen Square. I was so anxious I started yelling, "That's the wrong way! Where are you taking me?"

"It's no mistake," my elder brother answered. "Our mother has moved to Wukesong."

"Why does she live there?" I asked, now in a whisper. Then I suddenly understood. My brother and younger sister were being careful to avoid Tiananmen Square. My memories of that place were just too painful.

The bus circled around to Gongzhufen, where we got off. We got on another bus. We wasted a lot of time going that way, but finally we made it home. My younger sister knocked on the door. My mother asked through the door, "Who is it?" It was the thin voice of my mother, which

I had heard since childhood! The voice I had dreamed of for so long! I wanted to answer her, but it felt like a big rock was blocking my throat.

At that moment, when mother and child met, my ears were roaring like a passing train. Amid that roar, I cried out loud, "Mother!" and knelt down at the door. Eight years. On one end of the measuring stick of time, my mother had a full head of dark hair and was strong and healthy. Now, on this end, my mother's hair was snowy white, and she trembled and tottered. She helped me up and into the room, mother and child hand in hand, both crying. My mother could only keep repeating, "My child, my child, it's so good you've come back!" Over and over. "Mother . . . Mother . . . ," I said, "these years have been very hard on you, waiting for my return. I'll make it up to you. I'll be a good son. I won't be so hot-blooded and impulsive, and I won't waste my time trying to do something for this broken country."

My family all wept together. My mother and my elder brother's wife went to the kitchen to make dumplings, and I sat listening to their chatter. "My fifth-born loves my dumplings. Today I'll make dumplings for him with my own hands. Look how thin he's gotten over these years! Maybe he's even forgotten the taste of dumplings!"

I was a grown man, but tears streamed down my face again. When the dumplings were put on the table and everyone gathered round, I still felt an awful tightness in my chest, I couldn't eat a single bite. Mother sat pressed in very close to me. She kept trying to pick up a dumpling to put on my plate, but her hands were trembling and the dumpling kept slipping away. Finally she managed to pick one up and raise it to my mouth. "Fifth-born, at least just eat one and make your mother happy. Such is life. Look on the bright side, okay?" I managed a smile and bit down on the dumpling, then tried to swallow it without chewing, and I choked on it.

That night, during the reunion dinner, even as the dumplings got cold, none of my family ate much. It grew dark and soon all the streetlights along all three miles of Chang'an Avenue, the Street of Eternal Peace, were twinkling brightly. "Fifth-born, there's something that we've been keeping from you," said my brother when he saw that I'd calmed down a little. "Our father is dead. Just before he died, he kept calling your name. He said that he couldn't die without seeing you."

The news hit me like a thunderclap. I knelt down again. I looked through the windows to the sky outside and kowtowed three times to my faraway father. I said inwardly, *Father, although you were worried about me, the one you were thinking of most is Mother. I know why you kept calling for me. Rest assured.* He had died the year before I got out of prison, from late-stage lung cancer, a few days after going to the hospital.

It was only after a year or two that I was able to adjust, with a great deal of difficulty, to the changes in society. Once when I went to a gathering of classmates, one of them was shocked by my appearance. He looked me up and down. "Are you really Liu Yi? You aren't someone pretending to be him?" I didn't know whether to laugh or cry. "Weren't you shot and killed by the martial law troops?" he asked. "We all thought you died a long time ago."

"You could try pinching me to see if I'm a ghost," I said, and then he actually pinched me before confirming I was alive. Everybody laughed a very complicated laugh, full of regrets for all that had happened. In people's minds, I had been dead for many years. Now they saw me alive and appearing in public. Wouldn't that be disturbing?

How did you make a living after that?

Our old house had been torn down. I built a plastic shed nearby. On a low patch of ground, I laid a brick foundation just over three feet high, then made a small shop there. All year, in all seasons, I would eat, drink, and shit in that primitive shed.

You lived like a migrant worker.

That's right. The urban management officials kept coming to check up on my shop, and every time they came I would kneel down in front of the leader of the urban management team and call him whatever made him happy, even "Daddy," so long as he allowed me that small space to survive in. Later the street committee did a study and had me move to a different location, so I built a new shed there and opened for business. I worked from dawn to dusk for another year. Business gradually got better.

Weren't you like the great majority of Chinese people, brainwashed by daily life?

I was depressed. Nobody could stand to listen to what had happened back then. I could only go by myself to stroll around Tiananmen. Somehow or other I came to that spot beneath the flagpole, at the base of the Monument to the People's Heroes, where the tents of our Tiananmen Square Disciplinary Patrol Team had been pitched near the June Fourth headquarters. These days, crowds of people, several layers deep, gather to watch the raising and the lowering of the flag. Many people come from outside Beijing to watch with reverence and with hot tears in their eyes, listening to the national anthem and looking out at the marching soldiers. But I stand far away, puffing on cigarette after cigarette. I go through a whole pack each time. I think about how Chinese people are all like that fucking Ah Q, in the famous story by Lu Xun. They can't wake up. It makes me think that June Fourth was in vain.

In vain? It's hard to say.

I wrote about my feelings in a few articles, but I haven't found anywhere to send them. Later the police started paying special attention to me, sometimes visiting me several times a day, knocking on my door at night.

Everything I wrote was confiscated. I still remember one fragment of it. "With a clear conscience, I return to society. It is my fate to endure hardship. But what I see are people who have changed! What I smell is the stinking air of decay! What I run into is one corrupt official after another! I want to stand up and call out to the future, just as I did in the past, call out to my trampled compatriots to wake up and see their lives for what they are—a paralyzed present, worse than the life of a pig or a dog."

Then the police set a trap for me. They took advantage of a time when I was going to the Xijiao food market to ask for repayment of a 2,000-yuan debt to arrest me without explanation. After a quick trial, they framed me for burglary and sentenced me to four years in prison. Unbeknownst to me, they had set up a twenty-four-hour monitoring device on my small shop.

You were worth the trouble for them? How did demanding repayment for a debt turn into burglary?

I'd made arrangements to meet someone at his house. When I entered, it was completely quiet. I had just called out twice when I realized I'd been trapped: *I've been had! I've been had!*

That second time going back to "the palace" sounds like what happened to Lin Chong in the classic novel Water Margin, *unsuspectingly entering White Tiger Hall and being framed there. Many June Fourth rioters weren't even out of jail at that point.*

That happened in 2000. I was in Beijing Municipal No. 2 Prison for a year. Then I was transferred to the Chadian farm, where I joined a group of small-time crooks. That was a miserable and frustrating experience that I would rather not talk about. I sewed leather balls at Municipal No. 2 Prison and planted cotton at Chadian. Because I had skills, I was the in-house chiropractor for the officials in charge of discipline and education. They cut my sentence by half a year for that.

That time, when I got out, I had to go home by myself. Fuck, being sent away for burglary, I was too embarrassed to ask anyone to come and get me. I was flat broke. Even my clothes were a gift from one of the "team leaders" in prison. The prison gave me 40 yuan for traveling expenses, so I got on a bus and went back to Beijing. Besides family, I'd become distant from everyone else, so for a while I didn't know where to turn. I went back to Tiananmen again and sat smoking beneath the Monument to the People's Heroes. It was completely dark by the time I finished my pack of cigarettes. Tears rolled down my face. I felt like a stray dog yearning for his old home, the place where he'd pissed many years ago, always remembering the smell of urine in that spot ever since.

I walked around all night, stopping here and there, and didn't return to the western suburbs until the next day. When I finally reached home, I nervously went upstairs and knocked on the door. After a long time the door opened. My mother stared at me blankly until she said: "Fifth-born, you've come back! This time, even if you are a beggar, your mother will go with you."

Your family didn't know you were getting out of prison?

They should have known. I suppose they were just having an argument behind closed doors when I arrived. The faces of my elder brother and his wife looked darker than storm clouds. I forced a smile and went in to greet them, asking how the family was. "We're doing all right," my elder brother said. "Let's eat." We all sat around the table eating and fuming. I don't remember exactly why; maybe because my brother said something about my returning at a bad time. We exploded, pounding on the table and the bench. "It would be better just to leave," said my mother.

When my elder brother's wife in the kitchen heard that, she threw the pots and smashed the dishes, yelling, "Do you want to go? Then leave right now! Nobody's begging you to stay here."

"Come on now, sister-in-law," I said, "does that sound like something a decent person would say? I know what you mean. I've been in and out of prison twice and don't have a penny to my name. I'm also getting older. Are you afraid that poverty has destroyed my ambition, and that I'll just want to hang around here all the time to get free room and board? You would be ashamed even to have me as a neighbor. God knows, I only came here to see my mother for a moment. As long as she's well, I'll be at peace, even if I have the rotten luck to die in the street and be buried in some random place."

"If you two are so attached to each other," my sister-in-law said with a laugh, "then I'll do you a favor and let you be together."

What did your elder brother say?

He just hid off to the side. I went inside, helping my mother gather up some basic items and rolling them into a bundle. When the two of us left, mother and child, it was already past eleven p.m. All the shops had closed and the buses had stopped running. The once busy and noisy streets were now empty.

My mother was seventy-eight; she was used to what life might bring. And I had gotten used to the undependability of human relationships. I had fallen out with my friends and with my family. I'd gotten used to all that in the ten or so years since June Fourth. That night I had only 27 yuan in my pocket. My mother was having trouble with her asthma as she walked. I really didn't know where to turn.

You can't take an old person to go sleep in the open.

I looked all over for a public phone. When we got to Wukesong, I saw a small shop that was still open. By then it was past midnight. I thought of an old buddy I'd been on very good terms with for twenty years—from before June Fourth to just before I went to prison for the second time. Full of confidence, I called him up. The call went through. He was driving a cab.

"This is Liu Yi," I said, "and I don't have anywhere to stay. Where are you?"

"On the road, taking a customer somewhere," he said. "When did you get out, buddy? Why didn't you call? At the very least I could treat you to a meal."

"I just got out," I said, feeling a wave of warmth inside me, and then I told him everything that had just happened. Could he come and pick us up and give us a place to stay for one night?

He promised to do it. I hung up the phone. Twenty minutes passed. I saw my mother leaning against a wall. She could no longer stand up, so I put down her bundle and had her sit down. I called again and got through. "I'm on a long trip," my buddy said. "We won't get there for at least another ten minutes. Even if I drive pretty fast, it'll still take me another forty minutes to get to Wukesong to pick you up."

In those years, when people despised poverty but not immorality, as they say, your buddy's life wasn't easy, either.

After an hour had gone by, I called him again. He picked up the phone and apologized again and again: "On the way back, I picked up a short-distance customer, a woman. She hadn't been able to catch a cab, so I picked her up out of a feeling of professional responsibility."

"I can wait until the end of the world," I answered, "but my old mother is very sleepy."

"I'm sorry to let your mother down," he said. "Wait another ten minutes! This is the last ten minutes. I'll be on time!"

He wasn't going to come.

After another twenty minutes I called for the last time. His phone was off. Even the boss of the small shop couldn't help laughing bitterly. "You're really having some rotten luck. Take good care of your mother. I have to close."

My heart felt cold, very cold. It was past two a.m. I'd never thought this could happen. Still, I had to act as if nothing had happened. I helped my mother get up and said in a loud voice, "Let's go!"

We kept walking, I don't know for how long. The streets were completely empty now. We didn't see anybody else. A car passed by maybe once every ten minutes. The traffic lights blinked continually. Mother walked and walked until she was so tired and weak that she slid down to the ground like a slippery noodle. I quickly put her on my back and ran, covering two bus stops' distance to a small hotel near Gongzhufen.

The clock on the wall read 3:50 a.m. This hotel had been open for over ten years, and I used to go there often. Seeing an old man on duty, I put on a big smile and tried to charm him. "Is General Manager Liu here?"

"He isn't here."

"How about Mr. Qu?"

"Not here, either."

"Since none of my old friends are here," I said to him, "I want to discuss something with you. My mother and I don't have anywhere to stay tonight. As you can see, it's nearly dawn. Could you let my mother sit here for a while?"

"Did the precinct station give you a certificate?" he asked.

"We just had an argument at home and we haven't had a chance to go to the precinct station yet."

"I can't do that. If you don't have a certificate, then how do I know who you are?" he replied.

"May I use the phone?" I asked.

"What if you use the phone to commit a crime?"

I started getting flustered and angry. I controlled myself for a while, then I said, "You can make trouble for me, but not for my mother!"

"This has nothing to do with me."

"Don't you have a mother, too?"

"Swindlers may have mothers, but aren't they still swindlers?" That was his reply.

I was already too tired to argue with him. So I stopped arguing and said, "All right, after daybreak we'll continue theorizing about whether or not I'm deceiving you." And as I helped my mother down to the hotel floor to sit, I had an idea. I summoned up the courage and asked to borrow an old bicycle from the hotel, leaving my mother as security. "Mom," I said, "you stay here for now. Wait for me to get back. Don't leave until I come back."

I got on the bicycle and pedaled fast in a daze to You'anmenwai. Day was just breaking. I hadn't slept for two days and my eyes were red and stinging, but I saw some words written on a wall: "Room for Rent." I braked sharply and asked about it. The landlord happened to be squatting right there, barely awake and looking like a mess, his hands tucked in his sleeves. I didn't hesitate. "I want to rent a room," I said.

"Fine," he said. "Take a look to see if it suits you."

I had to bend over as we went through the low door, about the height of a child. After adjusting to the dark, my eyes started to make out the place: a microscopic room with a bed made up of some stools and a wooden plank. But there was enough bedding. And I wasn't going to be particular. All in all, it was a little nest where we could escape from the elements.

"How much is it a month?" I asked.

"Four hundred yuan," he replied.

"Four hundred is all right," I said. "I'll bring someone over now and give you the money at noon." He hesitated a moment. My heart jumped up into my throat. Luckily, the landlord agreed to give me the room. Then I hurried back and brought my almost completely exhausted mother there to rest. Nearly eighty years old, she'd never had to suffer like that before. I was an unfilial son. With 26 yuan in my pocket, I went to my younger sister's home. What do you think was the first thing my younger sister and her husband said to me?

They didn't need to say anything. Giving you a bowl of hot noodle soup would have been the best thing to do.

I told them about being out on the street with Mother. I didn't complain about my elder brother's wife. "A person like you who can't adjust to the times," said my younger sister's husband, "will be bad luck to whoever comes into contact with you."

"I paid for my younger sister's education," I said. "What right do you have to look down on me? Today, if it weren't for my mother's sake, I would rather die than walk into your house."

"But you didn't die, and still you came," he replied.

"Just stop," I said. "This is different from before. I, Liu Yi, swear by Tiananmen and before those dead brothers of mine, that if I can't make something out of myself in this screwed-up world, I will kill myself."

I couldn't hold back tears as I walked away back down the street. On an empty stomach, I borrowed a three-wheeled cart near our rented room and used my 26 yuan as capital to buy vegetables wholesale at the morning market, then took them to busy places and sold them retail. If heaven had wanted to destroy me, I would have run into the urban management brigade coming to confiscate my cart, and I would have fought them to the death. But everything worked out. I made three trips, and by noon I'd earned over 100 yuan, so I used it to pay part of the rent. Mother and son had a meal of noodles by the side of the road.

After selling vegetables for a few days, I found work for myself as the all-weather watchman for a company. That meant that while other people worked eight hours a day, I was on duty twenty-four hours a day. I didn't have a choice. Other people got 800 per month, I got 1,300. That's the law of the jungle, survival of the fittest. When they hired me, I took the place of two and a half people, so it made sense for them, too. After a month or so, I had enough for a cell phone. After three months, I had enough to buy a scooter. And so gradually I felt less aggrieved about the insults that I'd endured.

After working as a watchman for three months, I quit and started selling fruit. The local police station was kind enough to lend me a three-wheeled cart. Every day at three or four in the morning, I would head out to pick up some stock, because it was cheaper early in the morning. I wouldn't get home until past ten at night. I was so busy that sometimes I didn't have time to piss even when I really wanted to.

All in all, I sold at least two cartfuls every day. I had to sell out the fruit on the first cart by seven a.m. if I was going to make a little profit that day. Once I had made it in the struggle for existence, I needed to get a registered residence. For months I went to the district housing office at eight or nine a.m. every day. One day they simply told the security guard not to let me in.

I gritted my teeth and decided I would have to be hard to shake: I would block traffic. One day, when I was standing about three hundred feet from the district government building, I blocked a car. Looking at the license plate, I decided it was a high-ranking one. Grabbing onto the door, I asked, "Are you the district leader?"

"What do you want?" one of them asked.

"Are you the district leader?" I asked again. I was caught totally off guard when the driver put his foot on the gas and the car rocketed forward, dragging me along for about twenty feet. Both my shoes fell off. If it weren't for my strong hands and tight grip, I would have been slammed into the gatepost ahead and killed or crippled for life. They kept driving into an underground garage, yelling at me nonstop to get off. They went in circles around the garage a few times. I momentarily lost my grip on the car door and fell on the ground, terribly scratched up. They ran away and I limped along, giving chase for several hundred feet. That got me some attention. The district housing office finally allocated me a 100-square-foot place to live.

So you finally settled down. Have you gotten married? I noticed you took two calls during the short breaks in our conversation.

Speaking of my wife, I want to tell you how I really feel. She's really something. We've known each other for two years. She knows everything I do. She supports me in everything I do. When times were really hard, we've cried in each other's arms. She always says, "Don't worry. Don't be discouraged. You have me!" Yesterday we went to her family home, and I heard her saying to her younger sister, "Big Brother Liu really had a tough time. If any of you show him disrespect, I won't let you get away with it."

Does your mother still live in that first room you rented?

She still lives in You'anmen, but we rented a different, slightly better place for her. This year she's eighty-three years old. There isn't enough room for her at my place, so what can I do? We can only take care of her rent and her living expenses, and go over to check on her as much as we can.

I'm not counting on my brothers and sisters to help. I'm not angry about it, but who was it that told the Chinese people to move into this era of reform and opening when everyone would only care about themselves and would lose their moral integrity? So now is there any choice but to look forward to an era of flourishing corruption? Why in the world do ordinary people like us hustle every day doing exhausting, backbreaking work? So that we can eat! Early every morning, we rush out the door to go to work, we come back at noon to grab something to eat, and soon it's time to go out the door again. When evening comes, it's wok, bowl, oil, salt, and the other necessities of life again. Most of life we live in cycles. When the end comes, they say, "Sorry, it's your turn to be laid off."

I've seen for myself how many people in their thirties and forties are being laid off from work. I see them every day at the food market looking for rotting vegetables. I'm doing all right now, but some simple repairs to my small and shabby little home cost me 10,000 or 20,000 yuan. I now owe over 10,000 yuan. We have to live.

Following what Deng Xiaoping said back then, you went into business and were among those who "got rich first." But then you got involved in June Fourth, became a rioter, and then had a long rough road after that. Do you regret it?

June Fourth was the most glorious period of my life. More than when I ran around trying to make a living, and more than when I set out to make my "fortune." I don't regret it at all. Although I'm now in my early fifties, every part of my body is still in good shape. I have faith that I can hold out for the day when the people of June Fourth are rehabilitated and the wrongly accused ghosts of that day will finally find peace.

The Squad Leader

We were waiting in a distant Beijing suburb when a wan-looking forty-year-old man appeared, and Wu Wenjian jumped up. The two old rioters embraced each other tightly for a long time, like two hyenas locked in combat.

Hu Zhongxi readily opened up for two or three hours and at the end showed me a manuscript he had written, called "In Commemoration of the Fifth Anniversary of June Fourth," which contained the following words: "At that moment everyone had to make a choice: to be courageous and resolute, to flee, or to submit to tyranny and become an accomplice to evil."

After our interview, Hu got up and said it was time for him to go. "I'm surrounded by my wife, my parents, and my children. Every time I go out, they get very worried."

Hu Zhongxi: My life changed completely after June Fourth. During all the years that the Communist Party imprisoned me, my family spent a lot of money, made many trips, endured endless worries and sufferings all because of me. I owe so much to the love of my family. It's a debt that can never be repaid. My life is a total failure.

What did you do before the student movement?

I was working-class. The highest directive of Old Mao was that the dictatorship of the proletariat depended on us. My work unit was an import-export supply depot. On May 12, 1989, I went to the Beijing train station to meet a committee leader to discuss some business. But when I went there, I got swept up in the mass movement and took part in the street demonstrations, a lot like the angry patriotic youth of today.

But today the only place you see the angry youth is online.

There was no Internet in those days, and no such thing as virtual reality. If you were patriotic, you went out and showed it in public and actually did things. On May 19, army tanks started to enter the city en masse, taking different routes. At Liuli Bridge in Fengtai, some tanks were blocked by the people, and at other places, too.

The troops hadn't yet gotten the order to fire on people.

Right, many of the soldiers weren't even armed. We were all very excited, like we were celebrating a holiday. On the evening of May 20, I completely lost my voice from yelling slogans with the demonstrators. I was even at the front, holding a banner. After that, the leader of the Capital Autonomous Federation of University Students sought me out and asked me to be on the standing committee of the Beijing Workers' Autonomous Federation.

I didn't say anything, I was embarrassed. But on May 22, we independently established the "Black Leopard Death-Defying Squad." We had over fifty members, including workers, students, and people from outside Beijing. I was the squad leader. Our main responsibilities were maintaining order, providing moral support to the students, and supplying everyone, including local soldiers from the army awaiting orders, with food and drink. In addition, we maintained mobile sentry posts, made timely reports about any problems, and passed along information about the situation at various intersections.

You took care of the soldiers also?

Of course. When martial law had just begun, the Communist Party put those young peasant soldiers on the far, undeveloped fringe of the city, brainwashed them, and prohibited them from watching television or reading the newspapers. So the only authority for those soldiers was the word of their officers. When those ignorant soldiers were ordered to leave for Beijing, they had no idea at all of the true situation. So we civilians would patiently explain to them what was going on. The sacred duty of soldiers is to protect their country. What were they doing marching into Beijing? Why were so many soldiers needed in the capital city? Look around: Do these people look like counterrevolutionaries? On a hot day we give you Popsicles that we won't even buy for ourselves. What kind of scoundrels would do such things?

How did the soldiers react?

They just hung their heads like zombies. Water dripped from their faces. I couldn't tell if it was sweat or tears. They must have been ordered not to talk with the crowds. So when they couldn't refuse anymore and accepted the Popsicles, they would say "Thank you" or just nod and smile.

Who would have known that in an instant the whole world would tumble into darkness? In our squad we had a kid, just seventeen years old, who had grown up in an army compound. One day this very bold young man and his team of five or six ran into a soldier on the street. The team came to a halt. To their surprise, the soldier panicked, dropped his weapon on the ground, turned, and ran.

The kid got an assault rifle and 200 rounds of ammunition for nothing. I wasn't there at the time; I only heard about it later. I advised them to throw it away immediately. He refused to let go of the weapon, arguing that he was going to go into the mountains and fight a guerrilla war. "Just you and one lousy rifle?" I said. "That's ridiculous."

The kid didn't understand. We had to force him to throw away the rifle and bury the ammunition. He was very stubborn. In front of us, he buried a few bullets on the south bank of the river. Later, when we relaxed our watch, he disappeared with the gun. Most of the kids were young and hot-blooded and didn't think about consequences.

The day they captured me was my twenty-fourth birthday. What a birthday I had! I very nearly didn't live out the day.

Where were you when the troops started massacring people?

In Tiananmen Square. The southeast corner. I was walking by myself and ran into someone I knew. I greeted him and kept walking. Suddenly, I heard a hissing sound and a bullet brushed by my mouth. Instinctively, I tilted my face to the right, and immediately I saw stars before my eyes and hot blood rushed from the soles of my feet up into my brain. Stupidly, I hesitated for a few seconds. Oh, fuck, they were really shooting? And they weren't shooting those rubber bullets people talked about. I started running with all I had as the bullets pursued me. Waves of numbness came over my head, my arms, my waist. Where the bullets hit the ground all around me, sparks flashed everywhere. My pants felt warm; I must have pissed myself.

Fortunately I'm short, not a big target, so I escaped with my life. It was total chaos as many people fell around me and their blood squirted into one, two, and then many pools of blood. More than ten people lay on the ground around me. Their agonized cries and screams didn't seem human. Those of us who hadn't been hit kept running, with no time to look around and grasp the scene clearly. I remember yelling as I ran: "You can't aim your rifles at the people! You can't aim your rifles at the people!" That was the slogan of the chief of the "Black Leopard Death-Defying Squad" as he fled. Was that worth anything?

Another group, the "Northeast Tiger Death-Defying Squad," set up a machine gun at the Monument to the People's Heroes. Liu Xiaobo led a group of people to ask them to disarm themselves. Later, stubborn resistance didn't make sense anymore, so we dissolved the Black Leopard Death-Defying Squad. We pooled together some money and ration cards for those team members from out of town and sent them home.

The revolution ended before it could be proclaimed.

I thought so, too, so I continued going to work. On June 12, my birthday, I found a small restaurant and had a few cups of alcohol, two cold dishes, and a plate of chicken feet. I thought of how our patriotic efforts had failed and of the many people who had died. I thought I should treat myself well and celebrate my birthday. I was still thinking about that, and my cup had just been filled, when I felt a rifle at the back of my head.

It was like in a movie. "Don't move or we'll shoot!" they yelled. Then they held me down and took me to the second floor of the local police station, where they pushed me into a darkened room. Several policemen surrounded me and started beating me without explanation. I rolled on the ground and curled up into a ball and managed to protect the most vulnerable place on my body. The most vicious was a short policeman, who kept kicking me in the crotch. I screamed in pain, "You fucking bastard, why do you have to kick me there?" Well, the little bastard grinned hideously. He then pulled me up and hit me there with his knee.

Then it was electric prods, heavy boots, clubs, and the legs of chairs—whatever they could get their hands on. Sometimes they would have me kneel down, sometimes they would have me crawl, sometimes they would have me lean against the wall and give me a big kick. They would interrogate me as they tortured me. If my answer was a little too slow, they would hit me with two high-voltage electric prods, one in my chest and one in my back. That gang of beasts tortured me from six p.m. until three a.m. I half lost consciousness and stopped noticing the pain, nearly collapsing. Finally, even my tormentors were too tired to do it any longer, so they stopped for a while. They left someone to guard me at the door. When dawn broke, a guard teased me: "You got beat up pretty bad. Don't you want to escape?" I didn't say a word, just cursed him silently. *Escape?* I thought. *You're just waiting for the chance to kill me so you can earn some points.*

What questions did they ask you?

Who were the members of the Death-Defying Squad? What did you do? What division of labor did you have? What are the occupations, addresses, house numbers, and so on of the members of your gang? How would I know? We organized spontaneously. Before that, we didn't know each other. Much later I found out that the kid with the gun had gotten scared and given the gun to someone else. That person was even more scared and turned both the gun and himself in to the police, telling them how he came to get the gun. The police tracked down the kid, which led them in turn to many members of the Death-Defying Squad.

Early the next day I was transferred to a detention center in Dongcheng District. Every cell was crammed to overflowing. Even the corridors were full. We were all June Fourth rioters. During that special time, a total of twenty-six prisoners were packed into a space meant for eight. We were packed in tight, like spoiled canned fish. It was nauseating. Even my dreams were nauseating.

How did you sleep?

I had been beaten so badly that everyone had the heart to let me lie down. I lay down for about twenty days. After I got a little better, according to the rules, I would straighten up like a rod and sleep lying on my side, so that I would take up as little space as possible. I couldn't turn over. If I badly needed to turn over, I would beg the people on my right and on my left in advance and open myself up like a clamshell; then, once I had moved, I would close myself up again as tightly as I could.

With everyone packed so tightly, flesh against flesh, the steamy, stinky sweat turned the cell into a misty public bathhouse. But we never bathed. We couldn't even wash our faces or our hands. Fortunately, the food was very bad, and the hunger made us all lethargic, too weak to move. Later our bodies were covered with scabies, every single one of us. That gave us something to do. Everybody scratched themselves everywhere. Pieces of skin flew all over. Later, large sections of our flesh began to rot. The itching drove us crazy. Somebody who had been scratching for hours and hours without being able to stop the itching suddenly screamed at the top of his lungs, "Please kill me!" That got the government's attention. But except for applications of tetracycline, we got no medicine. Lice, fleas, and mosquitoes all had their way with us. It was torture.

Tetracycline can't stop the itching.

We got hungry fast. It shows that even when you put people in ratholes, they can still survive. We were supposed to get two steamed buns at every meal, but the police hated us rioters, so they cut it back to one bun per meal. When I first went to jail, I couldn't swallow those buns. I thought that even stray dogs on the outside wouldn't eat that stuff. But after being in jail awhile, that steamed bun started smelling better than chocolate. I couldn't just gulp it down in two or three bites; I would savor it in small mouthfuls.

Things went on that way for nine months. Many of my fellow rioters got their verdicts and sentences and left. Many more common criminals were put in the cells, and they ranked above us in the prison pecking order. The guards would tell them to supervise us as we mopped the floor and cleaned the toilets. Because each bed took up at least the space of two people standing, they ordered the rioters to sleep in shifts. If it wasn't your turn to sleep, you had to stand up straight.

The criminals even mimicked the police by interrogating us. They would pretend to be judges delivering verdicts and handing down sentences. You had to tell your story in detail. If you refused, they would find ways to have even more fun, like ordering rioters to slap one another. When it came to me, I thought to myself, *We're all brothers from the patriotic movement. You can hit me, but I certainly won't hit you back.* The jailer saw that I was disobeying orders, got angry, and punched me. The back of my head hit the wall hard and left a scar that still hasn't gone away.

Even stranger were the farting investigations. If someone was found to have farted, he would immediately be given a good beating. In there, they control your thinking, your behavior, your eating, drinking, and shitting, and even your farting is not spared. What kind of country is this?

A hermetically sealed country.

Later it got colder and a single layer of clothing was no longer warm enough. The detention center allowed family members to send packages to prisoners. Our jailers ordered us to write letters asking for good-quality soap and toothpaste, and then they stole the packages when they arrived.

From the Dongcheng detention center, I was transferred to the No. 7 Prison, where I stayed for another year and two months. The No. 7 Prison was a little better. At the very least, it was only one prisoner to a bed there. Just after I arrived, though, I was shocked by a cattle prod many times. They just wanted to show a new prisoner that they were tough. They trampled all over me and gave me shocks for a long time. They even stepped on my face, nearly breaking my nose.

(*Wu Wenjian interrupted to ask, "Did they shock your thing down there?"*)

Sure they did. I think they'd just shocked my mouth when they moved down to my anus, asking me, "Did that feel good?" Then they shocked my thing. All the hair on my body stood up straight, then I lost consciousness. I'm embarrassed to say it, but I also . . . I also lost control . . .

(*Wu Wenjian asked: "Shit or urine?"*)

Why do you need to ask about it in so much detail? Anyway, everything just came out.

When did you receive your judgment?

On November 17, 1991. My court appearance was the day of the U.S. attack on Iraq during the First Gulf War. The Communist Party took advantage of international upheavals and the fact that the West's attention was turning away from the June Fourth massacre to pronounce hurried verdicts on our group. That morning, still suffering from a fever, I got my ten-year sentence. The lawyer was very fair-minded and tried his best. I also tried to do everything I could. But things were going in a certain direction already, and there was nothing I could do about it.

When I was imprisoned at Qincheng, my lawyer made a special trip to see me. My crime was incitement to counterrevolutionary armed mass rebellion. What weapon did I have? Throughout the entire period of the student protests, I never yelled any reactionary slogans like "Down with the Communist Party." I didn't throw any bottles or bricks. But they just convict or kill whenever they please.

Although I was a low-level political prisoner, I stayed at Qincheng for two or three months before being sent to the Beijing Municipal Detention Center in Daxing County. About one hundred June Fourth rioters were jailed there.

Do you know what a *"weng"* is? It's a big rubber tube. Each time it's whipped, it makes a *weng* sound. Every time you committed an offense there, you'd get *"weng*ed*"* at least a dozen times.

We weren't beaten up as often, but we worked longer hours. Mostly we did garment processing. We worked ten or more hours a day sewing on buttons, cutting thread, and hemming. Even if we had worked until the end of the world, we still couldn't finish all the work. Working with fiberglass was the toughest. After finishing work, we'd lie down and feel all the stinging and itching on our bodies. By the time I got out of prison in 1998, I was in bad shape. I didn't have the money so I didn't go to the hospital, just bought some pills at random to take myself.

After my ten years in prison, society and people's hearts had all changed. I was pushed out to the margins of the margins of society. Nobody paid any attention to me. I had to depend on welfare to get by.

Did you stay with your parents?

They had an apartment that was about 200 square feet, with five mouths to feed in it: my parents, my elder sister, my nephew, and yours truly. I stayed put from 1998 until 2003, when the old house was to be torn down. Since I'd been in prison, my household registration was canceled. As a result, I didn't get the 96,000-yuan rehousing fee that I would have otherwise gotten as the occupant of a house being torn down. All I got was the 20,000-yuan low-income supplement. I panicked and went to the precinct station and the street committee office, but it was useless. I was so upset that I bought a can of gasoline and was going to go to Tiananmen to self-immolate. My wife found out, but couldn't stop me so she called 110, the emergency number. Then the police intercepted me and wrestled me to the ground.

"What are you doing?" asked the police.

"I'm not doing anything," I said, "just taking a walk."

"What are you doing walking around carrying a can of gasoline?"

"I found it on the side of the road," I said.

They didn't know what to do with me, so they confiscated the gasoline can and released me. I had a good wife.

When I got out of prison in 1998, a former colleague of mine saw that I was down on my luck and introduced me to her. She was a migrant worker from Chongqing. Beijing women looked down on me, so I had to look for a woman from out of town. We saw each other for ten months and then got married.

We have a six-year-old daughter. My wife later started a small hair salon. I also found some odd jobs and worked hard to save money. Life finally got better. But all in all I won't get anywhere in this life. I have no technical skills and no diploma. I can't do hard labor for long periods, either, because my arms and legs get weak and clumsy. Society is changing. Even some Party members are being laid off, so who would want to hire a low-level counterrevolutionary like me?

Can you go into business?

I don't have any capital. Anyway, if you're not a swindler, you won't make any money.

Do you regret what you did during those days?

Before I die, I want to tell my daughter how there came to be enmity and malice between her father and the Communist Party, and how I don't regret a thing. I refuse to concede defeat. Her father may be a poor good-for-nothing, but when the critical moment came, he kept his honor and proved himself a man.

The Street Fighter

The name Jiugong means Old Palace—several generations of Qing dynasty emperors kept a magnificent residence there—but today the place is just a distant suburb of Beijing, a dump.

The day Wu Wenjian and I showed up there, a gray mist was shrouding both heaven and earth. From time to time a few shafts of sunlight fell through the gaps in the dark clouds as if a filthy hand were scratching the surface of the clouds until they became bleeding scabs. A frigid wind hit us head-on and sent a few plastic bags scurrying into the air. A dark rain followed. We fought our shivering battle of attrition with the cold until twilight, when we finally sat down in a threadbare restaurant called Foolish Son's Hot Pot City.

We had an appointment to meet the Sun brothers. We waited until late that night, but there was still no sign of them. Fortunately, the slow-going Wang Lianhui did slink into the restaurant, looking listless. He worked as a security guard in a dance club. At first he shook me off, refusing to answer any of my questions, but after a few drinks he agreed to be interviewed in place of the missing Sun brothers.

———

Wang Lianhui: My family has been in Beijing for a long time. In 1989, I was twenty-two years old, doing temporary work in an electronics factory run by our village. I didn't know anything about politics and had no interest in getting involved in it, either.

But . . .

But I plunged right in when it came up unexpectedly. I made my own bad luck. On the evening of June 3, on my way back from my girlfriend's home, I happened to pass by my home village of Jixian, where I saw many people, angry like a raging storm, blocking the entire street. I got off my bicycle and hurried around the edge of the action. Just as I was about to avoid it all, and possibly could have gone on to live an uneventful life forever after, I ran into someone I knew. He called out to me from a distance, "Lianhui, Lianhui. It's still so early. Why are you going home?"

"It's already past nine o'clock," I replied. "I need to get up early to go to work tomorrow morning."

"Tomorrow's Sunday," my acquaintance said. "How can you be going to work? Let's join up with this patriotic demonstration."

I was astonished. He was right: it was Saturday night. I had been muddling along aimlessly. The gears of the factory machinery must have been wearing down my memory. So I turned around and followed the crowd. In the dim light I could see the crowd was getting bigger. They looked like they were walking to a fair.

There was no sign of soldiers at all. There was just one armored car parked crookedly at the side of the road. People said that several dozen armored personnel transporters had come from the direction of Nanyuan Airport. They rushed by in a gust of hot air and soon they were in the far distance. Nobody dared to block them. No matter how angry we ordinary people were, even if we had the heart, we didn't have the guts. This truck, however, had barely entered the highway before it came to a T-shaped intersection. It turned without slowing down and ended up hitting a big poplar tree. In a puff of smoke, a poplar tree the width of a washbasin was uprooted.

That guy must have been blind.

That chunk of iron was very solid! It could turn over without being damaged, but now the engine was stalled. The military situation was critical, so the army abandoned the car by the side of the road. It was very hot. Several university students stood on the armored car and made speeches with sweat and tears raining down their faces. They said that the martial law troops were shooting wildly, killing and injuring large numbers of unarmed people. That Tiananmen Square had become a river of blood. Who gave them the right to murder people? they shouted. Did Li Peng and Deng Xiaoping have the right to indiscriminately slaughter innocent people? These butchers called themselves the soldiers of the people, but in reality they were worse than wild beasts.

The speakers attracted a large crowd of at least several hundred people. Everyone was furious, but with no idea where to direct their anger they just ran around cursing. I don't know who it was who said in my ear, "Let's smash the damn thing!" I jumped on top of the armored car a few times. Many others, all young people, followed suit. We punched and kicked it for a while, but the iron didn't yield an inch. I got a brick and smashed it hard against the armored car but only succeeded in making my hand numb. The armor still didn't budge. Someone handed up a crowbar. I took it but could find no place to use it.

I wanted to pry the thing open, but there wasn't even the tiniest opening. Hot blood surged into my head, but I couldn't find anywhere to vent my anger. I smashed the scope of the antiaircraft machine gun mounted in front of the hatch and then smashed the two periscopes on either side of the vehicle. We wanted to paralyze that murderous machine completely. Then someone suggested dumping a few buckets of water on it while the machine was still hot. The parts would shudder and fall apart. But where would we find water along the edge of the road? "If we really can't find water," I said, "piss will do!"

I was kidding. Besides, we were in front of a few hundred people, both young and old. I wasn't crazy. Later the court verdict took that joke seriously, claiming that I was a congenital scoundrel who had pissed on an armored car, a crime that was especially serious. It claimed that my piss had nearly suffocated all the PLA [People's Liberation Army] soldiers inside the armored car . . .

There were still people inside the armored car?

They hadn't had time to get away. People said that after the armored car hit the tree it kept lurching forward for several dozen feet before the engine stalled. During those days, with everybody in Beijing raging mad, all it took was one person crying out and people from everywhere would rally together like when the Boxers fought the Western invaders back in 1900. The "people's soldiers," aware of the wrongs they had committed, feared that people would beat them. So they followed the example of the tortoise and stayed in their shell, determined not to leave it. But I had come later and didn't know that. Besides, that hunk of metal, once its iron pimple was locked tight from the inside, was totally seamless and watertight.

Later it became a joke in prison. Everyone would point to me and say that I was the June Fourth rioter with supernatural powers. "He pissed once and suffocated an entire car full of the government's 'revolutionary warriors'!"

There were about ten of them in that armored vehicle. They waited until everyone dispersed before showing their faces. People came and went all night as if it were a night market. The weather was like the people that night: hot and dry, lots of thunder but little rain. Inside the vehicle the temperature must have reached 100 or even 120 degrees. Most ordinary people would have fainted after only a short while. Even well-trained special forces would basically have turned into steamed meat. If only I had known that there were people inside of it!

Do you regret it?

I was only twenty-two, a very ordinary, ignorant person. It was really extraordinary that I could emerge from the crowd and be so bold. Most Chinese people are insulted all their lives but just clam up and suppress their anger. The political atmosphere of 1989 transformed everyone in an instant, making them noble and pure. They weren't thinking about anything, not even themselves, except stopping the martial law troops from going into Beijing to murder the students. If I had escaped that misfortune, some other hot-blooded youth, by some other strange coincidence, would have stepped forward to take my place.

Finally when I was exhausted, I jumped back down, squeezed through the crowd, and went home. On the way I met a neighbor who called out, "Lianhui, Lianhui!" I stopped my bicycle and walked with her to a secluded spot. She looked carefully all around but didn't look at me.

Suddenly she asked, "Did you smash the armored car?" I hemmed and hawed. "If you really did smash it, you should hurry out of town and hide until things calm down and then decide what to do."

I was worried, too, but still I argued with her. "Who saw me smash the armored car?"

"There were a lot of people around watching."

"I didn't see any police," I replied.

"Do the police have the word 'POLICE' etched on their foreheads? There were many plainclothes spies around tonight. The Daxing County police station and the precinct stations turned out in full force. Even the county police chief went out dressed as an old peasant to mix with the crowd."

I thanked that woman from the neighborhood. I said that I would give her a gift when I got my pay. She waved her hand at me. "Don't be an idiot. Don't wait to get your pay. Run away tonight."

Someone tipped you off and you still didn't run away?

I had never been in prison. I didn't realize how powerful the dictatorship of the proletariat was. When I got near our door, my mother also asked me about everything that had happened. Then she told me to go hide right away. But I was just a temporary worker. First, I had no connections; second, I had no experience in society; and third, I'd never traveled far before. Where would I go, even if I did run away? I said I would just have to accept my fate. What must be must be. If it's a calamity, I won't be able to get away; if I can get away, that means it wasn't such a calamity after all. Then I went to bed, but I lay awake all night.

On the day of June 4, everyone was jittery. According to a rumor going around, anyone who had anything to do with the armored car had been arrested. I secretly rejoiced that I had somehow escaped in time, because many people had climbed on the armored car both before and after me, blowing off steam. Some threw bricks at it, others hit it with crowbars or even with belts. Many more spat, punched, or cursed at it.

They arrested me on June 12. Somehow I felt ill at ease all day. My left eye was twitching and I was anxious. I managed to work until noon. The electric machinery in the workshop had broken down and the foreman said that we would be working extra shifts. I said, "I can't do that." I said, "I'm having trouble concentrating today." Just then the factory party secretary poked his head inside and called out, "Wang Lianhui!" It was very strange. There were three heads at the door, like three big heads of fruit, but none of them came in. *This is it,* I thought to myself, but I made a perfunctory response, saying, "Let me change my clothes first." "No need for that, just come," said the party secretary. I was led out like a zombie. I took off my dirty work gloves and followed. When I came out, I looked around. There were six or seven policemen with rifles lined up like a wall. The handcuffs clicked twice.

I was in a daze when we got to a detention center in Daxing County, where several hundred people were being held. We awaited trial in our cells, first getting a violent beating and then waiting to be interrogated.

Later I found out that there were sixteen other June Fourth rioters like me held in that detention center. We were all given the same indictment and bundled together as accomplices even though we didn't know one another. They decided to selectively prosecute people who had done actual harm to the armored vehicle, including those who had thrown bricks at it or attacked it with crowbars.

(*Wu Wenjian cut in, referring to similar cases: "There were also people who didn't do anything but still got heavy sentences for things like hitting a tank with his belt, creating a bad influence, then leaving the scene. Or eating roast chicken off an army truck."*)

Yes, the eldest among my group of accomplices was a man in his early sixties named Li Zexi. He was just making noise. He didn't have much strength to do anything else, so he just cracked a joke in front of the crowd: "Too bad this armored car isn't made of plastic. We wouldn't have to hit it. We could just light it up, and it would all be over." Wasn't he just talking nonsense? Who could have guessed, though, that the old guy would get a sentence of fifteen years for a "counterrevolutionary nonsense crime"?

Compared with people who burned army vehicles, set up roadblocks, and fought the armed police, what I did wasn't too extreme. Several hundred army trucks were burned in Beijing.

Several dozen trucks were burned in Chengdu, too.

That army truck in Daxing was the only one, and it didn't even burn. Still, my crime was considered the most serious. It was simply a matter of picking up a group of people and killing one of us.

Do you know why I'm still alive? Because of my clean family background. When they investigated my case, they found that I came from several generations of poor, long-suffering peasants who still nursed deep hatreds. As for myself, I was an honest kid who had been born in the new China and grown up under the red flag. I was a hard worker and my political record was unblemished. So they decided that I didn't fall into the category of idle people who should be punished quickly and severely.

The situation was very tense, Brother. Several dozen people were shot within a few days. Especially when I was transferred to the higher-level Beijing Municipal No. 7 Detention Center, namely the famous K building, where I thought I was just waiting to be executed.

Later, on December 26, 1989, Mao Zedong's birthday, a very cold day, I got my verdict. I was dumbstruck when I saw that I had gotten a life sentence. I spent eight months at Beijing Municipal No. 1 Prison until we were transferred as a group to Beijing Municipal No. 2 Prison. That was a so-called modern prison, with electronic monitoring and controls. It was built on top of an old graveyard. For a while just after we arrived, we would often kick up the bones of the dead as we walked around.

I was beaten up. Whenever you come to a new place, you always get beaten up. If you're young and from a poor background, as long as you're not so badly beaten that you're crippled, you can usually recover eventually. During the first two or three years, I still hoped that the June Fourth people would be rehabilitated. From time to time we would get together to pass along some uplifting little bits of news. Year after year we endured. Four, five, six years passed and the power of the Communist Party looked more solid than ever. Discouraged, we decided that we might as well steel ourselves and serve out our sentences.

I didn't have any special talents. I could only work as hard as possible and hope to earn some reduction in my sentence. No matter how tough, tiring, and dirty the work was, I could handle that, but the food was exactly the same every day. It was as monotonous as our days in prison. Cornmeal, noodles turning black, poor-quality flour mixed with various kinds of chaff. The same kind of thing, over and over.

Newspapers from outside revealed that heartless grain merchants took expired, mildewy old flour, added some chemicals to make it turn white, and then took it to the market to sell wholesale. That kind of spoiled food was the staple for us reform-through-labor prisoners. The food crumbled easily. Once pulled apart, it wouldn't stick together again. Strangely enough, none of the prisoners ever died from food poisoning.

As far as vegetables went, we had rotten potatoes and rotting cabbage bought at the lowest prices, including food swept up from the vegetable market at the end of the day. It would not be fair to them to say that they didn't wash the food. But their so-called washing was hitting it with water from a giant hose. Then they would cut it up into big chunks with a big knife and dump it all into a big pot on a stove, stir it with a large spatula, and drop in a few globs of grease and two or three handfuls of salt. That's what we ate for long periods of time. I don't think pigs would eat that today. Pigs these days don't even touch used cooking oil.

Prison life is hard to describe in just a few words. I finally got out in February 2005. I had been in jail for sixteen years and four months. It was a nightmare. At the age of thirty-eight, I had nothing to my name and I was completely cut off from society. I was trash. A burden to my family.

My father had died in 1990. My mother had died in 2002. I wasn't able to do my filial duty or say goodbye to them. [While I was in prison] I didn't even know if they were still alive. When I went home, I faced the portraits of my dead parents and cried for a while. My family became my elder brother and elder sister, as well as my younger brother and younger sister. I was the bachelor in the middle. At first I alternated meals at their various homes. My parents left our old home to me and my younger brother, divided equally between us. But my younger brother occupied it. All I could do was spend 300 yuan and rent a room nearby.

Society had changed very rapidly over that decade or so. When I was growing up there were eighteen production brigades in Jiugong. Now that whole system was gone. The commune and brigade enterprises were long gone. All the farmland had been sold off by the officials. The old way of living off the land, inherited from our ancestors, was gone. All the peasants had to find some other way to make a living.

Now I pick up and remove trash for Jiugong Township. These

days, like they say, people despise poverty but not immorality. Doesn't everybody want to drive a BMW or a Mercedes-Benz? People will be jealous of a whore, even if she is as worn-out as a public bus everyone has ridden, if they see her driving a BMW or a Mercedes-Benz. We June Fourth rioters missed out on a lot. My neighbors on the street say, "Lianhui, you are a good man. You didn't rob or steal. You didn't swindle anyone. It's nothing that you've been in jail. People know this full well in their hearts."

Do you think the people sent to prison because of June Fourth will be rehabilitated?

I don't expect it. Now I have a wife and kid. Stability is what I need most in life. History is too abstract; I don't pay any attention to it. In the future, if anyone says that they are going to get justice for me, I'll just tell them to get lost. I usually don't go to reunions of June Fourth rioters. It's too humiliating. I don't have the confidence to get together, with everyone asking one another what they're up to. What do I have to say? That I collect trash? That I rent the place where I live? That I'm supporting my family on 1,000 yuan a month? It's the humiliation. But I can't complain about being poor. No matter how poor I am, I'll carry on. It's for my kid, and if it's for your kid, there's no complaining.

The Hooligan

"We work two men to a shift," said Li Hongqi, standing next to a metal-frame bunk bed in his pitch-black bedroom. He was changing out of his security guard uniform while Wu Wenjian and I waited. "The guy who sleeps there was also born in 1968, and he's from Xinxiang County in Henan Province. But during June Fourth he was with the army, serving in an armored division of the martial law force."

"Did he kill anyone?" asked Wu.

"No. The people persuaded him not to," replied Li. "He turned against the troops he was with, climbed off the truck, and ran away. That's how he came to be so miserable, having to scrape by with rioters like me."

We went to a nearby restaurant and ordered *erguotou*, and soon time was flying backward. Sympathetic shafts of sunlight fell through the windows where we sat.

Li Hongqi: I was a ticket seller on the long-distance public bus that went from the exhibition hall to Mentougou. Normally each trip took two or three hours. When I got on the last bus on June 3, at first I didn't know what was going on. After a while I started hearing the passengers getting on and off the bus talking about where the fires had been, where the shooting was, the vandalism. I was puzzled. Then I saw over a hundred army trucks with their lights on, rumbling by, full of soldiers with live ammunition. Our bus had to stop on the side of the road to let the army trucks go by. We were delayed for a long time. Everyone was cursing but didn't dare curse out loud. Were those bloodthirsty bastards really going to fire into the crowd?

I think it must have been the first time that anyone in Beijing, young or old, had seen such a thing. So when I got off work at eleven p.m. and headed back to the bus company dormitory, I saw that many of my colleagues had gathered together, all in a high state of excitement, and they were saying that even back when we were fighting the Japanese devils, the Communist Party hadn't sent this many troops into the fight.

In those days the Communists were still guerrilla fighters.

The company phoned to tell us that employees in the suburbs should not go back into the city for the time being. They said that there were shootings in the city and the streets were flowing with blood. If anything happened, the company would not assume responsibility. But we wanted to get back home and we were worried that something had happened to our families. The company leadership couldn't say anything to that, so they sent a special bus to pick everybody up.

At first it was quiet, but later, as we neared the city, the atmosphere grew tenser. Near Pingguoyuan, both sides of the road were filled with burned-out armored cars. When we got to Xitaipingzhuang, the street was full of bricks and blood, and there were even more burned-out tanks and armored cars scattered along our way. Our bus turned this way and that, as if playing hide-and-seek on a battlefield, until finally, with great difficulty, we approached the intersection near where I lived. As soon as I got off the bus, three of my coworkers dragged me along to Tiananmen Square to go see what was happening. "I can't go," I said. "I'm afraid my younger brother might get into trouble."

"There's no way your younger brother is at home," said my coworker. "At this critical moment, none of us can stay home."

Were all three of you bus ticket sellers?

Yes, and all of us were about the same age. We got on our bicycles and reached an intersection where we saw a large group of university students waving flags, shouting slogans, and crying, saying that the soldiers kept shooting and were out of control. The scene filled everyone there with rage. I felt it, too. We continued on our bicycles to Xisishitiao Road. We could see a big crowd in the distance. The three of us went up on the bridge there for a closer look. Three soldiers lay on the ground, unconscious and bloody. I couldn't tell whether they were dead or unconscious. It was my first time seeing a body in the street like that.

As we pressed forward, the sight of bodies sprawled out in the street and burning vehicles became more and more frequent. When we got to Muxidi, we suddenly heard a loud bang. It was a soldier who had popped up out of an armored car and thrown a hand grenade into the crowd. It was a smoke bomb, and it released an eruption of poisonous smoke when it exploded.

We were furious. We began throwing bricks as we rubbed our eyes. Taking advantage of the chaos, the soldier quickly jumped out of the vehicle and ran. The crowd picked up bricks and gave chase. I was in the crowd. It was a chaotic scene. In an instant, my two coworkers and I got separated. I couldn't find them, so I just wandered around aimlessly. I ended up at the entrance to Fuxing Hospital. Many people were rushing in and out of the hospital. They all said that they had come to see the dead. I went in with them, too. Many Beijingers took out cameras and snapped pictures. The dead were covered in white cloth soaked with patches of blood. Someone brave lifted up the cloth, exposing dead bodies bearing student IDs, employee IDs, personal IDs, and military veteran IDs. They had been shot in the head, in the chest, in the stomach, or in the crotch. Their blood had congealed. Their faces were unrecognizable. It was horrifying. One of the students had half of his face blown away.

I saw more than ten dead bodies just in the passageway of the hospital parking lot. There were even more in the sickrooms. I felt nauseous, so I didn't continue inside but followed the stream of people out of the hospital, numbed and despondent like a zombie. I don't know how long I had been wandering, when I saw something like a thousand Beijingers surrounding and attacking the soldiers. The soldiers looked miserable, too, and they were arguing that they had no idea what the hell was going on. The army had trained them in isolation and forbidden them to watch television or read the newspapers. Before their emergency departure they were told that they were participating in an exercise. To be honest, I thought that the soldiers were to be pitied, too. They had no idea that they were being sent to confront the people.

Just then, not far from me, I saw several men with big iron picks taking apart an armored car, saying that they wanted to get some parts for souvenirs. I went up to them and said, "Something this bloody deserves to be smashed!" So I took one of their big iron picks and smashed the four mirrors on the front. Then I took the machine guns by the hatch off the roof. One mischievous man carried a military sack with many smoke bombs that he had found, took one out, pulled the string, and threw it inside the armored car. Smoke immediately erupted from the truck. I was intrigued, so I grabbed one, too, and pulled the string. I felt panicked, as if my whole body had caught on fire, as I hurriedly tossed it into the armored car. That, too, would later become one of the "charges" against me. I was charged with stealing machine guns, throwing smoke bombs, injuring several people, damaging army property, and so on.

There were many abandoned armored cars all around with large-caliber machine-gun bullets scattered both inside and outside the vehicles. Everybody was picking them up. I filled two pockets with ammunition from a plastic bucket. I also got a steel helmet. Many people picked up brand-new steel helmets. They joked, saying that they would bring them home to cook with, since the quality would certainly be better than ordinary aluminum pots.

It was about 10:30 by the time I got home. I had quite a haul. A steel helmet, ammunition, and tear gas bombs. A few days after June 4, on a whim I took out my souvenirs to show them off. My father said immediately, "Do you want to get yourself killed? Throw those things in the trash immediately!" The old man was a veteran of many political movements. He knew how terrible the settling of scores afterward would be. I was young and inexperienced. I went to work as usual and didn't take his words to heart. I thought that even if they detained street wanderers like me, it would only be for a few days, to teach us a lesson.

I was arrested on June 13. We reached the precinct station and ran into someone from the Joint Defense Command. "Let's settle dark scores in the dark for a little while," he said, closing the door. I became a football that many people kicked around. Before I even had a chance to scream twice, they stuffed two toothpaste tubes into my swelling cheeks, then a plastic medicine bottle, then they sealed my bulging face with tape. Blood and saliva dripped out. They took off all my clothes. No, they tore them all off.

An instinctive sense of shame made me want to cover myself and dodge their blows. I kept begging for mercy, but no sound came out. Exhausted from torturing me, they ordered me to kneel. As they kicked my private parts, they said, "Let's see you burn a military vehicle!" and "Let's see you kill a PLA [People's Liberation Army] soldier!" I had no mouth and no voice to defend myself with. I could only scrunch down as low as I could to protect the vital spot between my legs. Then they used iron clubs and rifle butts on me. After being hit a few times, I blacked out. They woke me up with a bucket of cold water and my nightmare continued.

Later, I lost consciousness again. I was sent to the Fuxing Hospital for emergency care. I had been beaten all over, and my head was bent out of shape. I looked like some evil ghoul. My thin body had become fat from the beating. I seemed to have swollen into someone two or three times the size of the original Li Hongqi. I had gotten a perforated eardrum in my right ear. I had ringing in that ear for years afterward and nearly became deaf. They took off the plastic tape and then forced me to eat burning-hot cigarette butts. Nineteen years have passed since then, but if you take a look, Liao, you can still see the scars they left on the side of my mouth.

After that they said that I was hiding pistols. They wanted me to hand over the guns. I said I didn't have any guns, only two bullets and one tear gas bomb. They didn't believe me. "If you don't give us the guns," they said, "you won't see the sun rise tomorrow."

In the next room, a little rioter—maybe just fifteen or sixteen years old—saved me. He was beaten senseless but suddenly bolted out of the interrogation room like a frightened bird. The police station had a courtyard-like layout. That skinny little kid ran around the courtyard with all the soldiers chasing him, just like a slippery eel. They couldn't catch him. A platoon leader from the police, shouting angrily, raised his pistol and was about to shoot him when the precinct police captain stopped him, saying, "You don't have a confession yet, and having him die in the courtyard would be unlucky." So it went on like that. Finally, everybody was so out of breath that they got tired of chasing him and let him run off. They waited until he got tired and collapsed on the ground. Then they grabbed him and continued the interrogation.

So they got distracted and stopped thinking about you.

In the early morning hours, the police van went out again, looking all over for rioters. I was handcuffed to the pole beneath a basketball hoop in the courtyard, feeling so miserable I wanted to die, but I couldn't.

A "leading comrade," a higher-up, came at four a.m. to interrogate the four of us broken-down rioters one by one. The first was the little kid who had run off and orbited the courtyard. He was like a little bird with broken wings now, collapsed and barely able to move. Still, his hands and feet were cuffed to the table legs.

The comrade squatted next to him and asked, "What did you do?"

"I burned a truck," said the little kid, as if he were talking in his sleep.

"Tell me, just how did you burn it?"

"I lit a piece of cloth with a lighter and threw it under the truck."

"Not bad. You were very brave," said the comrade with a smile, while at the same time a leg flew up and kicked the kid in the mouth, causing blood to gush out of his mouth and nose.

"You have all these black-and-blue marks," said the comrade, ignoring the kick and feigning concern. "What's that about? Did you fall?"

"You people hit me," said the kid.

The comrade made as if he hadn't heard. "Speak louder, child. Did you fall?"

"You people hit me."

He was knocked unconscious with a punch.

The leader sighed and moved on to the second rioter, chained to the next table leg. He asked him the same questions. This person was powerfully built but not very bright. He answered the questions about the same way as the kid had. The result was also about the same: he was knocked unconscious.

The third rioter was clever and saw that the situation was not looking good, so he said immediately, "I wasn't beaten. The People's Liberation Army is an army of justice. They could not be so cruel."

"Is that right?" said the leader. "Then how did you get those injuries?"

"I hurt myself. I hurt myself."

"Oh, you hurt yourself so badly?"

"Yes, yes, it was very dark. I couldn't see my own five fingers in front of me. I fell into a hole." He was spared a beating, and I followed his example.

What was the food like in prison?

We had two small steamed buns and a steaming hot bowl of the water they used to rinse pots. It was always the exact same thing every single day. Only one day did we have anything different—the day we had lamb. After going weeks without fish or meat, we felt as if we had grown iron hooks in our stomachs, but once we put the meat in our mouths, what a smell. It was meat that the police couldn't finish and it had been left around for a few days. Fly eggs were hatching in it, but they couldn't stand to throw it away, so they gave it to the prisoners to improve our diet.

The police knew we would have trouble eating it, so beforehand they gave everyone a lot of antidiarrheal medicine. Because we hadn't had any oil in our stomachs for so long, no matter how bad the meat smelled, we wolfed it down. That day, just after eating, we all felt a roiling storm in our stomachs and rushed to the toilet right away. We loosened our belts, sat on the toilet, and erupted with crashing sounds. Before the ones ahead had even finished, the next couldn't wait, holding their stomachs, screaming in pain, wishing that they could throw the person ahead out of the way. Many people couldn't wait and went in their pants. The whole cell stank with the thick smell of loose stool. The police gave us extra doses of antidiarrheal medicine, and everybody gulped down large quantities of it.

The government knew that the poorer people are, the tougher they are. Even if you were to die, well, what of it? You were less than a watery piece of shit. They would just throw you away. Those hot, hungry, and diarrhea-filled days in such a small cell, with all those bastards, skin sticking to skin, reeking ass next to reeking ass. If one person got sick, soon everyone was sick. Take scabies. If one person started scratching, soon everyone was scratching hard and skin was flying all over the place. Fleas were always poised to attack and everyone would wake up in the middle of the night to fend them off. Just like that, the torture went on and on until one day you got your indictment and then six weeks later your court verdict. I was charged with counterrevolutionary hooliganism, eight years. Robbery, ten years. Stealing ammunition and explosives, three years. The sentences added up to twenty-one years, but they made it twenty altogether.

During that murderous time, no lawyers dared speak for the rioters for fear of being implicated. I didn't dare appeal. I was afraid that they would bump up the severity of my crime by a level and my head would roll. When I got back to the detention center, I felt total despair. Several prison tyrants, in order to please the government, forced me to memorize the prison regulations. Suddenly enraged, I fought them. That astonished the police. They put me in handcuffs and leg irons. Several days later I was sent to Beijing Municipal Prison No. 1. There they put me immediately into solitary so I could do some soul-searching. It was the size of a doghouse, just nine feet long and six feet wide.

I burrowed in there and got right into bed. I wasn't allowed to sleep, though. I had to spend all my time memorizing the prison regulations until I could recite them fluently. The summer passed and fall arrived. From a crack in my door, I could see the withered branches and fallen leaves everywhere. I saw prisoners assembling in the yard, singing, "The stars surround you and the moonlight goes with you."

The June Fourth rioters stayed in Beijing Municipal No. 1 Prison for over a year doing odd jobs. Then we were sent all together to Municipal No. 2 Prison, where we made latex medical gloves. My job was trimming the edges. Everyone worked like machines, repeating the same two motions for over ten hours a day. For example, to test if a glove was airtight, you would blow into it first and then squeeze it with your hands, then put it in a box. Each box held 2,000 pairs of gloves. If three of the gloves in the crate leaked, you would have to do the work all over again and you would be beaten. And if you didn't fulfill your quota, the police would poke you with high-voltage electric prods and tie you up with thin hemp cord.

Many people's fingers were deformed by the work, leaving them crippled for life. Two of my cellmates were slow workers. They couldn't stand it. They broke thermometers and swallowed the mercury. They were sent to the hospital to have their stomachs pumped. Their suicide attempts failed.

When I was in jail, my private parts were burned with an electric prod. The same happened to you?

They poked me with the electric prod many times. It felt like tens of thousands of needles stabbing you at the same time. One time the section chief, Little Black Liu, shocked me for half an hour. I howled in agony like a wolf being slaughtered. Little Black Liu got angry. He poked my mouth with the electric prod. I foolishly bit down hard on it with all my strength, and it almost knocked out my front tooth. Later, there were big blisters on the inside and outside of my mouth. I was very hungry but couldn't swallow anything.

But Little Black Liu still hadn't had enough fun with me. He called over three collaborationist prisoners and wrestled me down to the floor. He then had a chair put over me and sat on it, so I was wedged between the legs of the chair, unable to move. They took off my pants, exposing my buttocks. Little Black Liu took the electric prod in his hands, holding it perpendicular to the floor, and aimed it right at my anus. I couldn't help squirming like mad, but besides my neck I couldn't actually move my body at all, as if everything had been screwed tightly together. My urine and shit all came out. Little Black Liu yelled over and over, "Bad luck, bad luck." He had me turned over and then shocked my cock. The pain was unbearable, like a knife jabbing into me. Those bastards got very excited. They were even singing.

Did that affect your ability to have sex?

This question is too humiliating. I don't want to talk about it.

The Prisoner of Conscience

In China, a prisoner of conscience is someone who dares to go up against the government, not because of any particular political program, but out of a simple sense of justice, an uneasy conscience about what's happening. Li Hai—fifty-two years old, still single, the hair on his temples going white—was a prisoner of conscience. Having been an older graduate student at Peking University, an epicenter of the movement, he was involved in it from start to finish.

To interview him, I was back at 798, Beijing's old factory district turned artist colony, where I had first met Wu Wenjian. Using the pretext of a visit with Wu and some other artists, Li and I quickly slipped away from the large group and found an empty room. I closed the door, and Li said it was best to lock it, so I locked it.

———

Li Hai: I used to have a good memory but now it isn't any good. I've forgotten many people and events. I recognize faces but don't remember names. I often get lost in my own neighborhood. When I have a conversation with someone, I suddenly feel that the other person is far away, as if he had just come from outer space.

What is closest to you?

June Fourth. June Fourth is yesterday. It will always be just yesterday for me. It's not like I have any thoughts. I have none at all. I got out of prison a long time ago but I'm still afraid. I'm afraid when I cross the street. I'm afraid when I go shopping in a little store. When I talk with my neighbors, I'm always looking this way and that, as if I were doing something I should be ashamed to be seen doing in public. One day a friend coming up behind me called my name. His voice was a little loud, and it frightened me, so I bolted. I'm not a coward, but I need to adapt to my environment.

Are you from Beijing?

I was born and raised in Beijing. I grew up in a nice environment. I liked to read books. After the Cultural Revolution ended, I passed the entrance examination for Nanjing University. After graduation, I taught for six years. In 1988, I passed the examination for the Peking University philosophy department. In 1989, I came into contact with the student movement and got involved.

Peking University was the center of the nation. The "Triangle" at the center of the Peking University campus was the eye of the storm. At the Triangle, that palpable sense of freedom of speech somehow stirs whoever passes by. When Hu Yaobang died, funeral scrolls, memorial essays, funeral poetry, and portraits of the deceased man covered the walls of the Triangle. Many people gathered there, lining up to go to greet the family of Hu Yaobang, going to the mourning hall to present flowers and bow three times before his portrait. I went there, too. I couldn't stop myself from weeping.

Hu was the symbol of Chinese reform. For Chinese people, he was like Gorbachev in the Soviet Union. But Deng Xiaoping played political games, supporting him for a while, then attacking him later. Hu died an angry man. But that phony dwarf Deng appeared at the memorial meetings and praised Hu to the skies.

He was also a tyrannical dwarf. He was Mao Zedong's plaything.
Now it was his turn to play with others as Mao had played with him.

That's why a movement to mourn Hu Yaobang arose spontaneously among the people. On April 17, marchers from all the universities in Beijing went out into the streets to demonstrate. Peking University was among the slower ones to act. It was about midnight, and people had changed to go to bed in the dormitories, when suddenly we heard waves and waves of wailing coming from the depths of campus. I'm not exaggerating one bit. It was as piercing as the howling of a wolf. It came from every building and every corner of campus.

Many people actually opened their windows, cupped their hands in the shape of a bullhorn, and made long, drawn-out howls. People in the opposite dormitory would howl back. Then people streamed through the corridors from all directions to gather at the Triangle until it was overcrowded. Some wore strips of white cloth wrapped around their foreheads, a traditional symbol of mourning. Someone emerged from the crowd to direct traffic. From the twenty-eighth floor of a building, someone unfurled a giant banner with the words "Chinese Spirit." We followed that banner and marched through the streets in great numbers, yelling slogans as we marched. More and more people joined our ranks as we walked for miles toward downtown. A little past four in the morning we reached Tiananmen Square.

That sounds like how, at the start of the Cultural Revolution, millions of Red Guards from all over China gathered at Tiananmen to be received by Mao Zedong. They also went to Tiananmen a little past four in the morning.

There's no comparison. The first time, they were gathering for a personality cult. This time, it was to promote democracy. The ghostly old imperial city of Beijing was suddenly overwhelmed by the excitement of the crowds. Some martial arts expert from who knows where took over the banner and, in a flash, leaped from the ground to the base of the Monument to the People's Heroes. They hung the "Chinese Spirit" banner where everyone could see it.

Then the student leader Wang Dan called an open-air meeting, attended by over a thousand people, to discuss what to include in the petition that would be presented to the Central Committee of the Chinese Communist Party. The petition started with eleven items and then was reduced to seven. If I remember correctly, these included ending restrictions on the press, eliminating corruption, and so on. Later we lined up to go to the eastern entrance of the Great Hall of the People. We sat there on the ground all day and all night, but nobody came out to receive us.

China is a dictatorship, so it doesn't have any mechanism for dialogue with the people other than repression. Everyone sat at the foot of the steps bored stiff, staring straight ahead. We didn't eat or sleep. The heat of the day alternated with the cold of the night. We held out with nothing but hearts full of passion and patriotism. Gradually, some Beijingers started coming to see us, then more and more surrounded us until we were completely encircled by layers and layers of people. Beijingers are more politically aware than people elsewhere in the country, so many volunteers came to give us presents of bread, fruit, and Popsicles. A disciplinary patrol organized on the spot formed a circle around us to keep order.

We were attracting a lot of attention. The officials couldn't stand it any longer and finally at dusk they opened the door a crack to receive our petition. We felt like a load had been lifted from our shoulders, so at first light we withdrew back to the campus. We didn't realize things were far from over. Wave after wave of protest arose after that. Another student sit-down strike took place at the New China Gate of the Zhongnanhai leadership compound. We rushed over to support them, but the People's Armed Police drove us back. The students naturally wouldn't stand for that, so there was a lot of pushing and shoving on both sides. The People's Armed Police got angry and started punching and kicking. I yelled, "Stop punching people!" A fist flew into my face, which swelled up fast, and I looked like a panda. Some students were beaten up much worse and had blood all over their heads. Others were kicked in the testicles and doubled over in pain.

That was the famous New China Gate attack. Afterward we withdrew. The official news we heard on campus was that the armed police hadn't hit anyone but had patiently persuaded people to disperse peacefully. What bullshit. My face was proof of that. That incident was a turning point. Tens of thousands of students started hurrying down to Tiananmen Square for sit-down strikes and demonstrations. On April 21 the Central Committee of the Chinese Communist Party held a memorial for Hu Yaobang in the Great Hall of the People. The students again sent Guo Haifeng and two others to present their petition. Nobody paid any attention to them, so they knelt down on the steps. After Chinese Central Television broadcast that scene live, it shocked the entire country.

The memorial was an internal meeting held by the Communist Party, and the people were not allowed to participate. Our tiniest shred of will was being completely ignored, so of course we knelt. We didn't imagine the Party could become so enraged when losing face. Shame can only lead to anger, so that led to the April 26 editorial in *People's Daily*, "We Need to Make a Clear Stand Against Turmoil." That folly poured oil on the flames, leading directly to the big march on April 27. All of Beijing emptied into Tiananmen Square. People say that a million people were there.

Then came the May 1 and May 4 demonstrations and the People's Armed Police mobilized hundreds of thousands of soldiers. To counter that, several million people from all over mobilized themselves. It looked like a tyrannical government was going to be drowned in a sea of people.

That's when they completely lost control. People say that there were demonstrations in dozens of cities, with tens of millions of people going out on the streets. People wanted reform, democracy, and human rights.

A graduate student in biology, Shen Tong, invited me to take part in the Capital Autonomous Federation of University Students, the major coordinating group at Peking University. Yang Tao was the chair and Chang Jing the vice chair. I was the liaison with outside groups, responsible for hosting visitors and communicating information. In all my life, I have never been so busy. I only got two or three hours of sleep a night, and I had no time to eat at all. I often felt dizzy and light-headed while hosting Western journalists; it must have been low blood sugar from not eating enough. On the eve of Gorbachev's visit, we debated at the base of the Monument to the People's Heroes whether we should temporarily pause the demonstrations to free up the area so the state could save some face. A dozen famous intellectuals also came to urge us to give up our hunger strike. The rock stars Cui Jian and Hou Dejian also came, and Liu Xiaobo.

A "Democracy University" started up in the square. Divisions among the student leaders sometimes led to fistfights. There was no way to keep track of all the things that went on. Nobody knew, and nobody could say what might happen the next day. What should they do next? They just kept on arguing. They were still arguing on the night of June 3 until about ten p.m., when we heard gunfire. That made everybody shut up for a while.

That day I was nearby in Xidan, when I got a telephone call from headquarters in the square, ordering me to take a few people to see what the situation was like near Xisi, to the west. It turned out that the trucks of martial law troops had been blocked by the crowds. The crowd had rushed forward to reason with the soldiers, urging them to withdraw and turn their guns around on the tyrannical government. It was a scorching day, and the armor plating of the military vehicles was burning hot. The soldiers were stuck inside, soaked in sweat, some hanging their heads and seeming to be suffering from heatstroke. Civilians came forward to give them water, Popsicles, fruit, and bread, moving them to tears. They said they hadn't understood the true situation before setting out. They said that, as an army made up of the "sons and younger brothers of the people," they would absolutely not fire at patriots.

But after that, they not only started shooting but killed many people—although I also saw many soldiers who abandoned their military vehicles, threw down their weapons and ammunition, and ran away. Some even gave away their weapons and ammunition to the people and told them how to resist. I suppose they must have been tried by secret military tribunals afterward. During that night of slaughter, I ran to many intersections. Bullets were flying, injured people were sprawled everywhere on the ground, while still others kept coming to help them, picking them up and carrying them to the hospital as bullets rained down. I went to Fuxing Hospital and then to Beijing Children's Hospital and saw there, with my own eyes, several dozen bloody corpses.

It was a scene from hell, with heavy gunfire sounding outside the walls. Inside the walls, physicians and nurses were frantic, rushing in and out. Amid the moans of wounded patients brought in earlier, the freshly wounded streamed in. By late that night Tiananmen was in the hands of the martial law troops. The only thing left for me was to hurry back to Peking University and pass on the news. I was too indignant, too exhausted, and too overwhelmed. In the dormitory, even as I sat straight up and talked and talked, I started snoring. My pants were bloodstained. In all my running around, I didn't know where the blood had splashed on me.

Early on the morning of June 4, a ceremony to mourn the dead was held on the Peking University campus. Chang Jing and I were in charge of hanging up funeral scrolls. Suddenly, an armored car braked sharply to a halt at the university gate. Two soldiers hopped off, smiled, and asked for directions. They acted as if, according to the old line, the army and the people were still as close as fish and water. Everyone was furious. Hundreds of people came rushing from all directions, surrounding and punching the two soldiers. Just as it looked like they were going to be killed, Chang Jing and I, without exchanging a word, dove into the crowd, pulled them off the ground, and rescued them.

At the time, any little mistake was an open invitation to further repression. During those days, there was wailing, like the cries of ghosts, everywhere in the Peking University dormitories. I decided to go home, which was not far away, in Sanyuanqiao. There was a roadblock there, too. Martial law troops were at all the intersections, so I went through some narrow alleys and circled around for six or seven hours before I finally got home. I locked the door tight, burrowed under my bed covers, and cried for a long time. Then, without telling my family, I packed a few simple things and prepared to flee.

Surprisingly, I got on the train without any trouble. I got to Shijiazhuang, and then, after some transfers, I made it to my relatives in the county capital near there. After hiding there for a while, I was depressed and bored and decided to go south to Sichuan. I even climbed Mt. Emei, one of the four sacred Buddhist mountains. During this period, many people escaped abroad and many others were captured. After another three months had passed, I received a letter from the Party branch general secretary of the Peking University philosophy department telling me that the troubles were over and I could come back to school.

They weren't tricking you?

Peking University generally had a tradition of protecting its students. Many people, however, felt that things were not so secure. In the months that followed, many people from other schools came to me privately to collaborate on a mourning ceremony for the dead of June Fourth. I couldn't resist participating and continuing my liaison work with foreigners. I was arrested on May 31, 1990. I had just returned to Beijing and I hadn't even settled into my chair in my dorm room when there was a knock on the door. The philosophy department Party branch general secretary was standing there. I had to go with him. First we talked for an hour at the school security office. Then I was put in handcuffs, loaded into a prison van, and sent to the Haidian District detention center.

Even though I was very anxious before entering the prison, I forced myself to be calm, with the righteous composure of a martyr prepared to be executed in a Communist novel. I went through the main gate, then a second gate and a third gate. Each gate was narrower than the last.

Then suddenly I was kicked. "Remove his belt!" someone shouted. Then it was my pants. I stood there naked as they completed their inspection. They didn't return my clothes right away but just threw them into a jail cell. In the cell were twenty other bare-assed guys. As soon as I entered, they surrounded me, making funny noises, and then they pounced on me. Kicks rained down as I rolled back and forth. I got a sharp kick in the chest that hurt like somebody was drilling my heart. I nearly spat blood. I collapsed onto the floor.

That is about what happened to me when I entered prison, too.

It hurt for several days. I heard a jailer say that a boy's urine can heal traumatic injuries, so I was constantly dreaming of drinking a boy's urine until I would wake up dying of thirst and couldn't get any water to drink. The rule of the cell was that every new arrival needed to be initiated with a beating.

It was long, slow torture after that. I was surrounded by petty thieves and scoundrels. They all laughed at my university student's way of talking. Naturally, the June Fourth slaughter was not long past, so everyone was sympathetic. A habitual thief told me that to support the patriotic student movement, he had taken part in the Beijing city-wide thieves' strike.

Eating, drinking, sleeping, and shitting were all difficult. The cell was too cramped and the prisoners were all packed in tight. We were rotting: one person touching another person, flesh touching flesh. There was no space between us. Sweat, smelly feet, and urine stank up the cell, but after sleeping there for a few nights you didn't notice it anymore. I had been a cleanliness freak. In my dorm room I couldn't stand even a spot of dust on my bed.

Now not only was I put in a stinking hole, I had to get up close and personal with those scabies-infested dregs of humanity, too. Surprisingly, after sleeping hugging my legs for a hundred days, I hadn't developed any similar problem. Everyone said that this counter-revolutionary's skin must be made of some special material, to be the only one who's not itchy when everyone else is.

Just five days after that, I suddenly felt an unbearable itch, which made me sit up in the middle of the night and scratch myself furiously.

Once I started, I couldn't stop. First it was small red spots, then small welts, then a series of blisters. Finally my whole body was covered with ulcers. My arms, stomach, genitals, and buttocks started to swell and continuously oozed yellow liquid. The government wouldn't issue any medicine. Toothpaste didn't help.

We could only use the sun to kill the disease little by little, during our exercise breaks. But sometimes the prison guards were too lazy, and we didn't get a chance to go out for more than twenty minutes at a time, and scabies would rage because it was so damp. Everyone was constantly scratching themselves from head to toe. Everyone was covered with ulcers, making us unrecognizable. People would roll around on the floor or rub up against the walls. Some couldn't bear the itch and squealed like pigs. When we were taken for interrogation, flies would buzz around us every time we moved our heads. Even the interrogators couldn't stand the sight of us. Holding their noses, they went to the prison authorities. After that they started thorough cleanups of our cells and sent us out to get washed up and gave us sulfur ointment, which we slathered all over our bodies. After two or three nights, a layer of skin peeled off.

I don't remember what my "crime" was. I signed a confession and a written pledge and then my case was considered closed. I was unexpectedly lucky to be released after 209 days.

But I didn't get off so easily the second time I went to prison. That was in May 1995. I had only been "free" for four years.

It's hard to escape one's fate.

I was careless and got on the Ministry of Public Security's blacklist. Peking University had expelled me. I couldn't study and I couldn't find work. I could only hang out at home and rely on my parents for support. In 1992, I got to know Liu Qing of the New York organization Human Rights in China and I helped him send foreign donations to the families of June Fourth victims all over China. I knew that was a little dangerous, but I couldn't get rid of my June Fourth obsession. Later, when the authorities discovered what I was doing, they called me in to discuss matters over a cup of tea. I answered frankly: "Yes, I forwarded some money. The money helps the state appease the people's grievances."

For several years I traveled to dozens of cities and personally distributed several hundred thousand U.S. dollars to over 600 family members of victims. Each person actually only got a little, maybe $200, $300, or $400. Some received $600 or $700. I was running around so much that I got completely exhausted. I often felt dizzy and vomited on long-distance bus rides. One time I fainted.

What got me in trouble was a woman. One time, right in front of me, she called Wang Dan and talked with him at length about June Fourth. That's how she and I got acquainted, and we stayed in touch off and on for about two years. Then she suddenly invited me to go to Guangzhou on vacation, saying that a "big boss" would arrange free room and board for us. I thought that was a little strange, so I politely turned down the invitation. She called a few days later to say that the police were following her and that she wanted to hide at my place.

"I'm just a 'clay Buddha' crossing the river myself," I said obliquely. "I'm not sure I can make it, either."

"The tiger's mouth is at once the most dangerous and the safest place," she answered.

"B-b-b-but . . . ," I stammered, panicking.

"But what?" she said. "I'm coming over right away."

"I'm going to visit an old lay Buddhist disciple this afternoon."

"I'll go with you," she said.

"You don't believe in the Buddha," I answered. "It won't do you any good to go along."

To which she replied: "How do you know I don't believe in the Buddha?"

I didn't know what to say, so I agreed and we went together to the home of a retired scholar, actually an old lay Buddhist disciple, and talked for over half an hour with him. Then she insisted on going with me to my place. "My place is too messy," I said. "Some other time." But she kept insisting, and somehow I couldn't refuse.

As soon as we entered, I asked her to sit down. While I was in the kitchen getting tea and making something to eat, she was inspecting my bookshelf. Among my collection of books were some notebooks that listed contributions received from abroad and when they had been delivered. My handwriting was very messy, but she took out the notebooks and inspected them, page after page, very focused, as if she were doing some kind of research.

I hurried back to stop her, saying, "This is private stuff and you shouldn't be reading it."

"What do you mean private?" she asked flirtatiously. "What is there that people shouldn't see?"

"Give me back my notebook!" I yelled.

She continued the flirtation act, hiding the notebook behind her like a lovely and innocent girl: "No, I won't give it back! I just won't give it back!" I went into a blind fury. I pounced on her from across the table, held her down, and pulled the notebook away from her.

Shortly after she left my home, the Joint Defense Command came saying that they had a report that I had assaulted a woman and attempted to rape her. It was a disaster. I couldn't have defended myself even if I had had a hundred mouths. They first took me to the Chaoyang police station, and then to the Chaoyang detention center. They made threats, demanding from me the details of our sexual encounter. There was nothing to explain, so they gave up on that. Then they made a thorough search of my home and confiscated all my notebooks, diaries, letters, and address books, and the large quantity of materials on the democracy movement that I had gathered over the years.

Then the intensive interrogations began. "Why doesn't that woman who had me arrested for indecency show her face?"

"Li Hai, don't beat around the bush with us," said the policeman. "Your problem now isn't indecency. You need to tell us everything about your ties to foreign reactionary organizations. How much intelligence did you provide them? How much did they pay you? How much money did you pass along on their behalf? Be frank with us and you won't have any problems."

"What nonsense is this? I don't know what you are talking about."

At least, thanks to my first time in prison and all the sufferings I had endured, I understood what I was getting myself into. I had to resist firmly. Because once I loosened my lips, many names and addresses would follow. Not only would many people be in trouble because of me, but the severity of my crime would also increase. The police raged at me several times and nearly beat me to death. Finally they put the leg irons on me, and that usually means the death penalty. I wore them for a full year. I grew emaciated, like a ghost.

I had been captured on May 31, 1995. My court date was May 30, 1996. With no evidence and no confession, I was convicted of revealing state secrets and sentenced to nine years in prison. I was ultimately transferred to Liangxiang Prison in Fangshan County, where nearly 2,000 prisoners were held. I was treated terribly there, tied up with hemp rope and shocked with electric prods. But they still didn't squeeze any secrets out of me. There was no reduction of sentence: I was released on May 30, 2004, after nine full years; that is 3,288 days. After I got home, since it was nearly June 4, I was put under house arrest for nine days. So the total comes to 3,297 days of lost freedom.

Now I have high blood pressure, conjunctivitis, and gallstones from doing hard labor day and night in prison. My memory has deteriorated. The only thing I can remember are numbers, but I can't remember the context of the numbers. I didn't speak for a long time, so sometimes I don't make much sense when I do.

Prison left me mentally disabled. Society changed dramatically during those nine years. When I go out on the street, I don't know which direction is north. I feel depressed at home and even more so when dealing with people in the outside world. My brain doesn't turn very easily. When I try to force it, it hurts. When I go downstairs to the little shop to buy bread, I open my mouth but I don't know what to say when I get to the counter. I forget what I came to do. The one thing that interests me now is Buddhism. In a few days I'm planning to scrape together a little money and go to a temple in Guiyang County in Chenzhou, Hunan Province, to see if I can become a monk there. I hope that might end all my worldly troubles.

PART II:

SICHUAN

The Animal Tamer

In a story by Gabriel García Márquez, a dictator arrests a rebel. Learning that the rebel is an animal tamer by profession, the dictator obtains a lion from a circus, locks it in a cage, and starves it for three days and three nights. When the lion has just about lost his mind from hunger, the dictator pushes the rebel into a cage right next to the lion's. The rebel can only huddle in the farthest corner of his cage as the starving lion charges him over and over, clawing the air just a few feet away.

Chen Yunfei is a man who tries to tame the wildest animals of all: Communist Party officials.

Chen is from remote Daxian County, in the Daba Mountains of northeast Sichuan. With his thick waist and large head, he looks like an incarnation of Maitreya, the Buddha of the future, every time he speaks or laughs. At the time of the June Fourth massacre, he was a university student in Beijing, and he heard with his own ears and saw with his own eyes the gigantic tanks that flattened people in the streets and the soldiers, like frenzied beasts, who fired into crowds of protesters. He calls himself "the animal trainer."

Several years after the massacre, Chen leased a small, cheap piece of unused land in a distant suburb of Chengdu and turned it into a nursery, where he cultivated flowers and trees. He also posted a sign announcing his other line of work.

CHEN'S LABOR REFORM FARM

Proprietor: Chen Yunfei

Political Affiliation: I have no idea what "Party" has meant for
the past twenty years.

Occupation: Animal Tamer

What We Tame: Officials or Police

Later, with a cardboard sign reading "Animal Tamer" attached to his chest, he traveled all over China helping poor people living on the margins defend their rights, free of charge. He didn't realize it, but the Chinese police and public officials he was taming were much fiercer than any actual animals anywhere in the world. Chen was beaten until he was black-and-blue on many occasions. The bruises he accumulated over the years, all over his body, did not go away. He was once beaten so badly that for months he couldn't get out of bed.

Later still, he added an additional line to his cardboard sign: "Please, public servants, don't initiate violence against 'public masters.'" That made people on the street gather around him and break into laughter, because, going back to old Mao Zedong himself, the Communist Party had always proclaimed that the people are the "public masters" of the state and that the Party serves the people. But according to the law, when the "servants" attack the "masters," the "masters" can do little else but report the incident. Striking back would be a crime.

I have great respect for Chen, not because he is fearless about getting beaten up, but because he says, "If I'm not beaten up, I can't get to sleep" in such a hilarious way that it makes people want to cry.

Another thing Chen likes to say is: "It was all because of that 'mining accident on 8964'—that is, June 4, 1989."

"Why do you call it a 'mining accident'?" I asked.

"Why *shouldn't* I call it a 'mining accident'?"

"It was obviously a great slaughter . . ."

"A great slaughter can also be called a 'mining accident.' Many years from now, when all the people involved are dead, the great slaughter will be called a 'mining accident.'"

"Why are you being so ridiculous?"

Chen winked at me, and a lightbulb suddenly turned on in my head. On a night as dark as coal, the hundreds of thousands of people who went out in the street to protest against tyranny were "miners," and the martial law troops had been sent out to save the "miners caught in a disaster."

The Communist Party always fabricates history according to this kind of logic. You have to go along with it. On June 4, 2007, Chen spent 45 yuan to place a simple notice in the *Chengdu Evening News*: "Respect for the resolute mothers of the victims of June Fourth!" Those fourteen Chinese characters, including the exclamation point, shocked the Party, government, and military from the local level on up through the city and provincial levels all the way to the Central Committee of the Chinese Communist Party in Beijing. They made solving the case a high priority. All they caught was one highly unconventional Maitreya.

I was astonished. "How could a Communist Party paper ever print this? What has the world come to?"

"Nothing."

"How did you trick them?"

"I didn't trick them. I just followed the infallible logic of our Party. I called the slaughter a mining disaster. In 2007, there were dozens of mining disasters all over China. Everyone had become numb hearing about them. The lady at the ad department was very nice and asked me if I was a family member of someone who had died in a mining disaster. I said yes. She sighed and said, 'That must have been very hard on your parents.' 'My father died,' I said—he really had—and I hoped that my mother would be strong. And that was it. Except for the words 'mining disaster,' everything else was true." Nodding in approval, I promised to stand him a little pot of warm *baijiu* down the line.

Another year went by, and soon it was another June 4. Chen put on a Western-style suit, a tie, and a pair of very short shorts. Out of the blue, he ducked into a bloodmobile parked in the city center, stretched out his sweaty neck, and asked if he could give blood. The nurse pushed away his neck and pulled on his arm so she could put a needle in it. "Today is June 4," he told her. "It's the anniversary of the Tiananmen Massacre. Do you know that?" The nurse shivered, and the needle went in the wrong way. Chen laughed. "A wronged ghost possessed you, right? You should call the police to tell them that June Fourth rioters are making trouble at blood collection points." The nurse was so scared that she started crying. Because she was young and naïve, she really did call the police.

Chen was detained for a few days after that. When he got out, his lips were swollen like the snout of a pig. A bunch of buddies invited him to a welcome-back feast. I joined in, too. I may be well versed in interviewing people on the margins of society, but I couldn't think of what to ask an interview subject like Chen. With other people—the family of a June Fourth victim, for instance—I could play up my writer's role and console them with the best words I could find. But I was at a loss when faced with this dude, who laughed and smiled cheekily like a thug whose attitude was that no matter how bad it got, no matter how deep the untreatable wound in his heart might be, he would stay cool. Everyone could only tease him and joke with him.

Chen was denied permission to leave China. He appealed to higher levels but lost. He returned from Shenzhen, near the border with Hong Kong, to his remote suburb of Chengdu. After helping his old mother boil a pot of congee, he took out his passport and travel permit for Hong Kong, Macao, and Taiwan and put them in a home-made paper coffin. He then wrapped a white turban around his head to show his filial piety, shed some crocodile tears, and held solemn funeral rites for his official documents. When he posted pictures of the mock funeral on the Internet, the Internet police roared with anger, but for the moment they couldn't find any pretext to retaliate against him. They swore, however, that sooner or later they would dig a hole in which to bury the goddamn "animal tamer."

In the end, before the wild animals even had a chance to dig their hole, the animal tamer fell into a trap. He even brought another twenty-odd people along with him. In a traditional gesture of respect for the dead, they had gone to Xinjin County, on the outskirts of Chengdu, to sweep the tomb of Wu Guofeng, a model student and brave photographer who was killed on June Fourth.

Chen had read my account of Wu's death in *The Corpse Walker: Real-Life Stories, China from the Bottom Up* and had long wanted to get to present a bouquet of flowers at Wu Guofeng's grave. He wanted to meet Wu's parents, one of whom suffered from migraines, while the other had lost a kidney, and see if they would take on the animal tamer as a kind of adopted son. But when the animal tamer got to Xinjin, he was surrounded and captured by over a hundred "police beasts." His crime, long ago determined by the relevant organs, was incitement to overthrow the government and troublemaking.

After being locked up for two years, Chen's animal taming case was taken up in court. The prosecutor read the indictment. When Chen's lawyer argued that he wasn't guilty, the judge constantly yelled and interrupted him. People from his home village, who had gathered outside the courtroom to support him, were put one by one into a mobile animal cage. When the time came for the animal tamer to make his final statement, the judge glanced at his watch and told him that he had one minute.

Chen took a deep breath and started reading his statement. "Dear lawyer and swindlers of the prosecution: I have been tortured for over two years now. I feel like the legendary Monkey King who was thrown in the furnace for concocting the pills of immortality. It felt so good in there. The prosecution, the beatings, the wearing of leg irons that I have gone through are like math problems: the more difficult they are, the more interesting they get, and the more significant they become. I want to thank the swindlers of the prosecution again for making me the man I am today. Thank you for making me into a household name for spreading propaganda throughout the whole world on behalf of the cause of freedom of speech and opposing dictatorship and tyranny. It satisfies my vanity, though in reality I am not so good or brave as a person—"

"Shut up!" roared the prosecutor.

"I always warn officials wandering near my prison door, for their own good: Ahead is a great abyss; retreat from it, repent, and be saved, or they will destroy you in the end—and they always do. People on the Internet ridicule me, saying that I am the black crow prophesying doom. Whoever I mention ends up going to jail . . ."

"Shut up!" yelled the judge, the prosecutor, and the court stenographer all together.

"Swindlers, stop before it's too late . . ."

"Seal his mouth! Son of a bitch!" they shouted, and the court became a combat zone as the roars of lions vied with the growls of tigers. The police rushed forward, but the animal tamer dodged them. The police swung their clubs and hit the face of the accused. Blood splattered in all directions, but he kept on reading his statement: "Lord, please forgive me . . . and forgive the swindlers of the prosecution because they know not what they do. I say this prayer in the name of Jesus, the son of our Heavenly Father . . ."

They pushed the animal tamer to the ground. Once again his lips swelled up like a pig's snout. The judge wiped the sweat from his face and sentenced Chen to four years in prison. Chen said he refused to accept the sentence, swearing to appeal because it was too light.

The Accomplice

One day, at home in Sichuan, I got a call from someone claiming to be my "accomplice." When I went downstairs to meet him, I saw a plump, ruddy-cheeked man entering the main gate of our apartment complex, opening his arms toward me from a distance. It was the former poet Li Qi, who once played a small role in the production company for my film musical *Requiem*, which landed us all in jail. Now he was in the "alternative book business," a gray market where people purchase excess print runs directly from the printer and sell them off on the side. There was no trace of the suave young man he once was.

Li talked about how other accomplices of ours—friends also sentenced in connection with *Requiem*—were doing. "Most of them have made some money, but there are exceptions like L, who still lives in the county capital. The woman he married snorts heroin. Whenever she's on the stuff, she starts cutting her wrists. The whole family hit rock bottom. Not to mention W, who lost two wives in ten years and now spends his days drinking, stuck in a dream world."

Li Qi: I don't think we've seen each other in ten years.

That's right. In 1994, a month or two after getting out of prison, I went to Chongqing to visit you. We were like two thieves standing at the end of the alley near your home. You suddenly gave me 200 yuan and found an excuse to hurry off. At the time I was hurt. I had spent more than ten hours on the train from Chengdu and you wouldn't even invite me into your home for a rest or a drink of water. But compared to other accomplices of ours, you and I at least met up. Z wouldn't even take my phone calls.

So many years have passed. Nobody owes anybody anything. You should be content with your lot. So many of your buddies were scapegoated and thrown in jail for your film musical, while you alone became famous as the ringleader.

So what if you had to spend four years in prison; in the end, it will ultimately be worth it. One day sooner or later, the June Fourth cases will be overturned. Then you will be the hero and get all the credit, demanding justice and decency and even material compensation from the state for your sufferings. What a beautiful prospect! Meanwhile, the rest of us caught up in the case were jailed for a year or two, some just for a few months. We went through the same torture, but we were just "educated and released." No credit for that.

That wasn't my choice. Nobody is willing to go to jail for four years for the sake of a poem or two.

What was I punished for?

I don't know myself. When we made the film Requiem, *I borrowed some costumes from you. You donated several hundred yuan and went with me to the Sichuan Institute of Foreign Languages dance hall to find some actresses.*

I wasn't even an official member of the film crew. At most I played a tiny role in the whole thing, but for that my home was searched, I was thrown into an interrogation center, and I was locked up for over half a year. I was interrogated in shifts for over ten days, grinning and bearing it as they slapped me around. I confessed everything and wrote up a pile of evidence exposing your activities. All I wanted was to get out of there as soon as I could. The interrogation center was hellish. Although I was a political prisoner and didn't have to go through the prison entry procedures, I had to sleep next to the toilet and ended up with lice all over my body. At the time, my daughter had just turned one and my wife, Xiaoxiao, needed someone to care for her. My life was ruined.

I would guess that all over China something on the order of several hundred thousand people were investigated, at least briefly, after June Fourth—more than the number detained in the Anti-Rightist Campaign of 1957.

Generally speaking, experiencing a few trials and tribulations in your life is not necessarily a bad thing, but I paid too terrible a price for it.

When I got home from jail, Xiaoxiao was sitting in a chair with the baby, not saying a word. I went over to her, thinking I would bend over and give her a kiss. Instead she got up and pointed to the change of clothes next to us. "First take a bath."

I walked into the bathroom like a zombie. The emotional reunion after a long separation, which I had rehearsed so many times in prison, just popped like a bubble. Washing and scrubbing in the hot bath relieved my frustration—it was something I hadn't been able to do for many months—and I relaxed. I understood that Xiaoxiao must be angry with me. Taking care of the child for so long without her husband had been hard on her.

I couldn't taste dinner. I kept stealing glances at her on the other side of the dining table. I wanted to hold her, I wanted intimacy, so much! What a long-suffering prisoner wants most is to spend the whole night hugging his wife, having sex, and pouring out his heart to her. But Xiaoxiao was quiet, without the slightest ripple of feeling. Whenever I tried to approach her, she would put the child in front of her chest like a holy woman's shield of chastity.

Later, I learned that Xiaoxiao purposely went and brought our daughter back—she was staying with Xiaoxiao's parents—so she could use the kid against me. Late that night when everything was quiet and she no longer had any excuses to keep puttering around, Xiaoxiao finally came to bed. The child was already sound asleep. I whispered to her, "Put Bingbing back in her little bed." She refused and put the child on the bed between us.

I nearly got down on my knees and begged, but she still said no. She turned out the lights and lay down with the child under her armpit, like a trench between us separating flesh from soul. I repeatedly reached out to stroke her hair, to feel her neck, to touch her breasts. But she kept shrinking away from me, saying, "Don't disturb Bingbing." Finally I couldn't contain myself any longer. I got up, crossed the trench, and pressed her under me. We wrestled quietly, rolling off the bed. The child woke up crying and called for her mother. From beneath my body, she called repeatedly, "Don't cry, Bingbing. Be good, don't cry."

Seized by lust, I pulled off her clothes and forced my way into her. She couldn't move. She just grabbed at me, called me an asshole, and sobbed. The child was fussing and her mother was crying. I had never expected our reunion to be such hell. I felt like I'd sinned. After coming quickly, I slapped myself hard on my face twice and roared, *"What have I done wrong? What have I done wrong?"*

"You didn't do anything wrong," said Xiaoxiao. "It's me and Bingbing. We're a burden to you; we're keeping you from achieving great things."

"I didn't want to go to jail, either," I explained. "I didn't want to leave you."

"I've had enough of you poets," said Xiaoxiao. "I'm vulgar. I'm sleazy. I'm greedy for money. I want a quiet life. If you can't live with that, you should leave now."

I said I would never leave them. I swore all I wanted in life was my wife, my child, and a warm bed. I repeatedly cursed your ancestors,

Liao Yiwu, going back eight generations. When dawn came, I saw that she had calmed down and I took the opportunity to ask if we could have sex. Xiaoxiao didn't resist this time, but she was like a block of wood letting me move her back and forth. When I was finished, she got up right away to wash herself off. I was an idiot, following her around with a smile on my face, until she turned around, irritated, and said, "You don't have any feelings at all. You're pathetic, Li Qi."

She was deliberately hurting you.

It's all because of you. Xiaoxiao got dragged into it, too. She was jailed for over ten days and interrogated almost every day. Just think about that: a naïve and simple girl, a college graduate whose character had been formed by literature and who, after she married me, wrote a love diary nearly every day. Suddenly all that was swept away. Locked up with her in the women's prison were prostitutes, thieves, pimps, perverts, and drug addicts. They were even more brutal in their torturing of new prisoners than the men. They would burn her vagina, use chopsticks to squeeze her nipples, and hit her buttocks with plywood. Scared to death, Xiaoxiao wept all day and nearly went crazy.

This disaster completely changed her outlook on life. She hated me, and hated you, the root of our disaster, even more. She decided she would reform me when I got out. She gathered up all the strange clothes I wore in my poet days and threw them out. Then she took me to a department store to buy a Western business suit, a tie, and leather shoes. I felt uncomfortable dressed up like that from head to toe. To be blunt, I had never dressed up since leaving my mother's womb. Even worse, she put a waxy wig on my bald head that made me sweat like a pig. But I didn't dare take it off, so I just frowned. Xiaoxiao took great pains with my appearance, putting me in front of the dresser mirror and examining me closely for a long time. Finally she laughed with satisfaction. "*This* is what a normal man looks like."

You are so miserable, Li Qi.

I didn't feel miserable, because I owed Xiaoxiao. The first time I went back to the school where I had been teaching, dressed up in all that nonsense, I found out that I had been fired. My secure source of income was gone. I braced myself to go to the street committee office to check my household registration and apply for a temporary residence permit. The police in charge told me in front of everyone I would have to report on my "thinking" to their office once a month. I accepted it. That was what society was like after June Fourth. No flowers, no applause, no demonstrations in the streets or yelling of slogans. In an instant the wind started blowing in the opposite direction. Everybody forgot everything.

Xiaoxiao arranged for us to go see her family. My mother-in-law laid a nice spread with food and drink and we sat around the table. Each spoke up in turn offering advice, saying things like "Li Qi, you're thirty years old. Now that you've learned your lesson, you should live a peaceful life." Or: "Your wife had a hard time. She not only suffered herself but had to take care of the child on her own while she waited for you." Or: "People with education are clever. They certainly can make a lot of money. Let's drink a toast to the future wealthy man Li Qi!"

I kept drinking alone until I collapsed. They carried me off to bed. In that half-conscious state, I heard someone say, "Get over this bump in the road and start a new chapter free and clear. Put the brains you've spent on writing poems to work earning money." I was forced to whore myself out.

*Literature was fashionable during the 1980s and business was
fashionable in the 1990s. Times change.*

Yes, the gunfire of June Fourth woke a lot of people up from a dream. They couldn't afford to love their country, or thought, or literature. Money was the only thing that overrode country, social status, literature, something they could devote themselves to completely.

Who wants to live for money? At first I couldn't find work. People weren't so open-minded in 1991 and 1992. Once they heard you were involved in the disturbances, they didn't dare hire you. I explained over and over how I had been wronged. They said without a letter from the public security bureau they couldn't consider me.

Chongqing was an old center of the Communist Party back in its underground days, so once people have a few drinks, they get frank. But they clam up completely as soon as you follow up with them on anything they promised over drinks. I wasted more than six months this way. Xiaoxiao suggested that I write to earn money. I got in touch with twenty or thirty periodicals all around the country. Some of my old contacts had moved up to deputy editor, director, or a similar position. In those dark days as a freelance writer, I devised seven or eight pen names for myself and, employing my old skills as a poet, started writing all kinds of articles. At first I was very exacting, weighing every word carefully, and I restricted myself to the literary world, writing lyrical prose, light essays, thoughtful pieces, book reviews, and short novels. I wrote at most two or three pieces a month, about 10,000 Chinese characters total. It was hard and thankless work. Editors kept rejecting my articles.

"Write something fashionable and send it to entertainment magazines," Xiaoxiao advised me. "Write about fashion, or makeup, or write love stories, or tragedies. It doesn't matter as long as the magazine pays well." I told her I couldn't do that, but that same evening I watched her churn out three 1,000-character essays about makeup in one sitting: "Why I Don't Worry as the Years Go By," "Twelve Secrets for Taking Care of Wrinkles," and "The Subtle Interaction of Perfume and Mood." I was astonished. If I could match her incredible pace of three articles a day, I would be a wealthy man within three years.

Everything I wrote from then on was trash. I could no longer express myself. Finally I stopped writing, not knowing what to do. I would sleep late and read literary classics until gradually I felt some creative inspiration. I started to write about my experiences in prison. Even though I had been out a long time, I always felt unsettled about it. I would often dream I was back in jail.

Although I wasn't the main person charged in the case, my scars are deeper than yours, Liao. You are destined to go down in the history of literature. In the future, in any discussion of the literature of June Fourth, "Massacre" and *Requiem* will have to be included. But as for me, my more than half a year in jail would be for nothing. If I didn't write about it, nobody would pay any attention to me.

Call it "history panic syndrome."

History always drowns out the voices of all but a few. Everybody has the right to struggle for himself. If I can manage to leave behind a book for my descendants to read, who knows, maybe it will become a bestseller and I will have become an essential part of that episode of history.

People who have been in prison are meticulous. Writing every day while Xiaoxiao was out, I would lock it all up in a drawer afterward. One day I forgot to remove the key from the drawer and went out to buy food. That was the day that Xiaoxiao happened to come back from work early. She looked around and dashed straight to my desk drawer. My forbidden literature was immediately discovered by the "home police."

I remember that when I got home and entered the room with pork and vegetables, my manuscripts had already flown all over the room and were strewn about the floor. "You cheater! Haven't you hurt me enough?"

She sat like a little girl among the scattered papers, crying bitterly, each cry stretching out into a long wail. I had never heard such miserable, desperate cries like that before. I was beside myself. I knelt before her like a criminal apologizing for his crime and begged her to forgive me. She just pushed me away and randomly picked up a page of criminal evidence to wipe her tears and her nose. She repeatedly muttered, "Do you know that the police are coming, coming to arrest you? *Do you know that?*"

We kept at it until late that night. Finally Xiaoxiao got up and stood at the dressing table wiping her face and fixing her makeup. Then she got her bag and turned to go out the door. I rushed to embrace her. No matter how hard she punched and kicked me, I wouldn't let go.

"I want a divorce!" she shouted.

"I won't allow it," I said.

"I'm afraid of you, Li Qi."

I gritted my teeth and said, "I'll burn it," but what I was really thinking was, *Can't I just bury it instead? Can't I just dig a hole and bury the manuscript in it?*

But I really burned it. Xiaoxiao stood watch in the bathroom, staring at me as I lit page after page. Then she took the black ashes, mixed them with the water in the toilet, and flushed down over a hundred pages. My eyes were bloodshot and my face was twitching. But I loved Xiaoxiao, that tyrant. I really was finished with all of it for the rest of my life.

For a long time after that I was very depressed. Xiaoxiao wouldn't talk to me. She would just assign me one fashionable topic after another to write about and say that it had to be finished within a certain amount of time. My mind, though, was filled with the destroyed manuscript. The flying ashes filled my brain like cancer cells, making it impossible to write anything else. "You have to earn your living," said Xiaoxiao. I still loved her, and the desire I felt for her increased with each passing day.

I deserved to be mistreated. For a whole month we had no sex. I was like a lion pacing back and forth in a room. I desperately wanted her to cause trouble and hit me. Late one night I woke up with strong desires and couldn't help putting my hand under the covers to touch her. With great trepidation my hand stopped for a moment on her breast. She didn't move, so my hand continued downward. When my hand reached her lower abdomen, she still didn't move. When my fingers slid into her panties and touched her, I was surprised she was wet. I was ecstatic. Tears rained down my face. Xiaoxiao was stirred by feelings of passion but she repressed them. The cold war between husband and wife was as thin as a piece of paper! So I cast the covers aside and, brimming with confidence, entered.

We've all had this experience, so there's no need to go into specifics. You got all excited, didn't you? Was it like watching an erotic drama?

Or a pornographic film? But this is the scene that followed. Xiaoxiao put up one of her legs to block me, saying, "I don't want to make love with you. My body feels it, but I don't want to do it."

"But you're all wet!" I exclaimed.

"I repeat," she replied, "I may be wet but I don't want to do it. Get off me." I became enraged. We started hitting one another and fell off the bed. I nearly tore her clothes to pieces and forced—

That's enough.

Yes, that's enough. When it was over, we didn't have anything to say to one another. After that we lived apart for two months and got a divorce by mutual consent. Our property and our child—it all went to her. I pay child support every month. And just like that, I became a bachelor wandering around without a penny to my name.

Do you still love her?

Feelings have their limits. Once you exceed the limits, the world changes.

You had changed.

Now I eat, drink, whore, and gamble. I swindle. I know all the tricks. I wrote for an independent book publisher for over a year and earned over 20,000 yuan. I decided that I would try to become a book publisher myself. I soon exhausted all my capital, so I borrowed money. I even cheated my mother out of her retirement pension. When she realized what I had done, she ran out the door and looked all over for me in the streets for a whole afternoon, crying and screaming. Fortunately, she wasn't hit by a car.

The first book I made money on was about the Indian meditation technique OSHO. I made 70,000 to 80,000 yuan on that. That book practically had me drowning in money. The famous poet N helped me get the book number the Chinese government requires for a book to be published. From the 1950s up to today, he has published several dozen poetry collections, so he knows the publishing world the way a fish knows water.

One day he invited me to come to his home after dinner to discuss something. I didn't realize that I would be entering a smoke-filled room with two mah-jongg tables. N didn't raise his head or give me a glance but just said casually, "You've come," and continued to rub his mah-jongg pieces. I stood to the side serving tea and pouring water, just keeping him company and smiling. That continued until the night was over and dawn broke in the east.

Finally N stretched and said goodbye to his mah-jongg friends. I was the only one left in the living room. I didn't know whether to stay or to leave. I gathered up my courage and grabbed my mentor, who was about to go off to his bedroom, and told him that I was there for business.

"Let's talk later," said N impatiently. "Call me this afternoon."

I went home with aching muscles, cursing in my head N's ancestors back eighteen generations. But unexpectedly the book number came through. If I had been a little impatient, I would have ruined a big deal.

Now that you've earned enough money, will you write your memoirs?

That kind of thing feels more and more distant to me now. It's like the way a child drops his beloved old toy in the water. The toy drifts away, never to be retrieved again. The child is still standing on the bank or running alongside it, chasing after the toy. I won't cry the way the child would, but the pain I feel deep in my soul, the pain from invisible but omnipresent fear, comes out of my prison experiences and my divorce. Talking with you about it today feels like a kind of emotional release or liberation, because there isn't anyone in the "alternative book industry" who understands these things.

One day, when I don't owe anyone anything anymore, I'll go off to be a hermit and really learn how to write. For now, all I can do is count money. Probably nothing would make Xiaoxiao happier than knowing that.

The Poet

One summer night in the prison yard, the poet Li Bifeng and I were gazing at the stars, discussing important issues like whether freedom is possible in the universe. The other prisoners were watching a classic movie from the revolutionary era. Out of nowhere, Li brought up a thousand-line poem he had written. Would I be interested in reading it and giving him some advice? I inhaled sharply and nodded.

Li, who had worked at the State Administration of Taxation, is one of the most talented writers of those imprisoned after June Fourth. He works in many genres: poems and songs, novels, plays, philosophy, political commentary, and letters of appeal. In between interrogations, he would sit in his pitch-black cell and ponder: Who invented mosquitoes as a weapon? He has a touch of the old Greek philosopher about him.

Of all of Li Bifeng's poems, the one that moved me the most is this one, which he wrote while he was in jail:

Winter comes too soon.
Our trees begin to wither,
since we can no longer feed them.
Our black hair frosts white,
in the years of passing snow
our skin cracking like parched earth.
Winter is here,

> we all love to hibernate.
> Our hearts are tired,
> our blood is tired.
> We hibernate under snow.
> In a country like this,
> all we have is hibernation.

The poem takes me back to the eighties, when I read the Russian poet Sergei Yesenin. In the prime of his youth, Yesenin wrote about the Russian winter and its clear bleak skies with metaphors like "patched calico" and "soiled kerchief." I also thought of the Chinese poet Hai Zi (Zha Haisheng), who threw himself under a train when he was only twenty-six, and of my own poetry, which used to pour out faster than I could write. Now even a single line is beyond me.

Shortly after Li Bifeng was released from prison, I went to interview my old friend the poet.

In the blink of an eye, your seven-year prison sentence is over and done with. I heard that you wrote over two million words while you were in there.

Li Bifeng: Most of it was confiscated, but I managed to hold on to several hundred thousand of them.

The more you suffer, the more imaginative you become. But how did you get involved in June Fourth?

The 1989 student movement spread first from Beijing to Chengdu and then from Chengdu to Mianyang. In May the university and polytechnic students were demonstrating in the streets. Seeing them there was very moving, so we hurried to the construction materials school in the Mianyang suburbs to get in touch with them and support them, but the school security patrol wouldn't let us in, saying we were "social chaff" plotting something sinister.

The next day we made banners in support of the students and persuaded some locals to participate in the demonstrations. Despite the blazing hot sun on May 21, 200 or 300 students held a sit-down strike in front of the city government offices. There were many people standing around, watching, but not one of them would give those patriots soaked in sweat so much as a cup of water. That infuriated me. I stood up on a rickshaw and started asking everyone to bring water and donations for the students. That day I was very eloquent. I talked for hours until I was losing my voice. Finally people started making contributions. Now that the students had the support of the people, their morale greatly improved. But as for me, because I had openly incited people to act, I had gotten myself in trouble. The public security bureau took note: "We'll have to detain that guy with the glasses from the taxation administration!"

Later, tracing the origins of my crime, the indictment quoted from a little poem I had published in the popular periodical *Seeking the Dream*:

> The sky is too dark
> I cannot see the volcanoes on the moon tonight

The prosecutor must have been illiterate, because he questioned just what it was I meant to say when I wrote that the sky was too dark.

"The sky is dark because the sky is dark," I answered. "That's all it means."

He pounded the desk, enraged. "You're being contentious. You're obviously slandering the socialist system by painting it pitch-black."

"My eyes are very nearsighted," I said, "so when I see that it's dark, I write that it's dark . . ."

Later, with the expert testimony of the editor Xie Zongnian, "The Sky Is Too Dark" became a truly reactionary poem and a solid piece of evidence against me.

After that day with the students in Mianyang, I caught wind from several sources that I was in trouble, so I fled. I headed directly to Chengdu to join the revolution. In the square by South Renmin Road, several hundred of us gathered and announced the founding of the Chengdu Young People's Autonomous Association. I was elected chairman of the association by majority vote.

What kind of activities did you organize?

I was in contact with a group from Peking University that was trying to spread the revolution. I went to the Sichuan Industrial College in the western suburbs and mobilized students there to participate in the May 30 Worldwide Chinese People's Demonstration. I was also planning to organize a "death-defying squad" to support the protests in Beijing. With a poet's intuition, I published "A Speech for the End of the World," predicting that the June of democracy would become a June of darkness. That angered some university students, who went to the police to inform on me and slander me as a "Taiwanese spy."

How did you know the end was near?

On the night of May 28, I was sleeping beneath the statue of Mao Zedong in the square, when I dreamed that six public security officers wielding police clubs came screaming at me like fiends: *"What are you doing?"*

A week later, on the morning of June 4, the dream came true. I was half-awake, half-asleep, lying under that same statue of Chairman Mao, and my eyes were open just a crack. By the dawn's first light I saw two ambulances and then some medical personnel. Behind them were several police cars charging up to the reviewing stand with horns blaring. A voice yelled, "Clear the square!" and several dozen people were led away.

Get this: exactly six public security men walked up the steps in front of the statue and prodded me with their batons, barking, "What's your business here?" Breaking into a cold sweat, I sat up and said, "Reporter," producing the fake ID card I had finagled through a backdoor deal. They thought it over before waving me off: "Go home and stay there."

After I escaped capture, I ran straight to Sichuan University to report to the underground student federation. A large group of students rushed to the square to give their support. I pedaled a rickshaw with a sophomore in it broadcasting our message. During the student-army standoff, we parked the rickshaw in the middle of the square and she rode on my shoulders, holding up a megaphone to plead our cause. Suddenly a swarm of green helmets and shields surged toward us. Exploding tear gas shot up to the sky, descending on us like a giant dissolving umbrella. My eyes started watering, and I fell off the rickshaw as the crowd stumbled in all directions. When the mist dispersed, both the rickshaw and our broadcaster were gone. Rumors went around that she was dead, and only years later were we able to verify that she had been captured, not killed.

We returned the compliment by throwing soda bottles at the police and scampering off like rats, running right out of our shoes. We were angry and sad beyond words. We went to factories to encourage the workers to go out in the streets, but we returned in despair. Back at the square, I happened to run into Yang Wei, a friend from Mianyang. Before I even had the chance to say hi, a tear gas bomb hit me in the ass with a thump. I howled; it was like needles boring into my eyes. My friend grabbed my hand and we ran blind. From near and far we heard screams and the dull thuds of batons landing on flesh. They must have flattened hundreds of skulls.

Meanwhile, Renmin Market was going up in flames, and many said the police had started it with their gunfire. Police and firefighters were on the scene, but they were chasing rock-throwing pedestrians instead of putting out the fire. A teenage girl yelled from a second-story window: "Don't beat the students!" A cop tossed a canister of tear gas into her window, and crimson smoke spewed out.

Smoke spread in all directions. We could only go back to Sichuan

University, but I was warned to leave immediately. Troops had already occupied Science and Technology University, and Sichuan University would surely be next. The students there gave me a rickshaw and a straw hat, and I took off running back into the streets, where I saw the most moving sight of the entire day. It was six older women kneeling in the middle of Dongfeng Road, begging the communications engineering college student support group not to go to the square. "Soldiers are everywhere," they said. "Don't go. You'll be killed."

Throughout that day and the following day, I wandered the streets of Chengdu. A seesaw battle went on between troops and the unarmed locals and students. A lot of blood was spilled. I saw many of the injured at the Chengdu Fifth People's Hospital and one female university student receiving emergency care. People say that the fire at Renmin Market burned all night. When I went back there on the afternoon of June 5, I could still see some smoke rising from the ruins. One person picked up a bottle of orange soda from among the debris and was promptly surrounded by bystanders, who gave him a good beating and scolded him for taking advantage of a national disaster. Others went and pried up concrete stakes used in the roadside railings, barricading entrances to police stations so that police cars couldn't get out.

By June 6, Chengdu was like a military camp covered in smoke. It was over. Seven or eight of us who thought trouble was coming for us—workers, students, and journalists—ran off together to Yunnan. I stayed in the home of a classmate in Kunming. Before I had a chance to catch my breath, the nationwide hunt for fugitives began on June 8. All kinds of people who had fled to Kunming from Shanghai, Beijing, and Chengdu converged and fled together to Xishuangbanna, heading to the southern border. When we got to Jinghong, we ran into the police. Most of us, including me, were captured. They kept me overnight at the Jinghong County Detention Center. I claimed that I was a journalist spending a few days looking into life in the border region and writing about local customs. Again I was able to get off.

After they let me go, I got in touch with a few others who had been able to evade capture. At Guangyun Temple we hired a monk to help us sneak across the border. Security at the border was touch-and-go. As we muddled our way through the checkpoint, we actually posed for a group photo. Soon after we entered the jungle, our monk-guide disappeared. I had always moved fast, and in my rush to get away I soon lost track of the others. *That's the way it goes,* I thought. I used the way leaves and branches grew as my compass and hurried in the direction I imagined to be south. I was on the run for three days and three nights, by which time I was teetering on the edge of complete exhaustion.

I figured the jungle would be full of poisonous snakes and wild animals waiting to ambush me, so I bought a machete to carry at my side. Later, I decided that it was too heavy and threw it away. After getting out of the jungle, I lay on the ground for a while. Faintly in the distance, I could see a Burmese village gleaming in the sun. Tears ran down my face. I slid down a slope through a dense undergrowth of giant reeds. I stood up, pushing away reeds as tall as a person, crashing and crushing my way forward, and then walked for about another thousand feet until I suddenly came to a fork in the road.

My instinct said to turn right. As if possessed by demons, I went straight. I had dreamed this exact scenario many times where my legs would not obey me. By now the leaves were so dense, it was impossible to take another step. A branch slid under my glasses and stabbed my eyelid. Voices began to echo right next to my ear, which made no sense to me. By the time the word had registered—"Freeze!"—I was surrounded.

Seven or eight people were pointing their guns at me. I heard the words, "Hands up!" and I obeyed. Suddenly I saw a beam of red light rushing toward me. It was the bright sun shining off the black nozzle of the gun. With a *wham*, my knees buckled, my soul fled, and I pissed my pants.

By the time I regained my senses, I was being carried into a village by two men, my two legs dragging behind me. Can you guess what happened? The guys who caught me were from Sichuan. They had been educated youths from Chongqing who crossed the border illegally in the 1970s to join the Burmese Communist Party's People's Army. At the time, China was supporting the People's Army in its guerrilla campaign against the forces of the Burmese government. So although they were from my own province, they still had to send me back.

No matter how much I pleaded with them, it made no difference. They took me past an ethnically mixed Chinese-Burmese village, hog-tied me, and handed me over to the Chinese border police. After loosening my bonds, eight border police lined up, spread their legs apart, and ordered me to crawl through their eight-groin tunnel. The squad leader gave me a kick that sent me flying until I landed facedown in the dirt like a dog eating shit. An excruciating wave of pain shot through my crotch. They left me with a hernia. In the summer, when I'm out cooling myself, a big lump can still protrude if I'm not careful.

I was nearly beaten to death. Later, a sentry tied me to the back of a tractor and started driving until my face was bent out of shape and my clothes were reduced to rags. That's how they dragged the "slave" back to Jinghong, where they locked me up in the detention center. The interrogator asked me, "How many army trucks did you burn? How many PLA soldiers did you kill? Did you steal anything?" I denied everything. They laughed at me. "Then why did you sneak across the border?"

I still stuck to my story: "I am a journalist. I came to the border to experience life on the border and write about local customs. I inadvertently got lost and crossed the border." They found my journalist's credentials and, surprisingly, let me go.

With only the 1-yuan compensation I got when I was released, I slept on the streets of Jinghong. I had nowhere to go, but I didn't dare contact anyone. I didn't dare go back to the temple, either, because if the monk-guide was exposed, the situation would get even more serious. All I could do was go back across the bridge over the Lancang River, walking a day and a night to the Simao District, up one long slope and then down another. After another day on the road, I reached Pu'er.

I spent my 1 yuan to buy food. I knocked on people's doors asking for water, but I was too ashamed to beg for food. There were mango trees and plantain trees along the way, but I couldn't climb them, so I couldn't steal anything. I threw rocks at them. I tried and tried until I was exhausted, but I couldn't get any mangoes to fall. The plantains were very bitter. I felt faint after taking a few bites, like I'd gotten food poisoning, so I didn't dare eat any more. When I reached Pu'er, I was completely exhausted. I couldn't move another step. Showing my journalist's pass, I shamelessly stopped a vehicle and bummed a ride, vowing to repay them extra when I got to Kunming.

When I got to Kunming, I found my classmate. Without saying a word, he cooked up a washbasin full of noodles. I slurped them down, rubbed my belly, and recovered enough strength to talk: "I can't serve my country and I can't escape, so I might as well just go home." My classmate gave me 20 or 30 yuan so I could spend the night somewhere in a hotel and then take the train back home. What I hadn't expected was that shortly after I left his place at ten p.m. that night, before I'd even walked very far, around ten plainclothes police would approach and arrest me.

All told, how many times were you caught and released?

I went to the Jinghong detention center twice. I was in the Kunming detention center for seven days and then released. They told me to go back to Sichuan and give myself up to the police there. Then I *really* got it in my hometown of Mianyang. When they interrogated me, the Mianyang police showed me photographs of myself during my escape and told me who I had been in contact with, all the evidence they had in my case.

My Kunming classmate got caught up in it. He was held for several days and then released after reeducation. In 1998, after I came to the attention of the authorities again, I went to see him once more. A few minutes after I left his home, I was caught again. The second time I went into "the palace," he was ordered to report to the public security bureau every day and was fired from his job.

For June Fourth, I got five years in prison for "propaganda and incitement." If you add on the time I was held for interrogation, I was held in detention centers for over a year. They punched and kicked me. They brought out other prisoners and gave them a good beating while forcing me to watch. They used electric prods to burn my tongue, which produced a blue curl of smoke and made me lurch forward. They would bring a basin of water, have me step in it, and then poke their electric prods in the water. As the electric shock wave coursed through me, my whole body would spasm and collapse. After repeating this a few times, my nose turned black and blue and my face got all swollen up.

There was heavy rain during the summer of 1991, and the Peijiang River overflowed. One evening while I was sleeping, I dreamed that a snake was licking the sole of my foot. I instinctively pulled back my foot. There was a splash, and I woke with a start. Floodwaters were already on my bunk. The prisoners were caught in the flood with no way to get out. We all yelled, "Turn on the light! Turn on the light!" The lights that were normally on all night were off. Everybody was splashing in the watery darkness. Nobody dared move, since if they fell off their bunks they might drown. The water in the small yard where we exercised was already over ten feet deep. We stood on our toes to keep water from getting into our mouths.

We heard noises at the door. A policeman swam into our cell. He told everyone to move out, hand in hand. We kept at it until dawn. We were out of danger, but the water still hadn't receded, so we were sent under escort to another place where we were packed in tightly—over seventy of us—into a 150-square-foot cell. The sky cleared and the hot sun appeared. In that steamy cell, people kept opening and closing their mouths like fish short of oxygen. That afternoon they drained the water out of the detention center and we returned to our cells, now full of mud that it was impossible to get rid of. We looked like a bunch of toads. But we could only make the best of our situation, and went on living. Afterward I was sent to Sichuan Provincial Prison No. 3 [in Dazhu County], where you and I first met, Liao.

Even after I was released, the police continued to harass me. My life was a mess. My family complained about me. To show that I had completely set aside my wicked ways, I got married and moved into my wife's work unit dormitory. It was a tiny room, without enough space even to turn around in, and we cooked in the corridor. Maybe my face was to blame—my eyes always darted around like a thief's—but no matter how much I nodded to the cops and kept my mouth shut around them, their suspicion of me never let up. Forced to be at their constant beck and call, I grew restless and rebellious again.

In the summer of 1995, when I heard that the Mianyang democracy movement figure X had gone to Shenzhen and fled the country from there, I was tempted. At the time, my son wasn't even 100 days old. We were very poor and I was in despair, constantly under the "special care" of the police. I talked it over with my wife and decided to give it a try. I immediately went to Shenzhen, where my democracy movement friends told me someone would meet me at the Shatoujiao Bridge. I had a newspaper in my hand that was supposed to be a signal so they would recognize me. I walked back and forth, trying to look like a gawking tourist, but I never saw whoever I was supposed to meet. Suddenly I ran into my high school teacher; astonished, I called out: "Teacher Wang, what brings you here?"

The police noticed me and ordered me to come over to show my ID. I forced a smile, but I already had a cramp in my legs. In less than three minutes one of the policemen ordered me into the sentry post. He made a call and after another three minutes he sent me to police headquarters, where they locked me up. By that time the Mianyang police were already expecting me back home. Without even setting foot on capitalist territory, I had to go back.

I didn't know until years later that a plainclothes policeman had been following me all the way to the border. Fortunately, I didn't have anything incriminating on me. That time I was held for only fifteen days for trying to cross the border illegally. After I was released, they stressed to me over and over that before leaving the Mianyang area I would have to report to them first.

To make my minders feel more at ease, I worked for several days part-time at a friend's company. In those days the democracy movement was more active, and many people were going to Beijing to file petitions. Liu Xianbin and other activists were operating openly in Chengdu and they often participated in discussions at Sichuan University. Wang Ming from Chongqing also got in touch. Wang wanted to make a "Citizen's Declaration." He only came a few times before our gathering place at Southwest University for Nationalities was shut down by the police. Call it rotten luck. I had just gone in there to rest at someone's invitation and was lying down when the police came knocking at the door. That time they arrested quite a few people. Wang Ming and I were both locked up and interrogated all night. When dawn came, they brought us outside to take mug shots. My heart jumped and I thought, *Shit. They're taking a picture to make a positive identification, which means they're going to send us away for reform through labor.*

At the time I had in my pocket "A Letter to Hong Kong Compatriots," which discussed the hoax of the 1997 handover of Hong Kong to China. I had waited for my chance to throw this piece of "evidence" out the window, but unexpectedly a policeman saw it and picked it up. Liao, you once wrote that "in those years, writing was creating evidence of your crime." Time and again my efforts to destroy the evidence against me failed at the last moment.

Yet again I was escorted back to Mianyang, held for a few days, and then released, but Wang Ming got three years of reform through labor. He had been in prison for five years the first time and had only been out for two years when he entered "the palace" that second time. That mishap cost me my job, so I worked it out with some friends to open a hotel called the Spring Water Fish at Chengdu's Beimen Bridge. Business wasn't bad, except that groups of hungry democracy movement friends came every day, some of them moochers using scheming and plotting for the movement as their pretext to stay for long periods at the hotel. As a result, the police would come looking for trouble. Liao, I remember on the day we closed for good, you and Wang came for a free meal. A customer had ordered fish, but I wouldn't sell it because I wanted to save the last fish for my friends in need.

My impression is that you have always been someone who comes and goes without leaving a trace.

People like us never feel safe. We're always running, even in our dreams. I was almost never at home. My wife and child would feel strange if I was there for a while. I wasn't a human being. I was a cornered "democracy beast."

Finally, they put you away in a cage again.

While working on my writing, I was also studying people's livelihoods. The old state-owned industries in the Mianyang region were in deep trouble. When a Mianyang silk factory was faced with bankruptcy, the heartless factory director took the funds the workers had raised for housing to invest in the stock market in Chengdu. He lost it all. People were furious. On the day things came to a head, in 1997, someone wrote on the blackboard, "Mianyang's Mayor Feng will come to the factory today to solve everyone's livelihood problems."

The workers waited patiently until ten a.m. but there was still no sign of the mayor, so more than 4,000 workers walked out of the factory gates, shouting and blocking the Shaanxi–Sichuan highway. Then the demonstrations got bigger as workers from the Mianyang silk spinning factory and other state-owned factories joined in, yelling slogans and coming over to lend their support. More than 10,000 people sat in the middle of the highway in the hot sun, blocking traffic for several hours. Naturally, a dictatorship resolves social conflicts violently. The police came and detained more than 200 people, and a curfew was announced.

When news of this reached the outside world, the Western media took notice, but the authorities claimed that none of it ever happened. When an official characterized the event as a "disturbance" in the local newspaper, I was livid and immediately wrote an appeal to the International Labour Organization at the United Nations, asking their help rehabilitating the people who had been arrested because of this "disturbance." I faxed my manuscript to the New York office of Human Rights in China. Soon a group at the United Nations was investigating it. All of the 200-plus people were released. The police, beside themselves with rage, came after me.

You were on the run for more than half a year?

I hid in an old fellow prisoner's home in Chongqing for a few days. Then Yang Wei came and took me to Guangzhou to prepare to cross the border into Hong Kong. However, T at Human Rights in China called to change the plan, saying that Hong Kong was too tense and that he couldn't go meet me there. I had no choice but to turn around and once again go back to the China-Burma border in Yunnan for a while. T again passed word that I should try to get across the border on my own. Someone would receive me at Chiang Mai in Thailand. It just went on and on like that, until eventually I went home.

People saw me as soon as I went in the front gate, but I was still determined to hurry up to the third floor and get through the door of our apartment. My wife was startled. "Why did you come home?" I hemmed and hawed and was about to head out the door, when my son suddenly hugged my legs and started crying, "I want Daddy!"

It was heartbreaking, because those were his first words. But there was nothing I could do: I had to harden myself and pry his hands off me, leaving with my eyes red with tears. I spent less than ten minutes at home before hurrying out into the street and hailing a rickshaw. When we reached the highway, I switched to a cab. I didn't ask how much, I just told the driver to drive toward Chengdu. Two police cars sandwiched us at a tollbooth, and the police dragged me out of the cab. The handcuffs clicked on my wrists.

I've now been captured more than ten times, caught red-handed each time. The last time I was caught, the case was about me alone, so I made a full confession. This time the authorities gathered many witnesses they had tampered with. I was sentenced to seven years in prison for "economic fraud crimes" and sent back to our old spot, Sichuan Provincial Prison No. 3. After a few months I was transferred to the Ya'an Prison in western Sichuan some 600 miles away. I was worn down, I had blood in my urine, my fingers bled, and I was as pale as a corpse. One day, when I had just woken up and eaten, I fainted. I spent several months in the hospital and feared that I wouldn't live to get out of jail. It was about that time that my wife asked for a divorce. I agreed for the sake of our son. Things dragged on there until 2003, when I met someone I knew in prison. We chatted for about ten minutes, but someone informed on us. Early the next morning I was transferred to the Mingshan Prison, about six miles away. There we made machine parts. The work was hard, awful. I was sick most of the time. My health improved slightly through better nutrition and exercise before my release. I wrote several million words' worth of poems and songs, novels and plays. Most of it was confiscated. I want to rewrite some of them from memory.

Running and jail; jail and running. Always back and forth between the two. Such is my life. I keep writing about life. But what is life? Now my son is nine years old and needs money and a steady father's love. But I have nothing.

After I got out, the public security bureau arranged for me to work at an insurance company. They said, "Don't you have a special talent for propaganda and agitation? Use it in that calling. Go from person to person and house to house and sell life insurance!" After two or three months I hadn't sold any insurance. I'm over forty years old and still asking my family for handouts. I have no shame. My way of earning a living now is writing. I want to publish books and articles abroad.

I've seen your poems, songs, and novels. It wouldn't be easy to make a living from them. In one of your poems you curse God, "that old landlord in the sky" who only wants to "use the gold coins of the sun to purchase humanity." Who could understand what that means?

You understand.

But I can't afford to pay authors' royalties.

The Prisoners

In the winter of 1992, two years into my sentence, I was transferred from a prison in Chongqing to Sichuan Provincial Prison No. 3, which was packed with June Fourth "counterrevolutionaries"; I met more than twenty of them there. The crime was always the same: "counterrevolutionary propaganda and incitement," but our sentences ranged from two years to twelve.

The shortest among us was Xu Wanping from Dadukou, in Chongqing, who, with his curving eyes and thin mouth, strongly resembles a laughing fox. The man is headstrong, and his thinking is totally naïve.

Xu was once an honest worker in a state-owned printing plant. His family had an excellent class background going back three generations—what they called a "brilliant red seedling background." In other words, he was a genuine proletarian. Who could have known the tricks fate would play? During the student movement of 1989, he followed the people into the streets and got mixed up in politics, chanting slogans and singing the Chinese version of the *Internationale*: "Overflowing with passion, we will fight for Truth!" With a black placard on his chest with the words "I am that son of a bitch Li Peng," he would stand on the street so the crowds could gawk at him and criticize him. All worked up, he was like a cross between performance artist and a red-cheeked fox.

He took advantage of the chaos to found the China Action Party. He was arrested a dozen or so days later and quickly sentenced to eight years in prison for incitement and for founding a counter-revolutionary organization.

Xu was frugal to the point of it becoming a vice. He often carried a big mug of sweetened water around with him, doling it out to himself one spoonful at a time, deliberately savoring every bit. He was interested in studying poetry, so we became friends and he invited me to enjoy some of his sugar water. Although I am a literary man, I am solidly built and have strong appetites. After a few polite words, I took the mug and drank it all in a few gulps and then in a grand gesture I wiped away the little pearls of sugar water from my mouth. Xu smiled and waited for me respectfully before saying, "Big Brother Liao, slow down a bit or you'll choke!" Remembering that scene many years later, I finally understood it a little bit better. Xu came from a very poor family. His father died young and his mother was retired, so they had just enough to survive on. The family would send small amounts of money, 20 or 30 yuan, to ease the hunger of their imprisoned, unfilial son.

Xu had a strong revolutionary will. He was punished a few times for his participation in prison strikes, hunger strikes, and other violations and locked up in that cramped little doghouse of a solitary confinement cell. As the chief negotiator for our group of political prisoners, he would go up to the prison office on the second floor. Before he could get a word out, they would force him to the floor and tie him up.

In 1997, Xu completed his sentence and was released. Without a way to support himself, he came with his poetry and other writings to visit me when I was down in the dumps. He spent over a month working in my mother's teahouse, attentive and ready to work hard, earning the appreciation of the middle-aged and elderly clientele. There was very little money to be made in the teahouse, though, so Xu had no choice but to eat less and less. Xu read a great variety of books and made many friends while he was there. He wrote a lot and his thoughts bubbled up like the water in a fountain. His ability and fame were growing, even as he grew more emaciated.

Then, in the fall of 1998, Xu became an activist in the China Democracy Party. During that very jittery period, he entered "the palace" for a second time, for the crime of subversion. This time, because the Chongqing police complained that the legal system was too obsessed with small details, they sent him directly to the Xishanping Forced Labor Camp for three years of reform through labor. Three years later, it was a fall afternoon when I got a phone call from Xu. His breathing was weak and punctuated by coughing. He said that Xishanping was the worst place in the world and that he had barely managed to get out of there alive. I didn't know what to say. "I was caught between common criminals and Falun Gong practitioners," he went on. "I didn't have a single June Fourth comrade in prison with me."

"You should write down your experiences," I said when I was finally able to interrupt him.

"They destroyed me in there," Xu panted. "Whenever I pick up my pen to write, my head buzzes."

Survival cuts like a knife, and human rights don't put food on the table. Xu, with his battered, bleeding, and buzzing head, had to start keeping a lower profile and join the hundreds of millions of other Chinese working to earn a living. He went around doing sales and ran a street stand. He even had the title "Business Manager" on his business card. On the eve of the SARS outbreak, he used a $500 donation from Liu Qing of the NGO Human Rights in China to open a noodle shop with another fellow sufferer, Jiang Shihua. Business was just starting to pick up, and Xu's morale was improving, when the SARS epidemic hit hard. In the blink of an eye, the government ordered Xu's noodle shop and others on the same street to close down.

Xu had invested all of his family's savings, and now it was completely gone. In desperation, he went to the police station, alone, protesting that he had a right to live, too. It didn't do any good. He made an overseas collect call and made unfounded accusations against various people for living off the sweat and blood of the democracy movement people. All that did was cut him off from the support he needed. One evening, Xu called me to say that he had just arrived at Chengdu's North Gate train station. After I gave him detailed directions to my house, I put down the telephone receiver and waited for him until late that night, but he never came.

Had the police arrested that crazy fucker? I lay on my bed wondering until I eventually fell asleep.

Just like that, Xu kept bumping along, eking out a living and finally even getting married, which was truly a wonder of wonders. I vaguely recall that his wife was a laid-off worker, too. The home the two of them made for themselves had all the distinguishing characteristics that Marx ascribed to the proletarian home.

On the Internet, I sometimes saw Xu's commentaries on current political issues, which must have earned him some royalties. Commemorations of June Fourth had started popping up in cities across China, and with the fifteenth anniversary approaching, Xu announced that he would organize one in Chongqing. I had seen plenty of them and didn't pay much attention to it. When Xu was arrested on June 3, I wasn't very surprised. During those years, democracy activists were always being detained and released.

But Xu had narcotics planted on him, and he was charged with drug trafficking. According to one report, someone walking by had slipped a bag of heroin in his pocket, and in short order Xu was videotaped and intercepted by police who were waiting right there in the shadows.

Just like some fucking Hong Kong movie, I thought angrily. Once the date of the anniversary was past, Xu was released yet again, but this time the narcotics division at the public security bureau had tortured him and tied him to a chair for forty-eight hours straight. How could he stand it? He didn't say. What was he going to do in the future? No one asked. Too much goes on in the world. In just a moment, it all becomes old news. *Xu is still alive,* I thought, *and in that sense he is doing pretty well.*

Not long after that, Xu was sentenced to twelve years in prison for the crime of trying to "overthrow state power."

———

Tall and thin, Pu Yong came from an influential family of practitioners of Chinese medicine in Nanjiang County, in the Daba mountain range of northeast Sichuan. He was a deputy town head in his early twenties and once had the prospect of a brilliant political career. Enraged after the Tiananmen slaughter, he took advantage of the nighttime stillness to distribute and post hundreds of leaflets condemning the Chinese Communist dictatorship. Swiftly sentenced to ten years in prison, he was just as quickly sent under armed guard to the Peng'an Prison in the Nanchong region. There he became fast friends with Lei Fengyun, who had gotten his own heavy sentence for attempting to dig up the graves of Deng Xiaoping's ancestors. They secretly tried but failed to build a political system inside the prison. Betrayed by informers, the two became the focus of a "struggle meeting" held in front of all the other prisoners. Then they were locked away in solitary confinement, in tiny rooms the size of dogholes, for three months. After getting out of the hole, Pu Yong was immediately transferred to another prison, where he became one of my fellow inmates.

To blunt his passionate spirit of resistance, the prison's cunning political commissar personally put Pu Yong into the lowest level of the prison, the automobile parts foundry and grinding workshop. Every day, for his reform-through-labor work, he did extremely punishing physical labor amid the constant dust of the foundry workshop. As a result, Pu contracted serious stomach and lung disorders for which he was never treated. He became as emaciated as a shadow, as bony as a ghost.

Despite all this, Pu studied hard every night. He read the classics intensively, especially Sun Tzu's *Art of War* and Liu Bowen's Ming-era commentary on the *Tui bei tu*, the famous book of prophecies. As he gradually came to understand these works better, he would often ask me for insights into them. Incapable of doing more than writing a few verses of clumsy poetry, I didn't understand them, either, so I introduced him to Li Bifeng, who was reputed to be an extraordinary fortune-teller.

As the sun was setting one day, Li Bifeng and I were strolling the prison yard as usual, when Pu suddenly appeared and asked, "Where are you going?"

"I go wherever I want to," I said.

"Let's imitate Old Mao," said Pu, "and play a game of mountain guerrilla warfare. Crazy Li, how about you and I discuss strategy?"

"Why in hell does a scholar want to fight like a guerrilla?" replied Li Bifeng.

"It'll be fun just to experience what it's like to carry out an armed uprising," replied Pu.

The three of us had a conversation ranging across 5,000 years of Chinese history, astronomy, and geography as we paced back and forth like caged lions. Our faces turned red as we engaged in a battle of words. One moment we were shouting angry insults, the next we were laughing. It went on until a jailer on the second floor whistled to alert us that the outdoor recreation period had ended.

During the last late autumn of the twentieth century, Pu was released after completing his sentence. His ambition was as high as the heavens, but his fate was as thin as paper. He huffed and puffed and ran all over the country, both north and south of the Yangtze, getting in touch and arguing with all the democracy movement figures he could find, and he returned home disappointed. Once Pu Yong visited me at home to ask about the whereabouts of my friend Yang Wei, who had fled abroad because of the China Democracy Party case.

Watching Pu's expression and choosing my words carefully, I told him about how Yang Wei had asked for political asylum at the U.S. embassy in Bangkok but was turned away. His face turning ghastly pale, Pu was quiet for a while before finally saying, "Then what can the unknowns like us do?"

I had no answer for him. During that long silence, Pu finally realized there was nobody to rely on besides himself as he struggled to live his difficult life. When we met again, Pu was enrolled as a student at the Chengdu University of Traditional Chinese Medicine. "I'm a bit older than the other students," he laughed, "but after studying for a few years, I'll be able to open my own clinic and rely on my own skills to live a normal life."

Later, we didn't have as much contact as before. I remember once when Pu was at my place, sitting and not saying much before suddenly sighing. "She Wanbao, Li Bifeng, and Xu Wanping are all back in prison again. Of all the others, you're the only one with a fixed address. They're all just drifting."

I tried to console him: "You'll soon lead a normal life."

Pu shook his head. "On the outside everything looks normal, but my heart just can't get past it, not until the victims of the June Fourth tragedy are acknowledged. I don't want anything. I just want them to be acknowledged."

After that, we didn't see one another again. My home wasn't far from where Pu was going to school. I would often walk over and ask after him, but I always returned home disappointed. Pu hadn't left a telephone number. All the political prisoners were like frightened birds when they left prison. Once they flew past, they were gone, leaving little trace in reality or in history.

Autumn passed and winter came. My father went into the hospital with a terminal illness. After fighting for over a year, he finally died in the cancer ward where Pu had studied. Once the funeral arrangements were complete, I returned home feeling like my skin had been peeled off. After beating up on myself for a while, I curled up like an insect and tried to get a good night's sleep. Just then, the phone rang. It was Pu's younger brother Pu Xiongwei: "My elder brother has late-stage stomach cancer and is in critical condition." My hands and feet started quivering so badly, like springs, that the call got cut off. I had to look up the number displayed and call back. At the other end of the line was Pu in his hospital bed. His life hung by a wavering thread, but his spirit was still fresh. Overcome by grief, I felt something blocking my throat, and for a while I didn't know what to say.

Pu consoled me instead. "Don't be sad. We'll meet again some decades in the future." Then he haltingly explained his medical condition. "My stomach gets bigger and bigger every day." He squeezed out a laugh. "But I'm not pregnant. It's just ascites."

"Can I do something for you?" I asked.

"There's no need now," he answered.

"The court verdict?" I asked.

"The prison confiscated it. There is a copy in the files of the public security bureau in my old hometown. When you have time, go to the library and read the October to November 1989 issues of the *Sichuan Daily*. There are reports in it about my counterrevolutionary crimes."

Two days later, Pu, following my father, departed this world. Xu Wanping (just out of prison), Lei Fengyun (who had always wanted to dig up the tombs of Deng Xiaoping's ancestors), and Hou Duoshu (just married) hurriedly got together and rushed to see him, but it was too late. All they saw were his ashes. When he was buried, the three cried by his grave, reading out names one by one and crying in bitter grief, to represent all who had suffered because of June Fourth. They heaped up flowers, burned incense, and set off firecrackers. Then in silence they wished him peace.

But Pu Yong can't possibly rest in peace.

————

When Yang Wei, from a poor family in Dujiangyan, was arrested at the age of seventeen, he was a callow student at a technical high school, with no prior involvement in national affairs. He had a heavy local accent and was no good at dealing with outsiders, but he was as alert as a civet cat and hard to keep tabs on.

In the aftermath of June Fourth, filled with righteous anger, Yang wrote a proclamation, which he posted in several hundred places through-out Chengdu. The poster openly called for rebellion, blood for blood, and the overthrow of the dictatorship. To make it look more authentic, he signed it in the name of the "Sichuan Branch of the China Democracy Party." The mention of that long-established democracy movement orga-nization, based abroad, made it a big case, which local, city, and provin-cial authorities reported up to the Party Central Committee. A group of experts was assembled to analyze the information. Several hundred police were mobilized and given a deadline for solving the case.

Absurdly, the footloose criminal Yang was able to remain at large for more than six months, carrying two large stamp albums and scampering around more than ten different southern cities as he sold the stamps off one by one. "I've been a stamp collector ever since I was just a few years old," Yang Wei confessed after his capture. "Every time I got to a new place, I would first go roam around the stamp market for a few minutes and soon have enough money to eat for a few days."

The state mobilized an impressive and persistent police hunt, but the criminal they caught was just a big kid with eyes so clear that you could see right down to the bottom. Exhausted by their investigation, the police were disappointed. What irritated them even more was that the kid had had no contact at all with foreigners. He didn't even know what the China Democracy Party was or where it was headquartered. When they asked about the "Sichuan branch organization," Yang confessed: "I am the chair-man, vice chairman, propaganda department head, and office worker."

This was too much for the public security bureau officials, the state prosecutor, and the courts to take. Yang was given a good beat-ing and thrown into a prison cell. "I made mental notes so I would be prepared to argue in court," Yang recalled, "but there wasn't any courtroom. They decided my case in an office. The verdict was al-ready sitting on the desk. The judge picked it up, handed it to me, and told me to scram. I wouldn't scram. He picked up the case record in his two hands and slammed me on the head with it."

Yang was sentenced to three years in prison for incitement to overthrow state power. He worked sanitation in the prison workshop, hanging around all day with an extremely tall murderer from Henan Province. Whenever they quarreled, Yang would glower from under the armpits of the giant, like a small mouse protesting to a tyrannical old cat.

One time, the criminal offenders, who were ten times more numerous than the political prisoners, ganged up on some political prisoners out on a hunger strike. Seeing his chance, the old Henan cat swaggered toward the little mouse and, with a swoosh of his hand, grabbed him by the collar and wouldn't let him down no matter how much he struggled. The prisoners all laughed. That scene came to symbolize prison life for me. Years later, the sight of Yang hoisted up in the air by invisible hands and suspended in the void, his feet dangling in the air, still comes back to me in my dreams so vividly that when I finally wake up, exhausted, it's as if I can feel the spasms in my own calves, too.

Yang returned home after his release in the spring of 1993. He worked as a laborer transporting beer for small merchants along the river with a tricycle cart. After he earned some money, he got restless again and started traveling up and down the country.

Later, he shut himself indoors and pored over banned democracy movement books as well as modern and ancient detective novels from both China and abroad. His thinking and his skills advanced rapidly. Not only did he find ways to fight the enemy through surreptitious communications by pager, fax, and public telephones, but he also managed to master, by persistent experiments, the extremely difficult art of using special chemicals to make invisible ink for secret communications. (In the novel *Red Crag*, set in the revolutionary era, using invisible ink to write characters that appear after the paper is immersed in water for a few minutes was the special trick of underground Communist organizations.) Unfortunately, up to this day, no one in the democracy movement recognized Yang's talent for using these secret techniques. "The police have become like roundworms in our stomachs!" he said. "They even know if you fart or have an erection." Yang was discontented, as men with unappreciated talents are.

For some time Yang stayed in secret contact with Liu Qing of Human Rights in China, based in New York City, exchanging information. He had also worked with me in helping fellow prisoners send out letters to the international community, asking for support. Unfortunately, the authorities found out about our activities and the two of us were caught and held for more than twenty days. Yang started worrying excessively that there were enemies everywhere, and his espionage skills became more elaborate than necessary. Once, choosing a time when I was away, he gave a pot of camellia flowers to my father, moving the old man to tears. My father watered and fertilized the plant and took extremely good care of it, never realizing that at the bottom of the pot was a letter of warning. Two months passed before Yang dropped a hint about it. Realizing that I hadn't understood him, I dug up both the soil and the plant. All that remained of his cry for help was a ball of paper nearly turned to mud, and a few earthworms.

In the fall of 1998, the actual case of the Sichuan Branch of the China Democracy Party erupted. Yang's old prank had come to life. The main culprits—Liu Xianbin, She Wanbao, Hu Mingjun, and Wang Sen— were arrested and sentenced to ten or more years in prison. Yang, as one of the seven core members of the group, was in his family's seventh-floor apartment, home-brewing Chinese medicine for his ailing father, when plainclothes special agents blocked his door.

The corridor outside their apartment was filled with black smoke and foul odors. The Yang family was very poor. Everything was in plain view. It only took the special agents a few minutes to turn everything upside down in their home. Yang knew he had been caught. He put down a bowl of Chinese medicine and laughed derisively. "I'm off to eat at government expense!"

With special agents pushing and cajoling Yang, the group twisted its way down many flights of stairs. Trapped in the middle, Yang staggered along, holding a metal bucket of coal ash and scattering irritating dust powder in the air as he went. The special agents couldn't dodge out of the way. When they ordered him to stop, Yang begged pitifully, "Let me first fulfill my duty to my father. Once I leave, I don't know how many months or years it will be until I can return home!"

"If you knew that before, you shouldn't have committed a crime," said the special agent in charge.

Yang kept on dawdling. When he reached the bottom of the stairs, he pounded on the ash bucket, creating thick clouds of dust. "Are you trying to cause trouble?" yelled the special agents. Paying no attention, Yang crossed the street and dashed into a trash collection station. At just that moment, a whirlwind's gust swept close to the ground. In an instant, the smoke from the knocked-over ash bucket blotted out both sun and sky. Yang seized the moment to run for it, and the pack of special agents had no way of chasing him. They could only stare at their own shadows and gnash their teeth in dismay.

Yang wandered aimlessly, like a dog without a home. He traveled north alone, trying to sneak into the Russian Far East at Jiamusi, in Heilongjiang Province. That didn't work, so he went back home, following the ancient principle that "a smart rabbit has three holes." He played hide and seek with the police in the Chengdu area for a while. Soon after that, Yang took a big chance. Using a counterfeit national identity card, he joined an international tour group and arrived in Bangkok. He pretended to be a sex tourist and kept insisting on going to the red-light district. He switched cabs on the way and, without knowing anything about his surroundings, made his way to the U.S. embassy, where he wept, soaked with sweat and overwhelmed by the smell of freedom.

That winter I got a fax from Yang. He wrote that the U.S. embassy had thrown him out and that he had nearly become homeless on the streets of Bangkok. Apparently, a Buddhist monk had taken Yang in.

Every day he swept the temple grounds in exchange for vegetarian food. Out of compassion for a friend in need, I contacted many foreign friends, trying to get help for him, but political asylum cases cannot be rushed.

Four or five years went by. Then one day Liu Qing, the human rights activist in New York, told me on the phone that Yang's status as a democracy activist had been formally recognized. The office for political refugees at the United Nations had accepted his case and arranged to send him 8,000 Thai baht, around $200, every month, just enough to pay for room and board. "Needless to say," Liu Qing said, "Yang won't be able to eat very well."

"What happens next?" I asked.

"I'll help him get in contact with a country that is willing to accept him. It's very difficult. There are many rules and regulations involved. After that, he'll have to rely on himself," Liu replied.

More time passed, until one day I was having tea with a writer named Wang, who told me that Yang had reached Canada.

"What else?"

"He says that your old phone number doesn't work."

"What else?"

"He wants me to give you his new telephone number."

At the end of 2011, after I, too, had followed Yang into exile, I was surprised to get a phone call from Sheng Xue, a friend in Canada, who told me that Yang's depression had developed into mental illness and that he was in a psychiatric hospital. "I'm on my way to visit him," said Sheng. "As his fellow prisoner and friend, do you want to say anything to him?" he asked.

"Please ask him not to be crazy."

"But nobody wants to be crazy. It must be that Canada is too cold and he can't get used to it."

"Even if it's hard to get used to, it's much better than living under the Communist dictatorship."

"He kept asking to go back to Thailand," said Sheng. "He believes that temple is his home."

Lei Fengyun, from Guang'an in northeastern Sichuan, is a tall, solidly built man full of poise and integrity—indeed an overall magnificence—incomparably greater than that of a much shorter man from the same county named Deng Xiaoping.

Young Lei was precocious and patriotic, and a great supporter of Deng—who had been championed by hot-blooded students in Tiananmen Square just thirteen years before June 4, 1989. When Deng came to power, he launched Reform and Opening and revived the university entrance examinations. Lei, from a humble background, rose with the times and passed the higher education entrance examination. He became a graduate student in English literature at Southwest China Normal University in Chongqing, which was something extremely rare in the 1980s, when very few people had any higher education.

Full of gratitude for these opportunities, Lei nonetheless cast aside a brilliant career out of righteous anger over the June Fourth massacre—and he held Deng responsible, feeling personally humiliated. "I wanted to avenge that humiliation," he told the writer Zhou Fengsuo, "but I couldn't get close to him. I felt the urge to dig up the graves of his ancestors. In our Sichuan, if someone commits a terrible crime that enrages both heaven above and mankind below, people would traditionally punish that person by digging up the graves of their ancestors."

So, on June 5, 1989, when the whole country had turned into an armed encampment, Lei and several other students from his hometown took a three-day train ride home. In the station waiting room in Guang'an, in front of some shocked fellow passengers, the group proclaimed their "Grave Digging Declaration" and promptly exited the station to buy shovels, spades, and the other tools they needed to carry out their plan.

They tried to board a bus, but the driver wouldn't let them get on.

Cabs refused to take them. Passersby came and went in a hurry, casting very suspicious looks their way. Lei felt something was wrong. He left his comrades, deciding to walk alone somewhere where he could get the lay of the land. A traffic policeman blocked his way, informing him that everything within a six-mile radius of Deng's home and his ancestor's graves was now under military control.

Lei was astonished. He didn't know yet that one member of the group had already betrayed them and that the police were onto them. To display loyalty to that iron-willed dwarf bandit Deng, the provincial government had even transferred an army battalion to the scene. Soldiers had already taken up positions all around, swords ready and guns loaded, prepared to annihilate in an instant any enemy who might dare to strike.

Lei hoped to hide out in a hotel, awaiting an opportunity to carry out his plan, but every hotel in the area refused him. There was nothing to do but go home. Some ten days later, Lei was arrested in his dorm room at the university and immediately placed on death row, where he was interrogated day and night.

The speed and severity of the sentence had everything to do with Sichuan Party secretary Yang Rudai. Yang, a trusted follower of the protesters' political hero Zhao Ziyang, had maintained an ambiguous attitude toward the student movement. Now he was protecting himself by demonstrating his loyalty to the government and distancing himself from Zhao. Yang intervened in matters not normally within his jurisdiction. He personally ordered that Lei be swiftly condemned to death and executed. His decision was reported to Beijing for approval.

"What saved us was that it dragged on for days and days," Lei told me three years later in our prison cell. "Once the peak had passed, the authorities ordered that the sentence be changed according to the law to twelve years imprisonment for counterrevolutionary propaganda and incitement." When I met him at Sichuan Provincial Prison No. 3, he was plotting to create a secret organization inside the prison, but someone seemed to inform on every move he made.

One time, the loudspeaker blared an announcement immediately summoning all prisoners to a meeting. We had barely squatted down, when we saw Lei being brought, all tied up, onto the platform. He had written a letter in English and paid a large bribe to a released former prisoner, who was still at the prison as a laborer, to sneak it out and put it in the mail. That man had informed on him and thereby won a little credit for himself. The prison's political commissar waved the letter and shouted at us: "We caught him red-handed. Bandit Lei is so shameless that he dared to get in touch with foreigners and betray the secrets of this prison. His counterrevolutionary nature is really hard to change. What else can we do but gather evidence and increase his sentence?"

Cries of "Down with him!" and "Smash him to a pulp!" resounded in the air, but Lei refused to give in. He tried to argue, but his mouth was sealed. He tried to get up, but his back was bent. Afterward, he was put in the doghole to await a decision about his fate. Nobody at the prison could read English, and they were afraid that the news would get out, so they secretly sent the evidence of his guilt to the Sichuan provincial reform-through-labor bureau, asking experts to decode the letter in the dead of night. What they found was that Lei had sent a New Year's greeting card to a foreign-language professor named Peter, who had once been Lei's teacher. In the letter, he asked Professor Peter about the differences in the pronunciation and spelling of some colloquial expressions in British English and American English. The letter did not mention the prison at all.

I didn't have a diploma, but my worldly experience was at least at the postdoc level. I wouldn't make the kind of mistake that academic types like Lei make of being too credulous and underestimating the enemy. Even though I had taken part in the June Fourth prison group's collective hunger strike to oppose Lei's confinement and had represented everyone in negotiations, I just used the same stubborn phrase over and over: "If you don't release him, I'll jump from the second floor."

Just then the United Nations released its *White Paper on Reform*

Through Labor and the prison authorities wanted to show that they were keeping up with the times, so they let Lei out of solitary early. Soon after, the prison authorities responded to Deng Xiaoping's call to "stimulate the economy" by allowing prisoners to have their photographs taken, albeit at five times the price of what it would have cost outside the prison walls. Nearly every one of the 3,000 prisoners, including the June Fourth political prisoners, rushed to sign up for photos.

The trickster in me saw an opportunity, so I had several photos taken, including a kind of prison graduation photo featuring six of us high-spirited June Fourth counterrevolutionaries in our prison uniforms, all of us with our arms behind our backs, three in the back wearing turbans and three in the front wearing glasses. Soon after, I smuggled them out through my mother and sister, and after I was released I sent them in a package to Hong Kong. All our "reactionary" magazines like *Baixing* and *Kaifang* ate it up, putting it on the cover, and a lot of innocent people got in trouble. The prison did a thorough search, immediately confiscating all photographs and letters, and interrogating each of the June Fourth political prisoners separately. It was the first time in decades of Communist Party rule that a group photo of political prisoners had made it to the outside world.

When Lei was released at the century's end, I arranged a gathering in Chengdu. He came with his wife and daughter, who had been waiting for him all along. During the meal Lei recalled the incident of the prison graduation photo and all the misery it had caused. I was feeling uneasy, but Lei said, "Thank you, Big Brother Liao, for letting the outside world know about us. The punishment was worth it." Feeling ashamed, I handed him the $600 in support that Liu Qing of Human Rights in China had sent. Lei was grateful but firm: "There's no need for this. Tens of thousands of June Fourth people went to jail. Those in need must number in the hundreds or thousands. I'm fluent in English: I can just live in obscurity and support my family by teaching English. I won't have any problem getting along." When the banquet was over and it was time to go, he added, "Before, everybody was patriotic. Today, since all people care about is money, it looks like it will be a long time before the Communist Party falls. You and I will just have to endure all that. Brother Liao, goodbye."

Goodbye, Lei. The seasons change and the constellations move to different positions in the sky. Since we said our farewells, we haven't had a chance to see each other again. I heard a rumor among my brother prisoners that Lei teaches in another part of the country and pays no attention to the outside world. But recently, some seventeen or eighteen years later, from my exile in a foreign land, I searched online and found that Lei had been interviewed by the former June Fourth leader Zhou Fengsuo. I could tell that the passions still run deep inside him. In the interview he refers to "butchers," "bandits," "digging up graves," and "avenging humiliation."

Still overly trusting and underestimating the enemy, I thought, counting his age on my fingers. Lei must already be well over sixty.

I felt a wave of emotion come over me.

———

Short and stout, Hou Duoshu, from Dazhou in northeastern Sichuan, was a well-liked teacher in his hometown when the Beijing student strike broke out. Electrified, he banged the table in his classroom and led a pack of young students to push down the school gate, which the president of the college himself had locked, so they could go demonstrate in the streets and shout slogans.

People in neighboring schools heard them and they, too, went out into the streets, which were like a bowl of boiling gruel. Amid the excitement, Hou was elected leader of the academics' outreach group. Above the turbulent crowd of thousands of people, he raised his megaphone and harangued the city's mayor for hours about the bloodbath taking place in Beijing and around the country. He called on the mayor to send telegrams calling for the overthrow of Li Peng and in support of the hunger-striking students in Tiananmen Square.

One evening in the middle of winter in 1992, with our heads pressed low into our necks like turtles in the biting wind, Hou Duoshu and I met at Sichuan Provincial Prison No. 3. We discussed our cases. He'd fled and wasn't captured by police until more than half a year later, in a small southern town. Tried back home, he was sentenced to eight years in prison for the crime of counterrevolutionary propaganda and incitement.

Soon, with the blowing of a whistle, all the prisoners assembled. As each prisoner's name was called, he would stand up straight and answer "Here!" and the warden would stare at him for a moment before moving on to the next. But when he called "Hou Duoshu," the warden's voice suddenly quivered, and Hou, with his arms crossed, grinned. Red-faced and dejected, the warden handed the roll call book to the prison group head and walked away.

"It's sad for a teacher and his student to meet in prison!" exclaimed Hou, and the entire group heard his words and started whispering among themselves.

"He was one of my favorite students, a hard worker from a poor family. In public, I treated him strictly, as I did all the others, since I was supposed to treat everyone the same. In private, I treated him differently, and tried to help him financially as much as I could." Later, Hou told me, "Our relationship was like that of Confucius and his favorite pupil Yan Hui."

One day, in an unobtrusive corner of the prison, a short, stocky prisoner—going against all regulations—shouted over to a tall, skinny man in a police uniform. The warden stopped, responding timidly, "Teacher Hou."

"Why are you here?"

"I was sent here after graduation."

"Why didn't you take the examination to go on to graduate school?"

"First I had to find a way to make a living."

"It's better to die than to become a 'running dog,' a lackey."

"What do you mean?"

"I mean your occupation. What makes it any different from being a running dog? What you should do is find time to review your studies and then take the entrance examination for graduate school."

"Thank you, Teacher Hou."

"No need to thank me."

Hou grew still more arrogant. One morning at three a.m., the shrieking sound of an electric buzzer woke us up. We formed into groups and made our way by the light of the moon and the stars to the reform-through-labor workshops almost a mile away. We started up the furnace while it was still dark outside and began to melt iron and mold automobile parts. Hou was with the group, but as soon as we arrived, he snuck off to the fitting workshop and went back to sleep. He didn't wake up until after the sun had risen, stamping his feet to get warm and taking out a copy of Bertrand Russell's *History of Western Philosophy*. The prisoners all around him were working hard; the machine tools were whirring. Sparks flew all around, but he ignored it all.

Envious people started to inform on him, but his former student the warden thought to himself, *How could a teacher be a teacher if he didn't read?* He sent someone to take Hou back to his prison cell and tell him there was no need for him to go out to work again in the future.

Instead, he was assigned to clean the exercise field, an area about the size of a basketball court. That was an extremely enviable job, since it left you with lots of free time, but Hou was the sort of person to take a mile if you gave him an inch. Every day he would do a cursory sweep for half an hour, swinging his broom like a Daoist priest scribbling an inscription, and then take a break to work on his English. That provoked even more envious informer reports. The young warden, in an awkward position, was eventually transferred.

Things quickly turned sour for Hou. Not only did he lose his sweeping job, but because he feigned illness, the prison leadership declared that he would be put in the doghole. That was a big disgrace for an educated man like him, so Hou grabbed onto the iron bars of the doghole, determined not to be put in there. A prisoner came by to push him in, but Hou grabbed onto him as he approached and they got into a fierce fight. Then Hou tried to cover up what he was doing by screaming "He's killing me!" so loudly that his voice echoed through the prison, but all that won him was a series of beatings with a police baton, plus a set of leg irons.

Just before I got out of prison, the warden-student, through self-study, did manage to pass the entrance examination of a graduate program at a university in another province. In violation of prison regulations, he went to the prison cell to say goodbye to his teacher. There was much to say, but his sobs prevented him from saying any of it. Hou laughed and said, "Confucius said, 'Everything is vulgar. Only study is noble.' I'm sorry that I cannot see you out. Later, when I am out of prison, we will meet again."

From then on, Hou's status in the prison deteriorated even faster. In the fall of 1995, together with Lei Fengyun, Pu Yong, Xu Wanping, and others—and with the help of an ex-prisoner who by then was working at the prison—Hou secretly sent a political prisoners' declaration to the United Nations, Amnesty International, and Human Rights in China. When they were discovered, each was put into solitary confinement for more than a hundred days. While down there, Hou screamed and howled and banged his head hard against the wall. He ended up tied face up to the four posts of a torture bed used for condemned prisoners, where he couldn't do anything on his own, not even eat, drink, or shit. Despite all this, when the prison authorities asked him if he regretted what he had done, Hou answered just as before, his entire body swollen up from his beatings: "Please allow me to read the Bible for a few days first before I tell you if I regret anything." The seeds of Christian faith had quietly taken root. Several years later, Hou was baptized as a follower of Jesus Christ.

In the spring of 1997, Deng Xiaoping died. The flag was lowered to half-mast throughout the land. Wardens dressed in mourning led a group of armed police into each cell to force the prisoners to participate in a memorial ceremony. Hou resisted. He lay on the ground like a scoundrel, cursing and spitting, saying, "That butcher deserved to die!"

That was going too far. The prison authorities strongly believed in the wisdom of the old saying "Kill one monkey to intimidate a hundred other monkeys," so Hou was ferociously beaten in front of the other prisoners. A special 175-pound leg iron was put on him and he was carried into the hole. The heart-wrenching pain made Hou howl bitterly like a pig about to be killed, a cry that blended perfectly with the solemn mourning music for the national martyr Deng Xiaoping.

That evening the prison's political commissar personally visited the cell and ordered him to write a self-criticism. Hou took the pen and paper handed to him through the prison bars and with a flourish of the pen he was done. "Honorable Political Commissar: I did not participate in the memorial for Deng Xiaoping today. I was wrong and I will behave better in the future. If there is a similar memorial meeting tomorrow, I promise to participate. Signed, self-criticizing person Hou Duoshu."

The political commissar laughed angrily at him. "You couldn't even write a self-criticism. What kind of education did you get?"

Hou sneered, "I didn't go to school to learn how to write a self-criticism." The political commissar turned around abruptly and left. Looking at his back, Hou resumed his murdered-pig howls. "God-awful sound!" said the political commissar, blocking his ears and ordering that Hou be let out of the hole.

The past is like a cloud of smoke. When I saw Hou again, the new century had already begun. "These last few years have been pretty rough. I felt ashamed to come to visit you," he said, laughing. "I heard from everybody that you had remarried. That's a fine thing, so I had to come." Then he took a pair of Nike running shoes, worth a few hundred yuan, out of his bag.

Living on the margins of society, it was the first time that I had ever had such a nice pair of shoes. I couldn't help but exclaim, "That's too much money to spend! What kind of business are you in?"

"I sell sexual health products."

"Is that a moneymaker?"

"This evening, let's keep things classy and not talk about things like that."

Then our conversation returned to what had gone on inside the prison walls. At the time, I didn't know that Hou had also married and had a child. In the predawn hours we talked about the sixth-century philosopher Boethius, sentenced to death by the Roman emperor. During some fifty days in prison awaiting execution, he finished his book *The Consolation of Philosophy*, and by coincidence it was just when he had laid down his pen that the executioner entered his cell. "Soon after Boethius's execution, the emperor died as well," Hou continued. "*The Consolation of Philosophy* was widely read and has lasted through the centuries, all the way up to us this evening."

Hou stood up to say goodbye. Seventeen years have passed since then.

The Author

This is a self-interview, from before exile. (Lao Wei is Liao Yiwu's pen name in China.) The third generation of my family to be honored with home searches and confiscations, I laugh it all off, play my flute, sell my art, and stand around screaming at the top of my lungs.

Lao Wei: So your home was searched again?

Liao Yiwu: The phone rang a little past six a.m. It was still pitch-black outside, and I'd had only two hours of sleep. It rang for four or five minutes without letting up. Then came the pounding on the door. Song Yu jumped out of bed, startled. I walked out of the bedroom, quickly pulling up my pants. It was like a scene from a horror movie, the duet of the ringing phone and the pounding on the door, while the lead actors blundered about blindly like headless houseflies.

Was your wife frightened?

She was relatively calm. Hanging around with someone like me, she's gotten used to dealing with the police. Remember the descriptions of arrests in the first chapter of *The Gulag Archipelago*? Song Yu can relate. For example, the day we made our first visit to her family home as a married couple, the groom suddenly disappeared before the feast, leaving her to put on a happy face while greeting the whole room of guests alone. And there was the time her husband made plans to go out for hot pot with friends but never made it back the whole night. There were many other similar disappearances. The only thing she could do in such situations was call the relevant friends to ask what had happened to her husband and wait.

So she kept her cool this time, looking in the mirror, brushing her hair, putting on her makeup, and getting ready for work. As the room filled up with plainclothes police, she turned to the top cop there and asked him for the court summons and search order. She read it over carefully, then smiled and asked, "Shouldn't there be a duplicate copy of the search order?" The section chief answered that there was only one copy.

"How could that be?" she asked. "When we go shopping, we always get a copy of the receipt. That makes things easier if there's a problem later and we need to look for you."

The section chief answered harshly, "Doing a search is not like going shopping. We will provide you with a detailed list of everything we confiscate, in accordance with the law." Song Yu wanted to talk back to him, but I quickly stopped her and told her to hurry off to work. Before she left, she put two tablets of cold medicine on the desk and reminded me several times not to forget to take it. "She's a young one," said the police admiringly, "but she is really tough!"

That afternoon at five p.m., because the police hadn't found the evidence they needed, I was released. A few days later Song Yu and I had a chance to really talk, in a way we usually didn't have time for. Questions like "What can we do in this life?" and "How is it we can have friends with ideals, ambition, and so much knowledge—like Kang Zhengguo, Liu Xiaobo, and Wang Lixiong—while I, Liao Yiwu, mostly just love eating and drinking?"

I argued strenuously with her, but my wife, who had been a student leader at school, stood in front of our bed and announced her conclusion after thinking long and hard about me: "You are not the kind of person who should get married."

How could you just laugh all this off?

When life is this tough, if you don't laugh a lot, you're doomed to be a bitter melon. Even if the laughter is just a mask, you need to keep the mask on. When we were little, we watched many times while condemned prisoners, all tied up, were paraded around in front of the people. We soon forgot all about them, but the image of one poor devil about to be killed, smiling happily at the crowd, will stay with us forever. People in the streets talked about him for a long time afterward. So if they are going to search, well, let them do it. What could I do when eight plainclothes police in two squads charged in? I still had to smile.

They took away my computer, including manuscripts of mine running to millions of Chinese characters. *Fuck,* I thought, *whether I like it or not, I'm the only writer in China who writes exclusively for the police. During repeated searches of my home, they have accumulated everything I have written from 1980 to the present, not to mention love letters, random notes, award certificates, old photos, and even smelly discarded manuscripts they fished out of the bathroom garbage can.* This time they had the honor of being the first readers of the third draft of my multivolume novel *Survive.* They figured out how to assemble my manuscripts for *Interviews with People on the Margins of Chinese Society* and *Unjust Cases.* They revisited my works "City of Death," "Requiem," "The Slaughter," and "Love Song of the Gulag Archipelago," and they systematically studied the news and reviews about each one.

They spent three hours methodically searching the balcony, the living room, my study, the bedroom, and all the hardest-to-reach corners of the apartment. After two of them had been in my study for a long time, I went in, with ulterior motives, to serve as their guide to my bookshelves.

"That's my elder sister. She died in a car accident in 1988," I said, taking back a picture they were holding.

"We wouldn't take that," one of the young guys said kindly. "Your elder sister was very pretty."

I took the opportunity to guide them through significant pictures, calligraphy and paintings, my vertical bamboo flute, and various other things. Intentionally or not, I was partially blocking their line of sight, but their eyes, used to taking in the smallest details, alighted on my complete collection of *Tendency*, an elegant illegal magazine printed in Hong Kong and bound in nine volumes; a copy of *Today*; and some things by Xu Wenli, Wei Jingsheng, and Liu Binyan, as well as printed materials from the China Democracy Party. One of them picked up a book by Huang Xiang, flicked through it, and then put it down. There was also a copy of the "Appeal to Compatriots Throughout the Country," which they had fished out of some drawer. "Was it mailed to you?" they asked, excited. "Where's the envelope?"

Years ago, I had lost all interest in collecting envelopes, so I felt that I had let down the People's Government. To express my sincere apologies, I praised them, talking about how times had changed and how our comrades from the police force had changed their traditional style of acting like devils and monsters into something much more approachable, meticulous, and patient.

"I can see this by the way that you're searching my home," I went on. And then I took the initiative and stuffed a big pile of illegal materials right into the tiger's mouth, hoping that a few bits would fall out again from between the tiger's teeth. When they offered to help me put things back in place again, I thanked them several times, but actually I was afraid they would turn up more things. I praised them shamelessly: "The police are more fit to get married than vermin like me, who go around harming people. Assuming the comrades are just as sensitive and solicitous in their personal lives, surely any woman in the world would fall for them."

The police must have been moved by my praise, because before they left they reminded me to lock the door securely to keep burglars from getting in. Together we descended seven floors in force and piled into three police cars. Every pair of eyes in the neighborhood saw us. Fortunately, there were many criminal cases going on that year, so people didn't think much of it. When we got to the police station, the police divided into two groups, one interrogating my human brain and the other interrogating my electronic brain, my computer. Apparently there were more problems with the electronic brain than with the human brain, so a group of specialists went about examining it to determine my guilt. At the time, I was suspected of having signed on to a group that had published *China's Wrongful Cases* and a political series that was coming out online in installments. But as to the question of how many websites were carrying my articles and signature, a computer-illiterate person like me just had no idea.

Just now you said times have changed. Has the traditional way of searching homes changed, too?

Forget the innumerable cases of home searches and confiscations mentioned in premodern Chinese writings or the early twentieth century. Even just over the course of the several decades of our "new society," including hundreds of political movements large and small, I'm afraid that up to 80 percent of all Chinese homes have been searched at one time or another. Ba Jin once openly proposed building a Cultural Revolution Museum, but I think that would be too narrow. I believe one day a Political Movement Museum will be built in this country, with the Cultural Revolution Museum as just one of its sub-museums. Some people have suggested erecting a Monument to the Ideological Criminals to take the place of the Monument to the People's Heroes now on Tiananmen Square.

On that future monument they should engrave the names of tens of millions of ideological criminals, with every name enclosed in a teardrop-shaped crystal. Seen from a distance, it won't look like a monument but like a mountain gleaming with the cold light of eternal tears, one piled on top of another. I hope Liao Yiwu's name will be among them.

In the future Political Movement Museum, I firmly believe that home searches, custody, and struggle sessions should be categorized as separate subjects. At least there should be specialized fields of study, like home search studies. More than 1,000 professors and staff will be needed for the vast project of collecting, sorting, classifying, identifying, and researching all this material.

If we go down this road, then China in the future will have to conjure an array of museums and monuments out of thin air—a Land Reform Memorial, a Monument to the Three Oppositions and the Five Oppositions, a Monument to the Hu Feng Case, and monuments to the Anti-Rightist Movement, the Four Cleanups Movement, the Great Leap Forward, and the Great Famine. We couldn't do without monuments to the Cultural Revolution, to April Fifth, to Bourgeois Liberalization, and to June Fourth. You write about unjust and mishandled cases involving ordinary people. Shouldn't there also be a monument to the marginalized people in Chinese society and to the people who were unjustly wronged? Naturally, we can't leave out monuments and museums for Falun Gong, the China Democracy Party, Tibetan independence, and Xinjiang independence. In short, one monument for each debt the government owes. Our Party already has lots of rotten accounts. How many monuments will have to be built? Will our children and grandchildren find a place to live in a country crowded with so many monuments?

It's human nature to forget our wounds as soon as they heal. Two days after they searched my house, I can stand before you, smiling and grinning. People don't like to talk about troubles. Once people hear the same old sad story several times, they curse you in their hearts as if you were Xianglin's wife in the famous Lu Xun story, who was always telling the tale about her son A Mao being eaten by wolves. Three generations of my family have had their homes searched and their possessions confiscated.

My grandfather was an old landlord. Nothing about him left a stronger impression on me than his stinginess. Rats and king rat snakes had been nibbling forever at the aged, cured meat he hung in the rafters of his house, but he never took it down to feed anybody. Walnuts and peanuts sat in his pantry for seven or eight years getting eaten by worms and moths, but even when nothing was left but empty shells, he still couldn't stand to bring them out to eat. He wore the same clothing winter and summer and rarely changed to wash it. When I was little, I once spent two days in the old broken-down courtyard of my grandfather's house. I was itching and wanted to change my clothes and wash them, but there wasn't any soap. Finally, my older cousin knocked some pieces off a Chinese "soap pod" locust tree.

My grandfather never rode in a car. Even when he was nearly eighty years old, he still walked miles and miles on mountain roads to my father's middle school in the county seat. On sunny days he would open up his pants as he walked so he could pick out the lice. If he wasn't careful, his pants would fall down to his ankles. I never understood how there could be such a hardworking and plain-living landlord. My father said that when land reform began in 1950, my grandfather was really out of luck, because he had just worked himself nearly to death to buy 40 mou, or 6.6 acres, of land. Forty mou put him just over the line to qualify as a "landlord," so everyone went after him. My third granduncle from the same branch of the family had lost all *his* family property smoking opium, so he was honored as a poor peasant. He even led the masses to his elder brother's home to search it and confiscate what he owned.

Two plow oxen, five fat pigs, and several dozen ducks and chickens were confiscated and divided among the poor. Everything was taken—all the cabinets full of grain were opened, all the white rice and white flour he was normally too frugal to eat on a daily basis. Then people filled their sacks with old millet, wheat seeds, corn, and garden peas, and carried them away. The cellar, filled with over 2,000 pounds of sweet potatoes, was emptied. That day the poor people of Lijiaping lived like they were having a festival. They swarmed all over my grandfather's home, taking whatever they wanted. At first the head of the working group kept accounts of what had been confiscated. Later there were just too many people and there was just too much chaos, so he stopped keeping track.

That evening, something like a hundred people had come with

only one or two lanterns between them. In the dim light, all my grandparents' woks, cups, and ladles vanished. Naturally, "policy work" had to be carried out. Everyone dug all around, more than three feet deep into the soil. When they dug up a box full of gold and silver jewelry and two bolts of indanthrene blue cloth, the working group leader announced to the crowd that it was all being confiscated. My grandmother was paraded around the village and criticized and "struggled against" for hiding it all. Some young men the same age as her nephews even tied her up with a rope.

In the late 1980s, I went back to the family home with my father and took pictures in front of the ancestral graves. Grandfather had just died. Grandmother had died in the famine thirty years earlier. People say that during the famine people tottering from hunger still didn't forget the class struggle. They broke into the old landlord's home to search for food. They took corncobs kept as fuel next to the kitchen stove, broke them down to bits, and ate them. They even emptied my grandfather's pickling jugs. Finding no vegetables left, they scooped out the pickling juice one spoonful at a time and passed it around.

Before she died, my grandmother rolled out of bed and crawled to the main hall, sat on the threshold, and cried for a long time. The fields had been divided up. Five households had moved into the courtyard left to my grandparents by their ancestors. The newcomers took up a dozen of the rooms on all four sides of the courtyard, leaving only the side room on the southeast corner to my grandfather and grandmother. Father said that when land reform began, he was teaching over in the county seat. Someone from home came with a letter bearing the bad news. He didn't dare go home to see what was happening, fearing someone would report him for not drawing a clear line between himself and his exploiter-class family. It was only once the storm blew over that he quietly returned to Lijiaping to give my grandfather some money to help him get through. Not a single chair was left intact in the entire house.

I was seven or eight when the Cultural Revolution broke out, old enough to remember it. During that "spiritual" revolution dead set against property, books—old and new, Chinese and foreign—were the main target of searches and confiscations. My father's home was searched because he was too good a teacher. He was particularly good at teaching that famous article "The Style of the Pine Tree" by Tao Zhu, who was considered the number three supporter of the political line espoused by Liu Shaoqi and Deng Xiaoping. For that, he was labeled a reactionary academic and a member of a sinister gang. Frequently beaten, he had to write self-criticisms every day. At the time, he had a salary of just over 50 yuan a month. With four children to raise, there wasn't any chance of saving any money.

When the Red Guards came to search our house, they were indeed more honest than those poor people and police who came to my grandparents' place after Liberation in 1949. The Red Guards turned our house upside down, but all they carried away was basket after basket of my father's books, including his teaching materials. At the school exercise grounds, they burned all the feudal, capitalist, and revisionist works they had collected, including my father's lesson plans, and the fire burned for nearly an hour. While the embers were still warm, they held a criticism and struggle session, pulling my father up to the platform together with the school principal, the department heads, and other forces of evil. Black placards were placed over their necks, and they were made to bend over 90 degrees. I was just a skinny kid standing stiffly at the door of our house, sucking on my fingers and looking on while several Red Guards painted their big-character denunciation on the wall.

But let's talk about your own experience with home searches.

Even before 1989, the homes of many Sichuan underground poets were searched. At the time, there were many channels for publishing underground poetry, and some were very influential. As a result, the Sichuan public security bureau kept a special dossier on underground poets, Zhou Lunyou, Shi Guanghua, Wan Xia, and Song Wei among them.

In 1987, I was working at the Fuling District Art Museum, where I tried a little sleight of hand, turning the museum publication *Sichuan Literary Style* into the *Sichuan Contemporary Poets' Group*. I spent two months running back and forth to the printing press every day, checking the lead type myself. On the day the publication was supposed to come out, several dozen police raided the press. I was on the second floor, happily inspecting proofs and supervising the binding, when I heard the police sirens down below. I grabbed a copy that hadn't yet been bound, opened a window, and jumped out. Fortunately, the road below was just a country-style dirt alley, so I was completely covered in mud but I wasn't hurt, and I ran for my life. Only after I reached the docks did I turn around to see if anyone was chasing me.

I took a boat and then a bus, bumping around until I finally reached Zhou Zhongling's home in Chongqing. He was the boss of a local printing shop, so it was a simple matter for him to duplicate and bind several dozen copies from that one original I had taken with me. We sent it off to poetry hubs all over China with a handwritten note that the matter was urgent.

All the poetry fans who got a copy treasured it, solemnly footing the bill to make more copies, so that even more third-generation copies were distributed. In fact, the number of copies in circulation increased geometrically, with ever more copies being made and distributed, even as later generations of the collection became harder and harder to read.

I spent a few months wandering around, getting free meals and free drinks like some kind of hero out of a legend. By the time I returned to my work unit, the political winds had already shifted. I learned that on the day of the raid, the head of the printing press had been fired and 2,000 copies of the book had been sent to the provincial cultural bureau to be locked up forever. My home got a symbolic search as well. According to my ex-wife, the police officer who led the search loved reading and writing and was secretly a fan of my work, so he kept the search pretty cursory.

Despite that brave act of jumping out of the building, it was only a scare and nothing really happened. That doesn't really count as a home search.

But the episode I just mentioned is directly related to something that happened later. Michael Day, the Canadian who became my accomplice, managed to get hold of a third-generation copy of that book of poems at the home of Liu Xiaobo. That prompted him to write me a letter and travel a long way to see me. Over the two following years, he was a frequent guest at my home. On the morning of June 4, 1989, I used his tape recorder to add in background music and, through tears, I committed my crime of reading my poem "The Slaughter."

Originally there were two copies of "The Slaughter," one for me and one for Michael, and both copies passed through many different hands. The next year a few colleagues and I filmed *Requiem*, a kind of companion piece of which I was the main performer and author. The very day we finalized it and distributed the master copies, the Ministry of State Security raided us and the entire *Requiem* group was taken into custody.

It was then that I witnessed the true power of the dictatorship of the proletariat. The dreams I had cherished for over a decade of making poems and songs ended in an instant. A little after ten in the morning, with "The Slaughter," *Requiem*, and other criminal evidence on my person, I boarded a bus from Shapingba to Niujiaotuo. I was just about to cross the street to catch another bus, en route to the train station, when I heard someone call my name. As soon as I turned to look, a group of military-issue raincoats pounced on me from all sides.

They took my backpack, cuffed my hands behind my back, and stuffed me into the back seat of a police car. The plainclothesman beside me gritted his teeth and wiped his bloody nose. I had instinctively thrown a punch at him. "You dare resist!" he roared at me, and tightened the handcuffs behind my back until the steel barbs bit into my flesh. "No. 1 in custody," said the fat policeman, sitting shotgun, into his walkie-talkie. "We are escorting him to Songshan."

As I later found out, several dozen police, methodical as sappers, had sifted through the workplace and the room of our photographer Zeng Lei's dormitory. Before they got into the car, Zeng Lei and Wang Xia were made to hold tapes and books in their handcuffed hands so they could be photographed with the criminal evidence. The two men's eyes were dull with sleepiness, and bits of toothpaste were still sticking to the corners of their mouths. The evidence filled a whole van, including all of Zeng Lei's photographs, tapes, books, and letters, as well as makeup, costumes, and props.

More than twenty homes were searched across the province, including the homes of Liu Taiheng, Wan Xia, Gou Mingjun, Li Yawei, and Shi Guanghua. At Zhou Zhongling's place, they emptied a giant bookcase and tramped back and forth over a pile of his books several feet deep. At Ba Tie's they confiscated all the avant-garde poetry, materials, notes, books, publications, and letters exchanged with literary figures that he had spent years collecting. Two years later, released after detention, he was so discouraged that he decided to leave the world of literature that he had loved for half his life.

The police also patronized my home and my in-laws' home. Within the space of three days, my living quarters were searched three times. Cassette tapes, photo albums, my then wife A Xia's diary, pen-and-ink drawings, books, a tape recorder, and manuscripts were all taken away. My wardrobe, bookcase, sofa, bed, and tables were all turned upside down and soon had big holes in them, thanks to iron clubs.

A Xia, then three months pregnant, was taken away and locked up in the public security detention center for over forty days. She was interrogated every day to make her inform on her husband. By the time she was released on bail, she had a bad case of pulmonary disease. She couldn't stay home anymore, because, according to our neighbor, thieves had entered and ransacked our home several times, taking anything the police had left behind: jewelry, clothing, furnishings, electronics. Our dressing room mirror and bed were smashed. There was also some shit left behind in the living room—probably the thieves' revenge, because the pickings in our home were so slim.

I have no clue how much I lost between everything that happened. Everything I had with me—all my manuscripts from 1980 onward, many audio and video recordings, a mini–tape recorder, photo albums, collections of underground poetry, along with more than 1,400 yuan— was confiscated. I was taken to the Songshan Detention and Interrogation Center in the Geleshan Mountains, an old-fashioned prison near Baigongguan. As soon as I entered, five ferocious reform-through-labor prisoners pounced on me and stripped me naked. On that overcast, rainy day in March, I stood for a long time in the corridor, naked with my hands over my crotch, while the prisoners thoroughly and skillfully squeezed and shook and took away everything in my pockets and the seams of my clothes. Then they took away my belt and used pliers to remove any metal buttons from my clothes and zippers from my pants.

At that point they held me down on the floor, stepped on me, and shaved me until I was bald. Then they ordered me to hold up my ass while the head prisoner stuck bamboo chopsticks up my asshole, making a great show of shining a flashlight to ensure I didn't have any contraband hidden inside.

To be honest, I wept as they did all that. My dignity as a poet had been stripped away from me. When I numbly put my clothes back on and was locked in the cell, I was already just like the other prisoners in there: shoulders slumped, head shrunken, worn-out shoes on bare feet, shocked, holding up with both hands pants that would otherwise have fallen down. I thought that I was finished, that I had no way out.

Sometimes, when I wake up from a dream, I think it's strange that I was able to go on living. During those four years in prison, searches of our cells and bodies were commonplace. After being violated so many times, you become like a prostitute with clients. You get to thinking that all the perverted demands of the police are completely normal and just a regular part of law enforcement.

When I finally got out of jail, the black mark of having been a political prisoner was always with me. It meant that as long as I still lived in China, I would never be free of subpoenas and home searches. In June 1995, I was detained for a month because I was one of fifty-six people who signed a statement initiated by Liu Xiaobo about June Fourth. They also searched and confiscated my belongings in the tiny room at my parents' place where I lived.

In October of that year, because I had attempted to deliver a "declaration" by political prisoners still in prison to Amnesty International, I was detained for a day and a night and then placed under household surveillance for twenty-four days. Among the books and letters they confiscated were the handwritten manuscript of *My Eyewitness Account of June Fourth*, over 300,000 words long, and all the source material for *Interviews with People on the Margins of Chinese Society*.

In June 1997, I was subpoenaed and detained for a day and a night for starting a journal called *Intelligentsia*, unofficial and run by ordinary people. Rewritten and this time over 200,000 words, the manuscript of *My Eyewitness Account of June Fourth* was confiscated once again.

In September 1998, my temporary quarters in Beijing were searched because I had conducted "illegal interviews." The following day the police put me on a train and ordered me to leave Beijing. In February 1999, because my collection of material for *Interviews with People on the Margins of Chinese Society* had alarmed the State Security authorities, I was detained for two hours before I was supposed to return with my new bride to her home for the traditional banquet; we were detained and interrogated for twenty-four hours. I lost more than forty chapters of the original manuscript for *Interviews with People on the Margins of Chinese Society* and my address book.

Looking back on the whole series of house searches and confiscations, I can see signs of social progress. Judging by both their words and deeds, the police were getting more civilized each time. In fact, I realize that, in a country where thought can be criminalized, writing itself creates criminal evidence when a writer in all good conscience tries to express social realities. To date, I have already written several million words of criminal evidence, which several generations of Sichuan police have studied and read.

Up until now, the police have never returned anything they took except for a dozen letters. When a big group of brawny, brutal policemen smash their way into your home and force you to submit in the name of the law, treating your private space like a free supermarket, grabbing whatever they like and poking into everything, all you can do is insist that they scrupulously follow the procedures stipulated by law and that they make a complete list of everything they take, although they almost never return anything.

What good is a list?

I keep it as material evidence—as a reminder to myself and to people who will come after me. Besides, I like to make that request as a small way of getting the upper hand. The day I went to jail, Liao Yiwu the poet was already dead. Today, standing here, there is only Liao Yiwu the witness. It doesn't matter if you search me, strip me naked, or violate and search my asshole. I have more dignity than any policeman, because I write, I record, and I do my own countersearch of their filthy, perverted souls. If one day I am stripped of the ability to write, then I can still play my flute, I can still sell my art, and I can stand around screaming and yelling at the top of my lungs. It gives me a reason to go on living.

The Last Moments of Liu Xiaobo

L iu Xiaobo (1955–2017) was a writer, critic, philosopher, and political activist who returned to China from the United States, where he was a visiting scholar at Columbia University, to support the protesters in Tiananmen Square in 1989. He began a hunger strike with three others on June 2, and his actions saved many lives during the crackdown that followed. As the central figure behind Charter 08, which called for democratic reform in China, Liu received an eleven-year sentence for "incitement to subvert state power," and his wife, Liu Xia, lived under house arrest. In 2010, he was awarded the Nobel Peace Prize while incarcerated.

The following essay, translated by Michael Day, is an account based on recorded telephone conversations, held under extraordinary circumstances, between the author and Liu Xia. Chronicling the last days of Liu Xiaobo and the attempts to get the Lius out of China, it makes clear how hard it is to save a single person. I began writing it on October 14, 2017, revised it continually, and only finished it after Liu Xia's miraculous arrival in Berlin on July 10, 2018. Wolf and Pamela Biermann subsequently agreed to disclose some of the "secret letters" between us. My poem "A Dirge for Liu Xiaobo" was translated by David Cowhig. Thank you to the German Ministry of Foreign Affairs, the Chancellor's Office, and Mrs. Angela Merkel for their unremitting efforts to help the Lius.

On the afternoon of August 29, 2017, I got through to Liu Xia on her landline at home in Beijing. It was the first time since Xiaobo had left us. As before, Liu Xia was being strictly monitored. Two days earlier, the police had finally allowed her to return home from eighty days of internal exile in distant Dali.

I shouted her name into the phone.

"Who?" she responded feebly.

"It's old Liao."

"Oh, it's you," she said, followed by a couple of hollow laughs and a pause, and then she began weeping uncontrollably.

There was sobbing on both ends of the phone, but I finally forced out a question: "How did he go?"

"After saying goodbye to all the doctors, nurses, and assistants in attendance, he kept saying again and again, 'Thank you, I'm going now.' So peaceful, so decent. When I told him he was still breathing without the tubes, he responded clearly: 'Oh, I know.' And then: 'You should go out, go out . . .'"

Hearing this, I couldn't help but lean on my desk in Berlin as I bawled. I heard Liu Xia say: "He hated my crying. Every time I'd cry, he'd hug me, stroke my face, hover around me."

Since crying wasn't solving anything, I said, "You need to recover your health, start a new life."

"I'm taking care of myself," she said. "I'm taking Chinese medicine and I'll go to the hospital for a checkup in a few days, but I often have sudden fainting spells. I pass out on the floor for who knows how long, and when I come to, I discover injuries here and there."

"You have to keep fighting to leave the country," I told her. "That's the only way Xiaobo can rest in peace. A few days ago the Müllers [the writer Herta Müller and her husband, the dramaturge Harry Merkle] and Peter Sillem [publisher at S. Fischer] came to visit and were very concerned about you. Herta was here in my home when she started writing that appeal letter for you and Xiaobo signed by more than 100 Nobel laureates. According to Chinese law, you're free."

"What law? If there was law, we wouldn't be in this situation now. Everything must be approved by them."

"Still, you have to make a written application."

"They say they'll talk about it after the Nineteenth Party Conference. It feels like they'll let me go. It does no good, you being anxious about it; you'll pressure me to death. Anyway, I'll fight for it. Relax.

"Before, every time I visited Xiaobo in prison, I still had hope," she said, "but now there's nothing at all. Going into a supermarket, I stand there in a daze. Before, I'd always be thinking about buying him this and that; now there's nothing I need to buy."

"You can't go on like this."

"I know I can't. Gradually I'll get my health back, I'll paint, find some distractions. Oh, my phone's running out of battery."

"I'll call again."

"Call when you have time."

The last time I heard Xiaobo's voice was nine years earlier. I received his email with the Charter 08 attachment indicating it was infected. I didn't dare open it. I was surprised when Xiaobo followed up with a phone call, asking whether I had signed it or not. I hemmed and hawed as I typed "Liao Yiwu, writer" and hit reply. When Xiaobo saw it on his end, he chuckled. "Thanks, baldy."

Inside and outside prison, both Liu Xiaobo and Liu Xia were largely cut off from the world. It wasn't until early 2014, after I escaped to Germany, that I was able to reach Liu Xia on the phone. She was weeping uncontrollably and aside from the crying, very little was actually said. The past is like water that flows late at night, like a single boat that disappears into the distance.

In Berlin, I started working with Herta, Harry, and Peter to find a way to help Liu Xiaobo and Liu Xia, exchanging emails almost every day, and a few times all of us gathered at my place. The birds outside were chirping as we went deep into fierce, naïve discussions, drafting a letter to Chancellor Angela Merkel. "Should it be 'exile' or 'medical treatment'?" I asked. Herta paused a moment. "Change it to 'leave China for medical treatment.'"

Dear Chancellor Merkel:

Please forgive me for addressing you directly with this letter, but I have no other choice.

It's about my close friend Liu Xiaobo, the 2010 Nobel Peace Prize laureate, who has been imprisoned in China since 2009. He has recently expressed a clear desire to go into exile in Germany and I very much hope for the support of the Federal Government in this matter.

On March 30, 2017, his wife, Liu Xia, took a train from Beijing to Jinzhou, in Liaoning Province, where Liu Xiaobo is being detained. There she told her husband for the first time about her clinical depression, her heart disease, her terminally ill mother, her brother Liu Hui, now also sentenced to eleven years imprisonment for complicity, the whole depressing situation, including her own seven years as a hostage under house arrest. Liu Xiaobo had known nothing about any of this. He was shocked, of course, and felt guilty. Given that his wife and her brother had to endure this ordeal because of him, his response was that from then on he would do his utmost to come to Germany together with them.

Previously, Liu Xiaobo, the most influential political resistance fighter in China, the author and disseminator of Charter 08, who has been imprisoned four times for political reasons, had never wanted to turn his back on China, but wanted to continue to fight in-country for a future democratic China.

That Liu Xiaobo wants to come to Germany and not any other country is mainly because he knows about my situation in Germany. In the last six years I have had six books published by the S. Fischer publishing house and have been awarded the Peace Prize of the German Book Trade. I have received recognition and support from this society in every conceivable way. Three years ago, German diplomacy led to Liu Xia, under house arrest, being allowed to resume telephone contact with the outside world after four years with no such contact. Since then we have been in close contact with each other.

Liu Xia's physical condition is worrying. Several times she has suddenly lost consciousness and been hospitalized, but under constant close surveillance by the police, healing is not possible. In addition, she was not allowed to tell her husband in prison about her health, under threat of retribution.

Now she has been allowed to tell him the whole truth for the first time. Against all expectations, Liu Xiaobo unhesitatingly decided he would like to leave the country with his sick wife and her wrongfully convicted brother. I think that through discreet, active mediation by you, Mrs. Merkel, and the German Foreign Ministry, Liu Xiaobo and his relatives may be able to safely reach Germany for the following reasons: two years ago, Liu Xia would have liked to convince her husband that they should go to Germany. She told me this repeatedly on the phone. I have also discussed this wish several times with Herta Müller, Peter Sillem of the S. Fischer publishing house, and others who are all very worried about Liu Xiaobo's situation. On March 22, we all got together again and talked about the case. We agreed that, despite the likelihood that the Chinese authorities would not give their approval, Liu Xia should seek permission from the security police in charge of her surveillance to tell her husband the truth about her condition and allow her to leave.

Unexpectedly, the interview was approved by the authorities.

That is a clear signal: if the Chinese authorities were opposed to Liu Xiaobo's departure plans, they would not have allowed Liu Xia to visit and speak of this. In addition, they would certainly have prevented the closely monitored international telephone contact between her and me. They would have prevented any contact with the outside world to keep these plans from leaking out.

Madam Chancellor, you helped me come to Germany, and the late Foreign Minister Guido Westerwelle even made a public statement. I will never forget that. I have also recorded these memories in my book about my escape to Germany, which will be published in 2018. Today it is Liu Xiaobo and his wife who are worthy of more of your help. The name Liu Xiaobo is a symbol of the Chinese democracy movement; it stands for China's future . . . I sincerely hope that you and the Federal Government, by whatever means, together with the Chinese government, can negotiate for the departure of Liu Xiaobo, his wife, and her brother so that they can come to safety and freedom in Germany.

We have met with each other several times, and out of my deep trust in you, I personally ask for your help. This is the most important letter I have ever written in my life. I therefore will have it conveyed to you through our mutual friend Wolf Biermann.

If you undertake this task, I will be most grateful, as will Liu Xiaobo and his wife.

I remain in hope of your response

with the highest respect

Yours,
Liao Yiwu,
Berlin, April 15, 2017

The eighty-one-year-old troubadour of the Berlin Wall, Wolf Biermann, was to be the bridge, as the Merkels and I were all good friends of his and fans of his music. And so I wrote:

Dear Wolf Biermann and Pamela,

Liu Xiaobo, my loyal friend and one of China's main political resistance fighters, has recently decided to go into exile in Germany, if possible.

For this reason, I have written a letter to Chancellor Merkel asking for help. I don't know who else but you would be able to pass this letter on as quickly as possible to Mrs. Merkel.

This reminds me of the lines you wrote to me seven years ago, the song "China Under the Great Wall," which a friend translated into Chinese for me . . . and then, a while later, I was actually sitting by a bonfire next to your home, listening to you sing it . . . Time has passed quickly since then, dear Wolf.

Today it is up to me to give my friend Liu Xiaobo a helping hand out of China, but that is only possible through your mediation. I hope that you and Pamela will one day meet Liu Xiaobo and his wife, Liu Xia, and that we can all make music together.

Warmly,
Your Yiwu

Early on the morning of May 3, the sky was overcast and a drizzle was falling. I'd been awake all night, only slipping into a deep sleep just when the doorbell rang. A white-bearded old man suddenly appeared. Filling up the doorway, he passed me a letter. I turned my head to call my German-speaking wife, to ask what was going on, but the old-timer was already gone.

I opened the envelope and saw in it a copy of this letter to the chancellor, with Wolf having made a note in red in the upper right-hand corner. In a rush of excitement, I ran out to catch him, but the messenger had vanished without a trace.

It was like a scene from another lifetime, as if I'd returned to China, or the former East Germany. Later, Pamela said that many years ago this was Wolf's favorite way of doing things.

Dear Angela,

You probably know what it is I'm writing about . . . China's bravest dissident Liu Xiaobo, now stuck in possibly the most bitter situation of anyone, has told us through his mutual friend in Berlin, Liao Yiwu, about his own life in prison and his seriously ill wife.

I understand the reasons that Liu Xiaobo, after so many years of imprisonment, wants to escape this now utterly hopeless conflict. Thinking it better than being buried in a mass grave in prison, he now wants to try for a comparatively unpolitical life in Germany. Incommensurable forces! Liu Xiaobo must now apparently give up his struggle so as not to have to give up his life and his wife. Even if martyrs unrelentingly struggle, they also have moments when they need to pull back. The thinking of the Chinese leadership might be that it's better to have one less inspiring martyr around to bother them as they build their turbocharged concentration-camp capitalism. In that case, it could be a win-win situation . . .

Maybe we can make Liao Yiwu's friend laugh again . . . maybe at our home by the fireplace in Altona. Pamela has invited Liao Yiwu to join us and the old Free Jazzers of the Central Quartet to give a benefit concert at VEB-Knast Cottbus before the elections in the fall.

Warmly,
Wolf
on the 27th of April 2017

Later, there was a time I got through to Liu Xia by phone when Herta happened to be at my place, and the two of them spoke with each other for the first time. The storied old city of Karlsruhe had started a movement where a free writer would "adopt" an un-free writer and speak on their behalf over an extended period of time. I took on Li Bifeng and Herta adopted Liu Xia. So Herta was aware of everything to do with Liu Xia, as through a translator they spoke of life, poetry, Paul Celan, and so on. Herta felt that Xiaobo should leave China, teach at university, lecture all over the world, and enjoy freedom, and that freedom would greatly stimulate his creativity.

Liu Xia was so happy, her voice trembled. Again and again she said, "Just wait a bit, wait a bit. Xiaobo loves me; they have no reason not to release him." I told her the German government was hard at work, that secret negotiations between China and Germany had been under way all along.

———

When Liu Xia and I spoke by phone in May, she laughed like a bird in a forest: "It won't be so quick." She actually comforted me. Peter Sillem's news from the German Ministry of Foreign Affairs was the same: "It won't be so quick."

And then, on June 6, Liu Xia was struck by a bout of depression, her heart beating like a drum; she reached out for her medicine, but there wasn't enough. She clutched at the phone, but she fell to the ground. When she came to several hours later, the phone rang and she struggled to pick it up. It was Jinzhou Prison, and they wanted her to come immediately. She cautiously asked why, as it wasn't time for the monthly visit. But the caller was noncommittal, so she immediately rushed there.

After that, we lost contact. I asked everywhere, but there was no news. I sensed something was wrong. On June 16, at 4:30 in the morning, I received a call from someone in Liu's immediate family.

"Uncle has liver cancer, late-stage."

Not hearing clearly, I thought I heard "aunt," and was shocked: "What? Liu Xia has liver cancer?"

"No, no, it's uncle with late-stage liver cancer."

I was stunned for a moment, and then yelled at the top of my lungs: "Xiaobo? HIM?"

"Yes, Aunt made me tell you as soon as possible, but you can't tell anybody, especially the news media."

"I guarantee I won't. But can I go through channels and tell people in high levels of the German government, like Chancellor Merkel?"

"Yes, this is precisely what they want you to do."

"Xiaobo and Liu Xia want me to do this?"

"Yes."

"I need to understand more of the situation. Where is Xiaobo now? In the prison hospital? Or will he be secretly moved to Beijing?"

"He's stuck in a Shenyang hospital. Nothing can be done about this."

"My dad had cancer, so I know liver cancer is the most painful type."

"That's why Uncle and Aunt want to go to Germany. As soon as possible. If he has to die, it would be better for him to die in Germany."

Tears welled up in my eyes.

"Aunt knows Xi Jinping will be visiting Germany next month. Please ask Mrs. Merkel for urgent help. Plead with her to bring this up specifically when talking with Xi Jinping, to let Liu Xiaobo go to Germany as quickly as possible . . . no, to save him.

You've told Aunt that Merkel is the most humane and compassionate of politicians today, that she's helped you and many refugees, even when it has caused her great difficulties."

"May I reveal to Merkel the source of this information?"

"You may. These past two months, after all Aunt's applications and struggles, the government finally allowed Uncle to learn what happened to his family [while he was in prison], but now he's dying."

"I understand. Please give me your contact details . . ."

Without pausing for breath or thought, I wrote an email to the Biermanns, telling them the situation described above. They were shocked, Pamela saying she would inform the Chancellor's Office as soon as possible and that she might come to Berlin to see me, but that today it wasn't possible to determine a plan of action.

Given the abrupt change in circumstances, I took up my pen and wrote:

Dear Mrs. Merkel:

Please forgive me for taking this liberty! But matters are urgent, and I have no choice but to send you a second letter asking for help.

My old friend, Liu Xiaobo, the still-imprisoned Nobel Peace Prize laureate, has been diagnosed with late-stage liver cancer and is now at death's door.

This shockingly bad news was entrusted by Liu Xiaobo's wife, Liu Xia, to an immediate family member, and at 4:30 this afternoon she risked calling me to tell me about it. Liu Xiaobo and his wife asked me to represent them and to ask you and the German government to rescue them from totalitarian China. Liu Xiaobo, though wracked by pain, had the strength to say: "It would be better to die in Germany if I have to die!"

At this point, my face is drenched by my tears. I can't write anymore. I know that Xi Jinping will visit Berlin early next month. I beg you in the names of Liu Xiaobo and his wife that in your talks with Xi Jinping you use your compassion and political wisdom to urge the Chinese government to release Liu Xiaobo to Germany as soon as possible; no, call it a humane rescue. Liu Xiaobo is now deathly ill and cannot "subvert the country" anymore.

If you are unable to help, please reply, and I will convey the news to Liu Xiaobo and his wife.

If you need to meet with me for more details, please pass this information along by way of our mutual friend, Wolf Biermann. I will be awaiting news at home.

Respectfully yours,
Liao Yiwu, writer in exile
in Berlin on the evening of June 16, 2017

From the frequent feedback I received through the kind offices of the Biermanns, as well as the German Ministry of Foreign Affairs and the embassy in Beijing, I learned that the talks between Germany and China about the Lius were extremely difficult. And then on June 26, with tacit permission from the authorities, Liu Xiaobo's former lawyers, Mo Shaoping and Shang Baojun, suddenly revealed to the global news media the shocking news that the imprisoned Nobel Peace Prize laureate had late-stage liver cancer. Our good friend in China, Zhou Zhongling, took the risk of posting a short video announcing that neither chemotherapy nor radiotherapy could be used to cure Xiaobo's cancer. Shortly after this, Liu Xia and her husband vanished. I did everything I could to find news of them, but everybody said they were inside a heavily guarded building in Shenyang and nobody could get close to it. Still later, Jinzhou Prison announced that the convict Liu Xiaobo had been approved for "medical parole." According to the law in China, medical parole implies a return home, but the Lius were not allowed to return home. The authorities guaranteed they would gather the country's foremost cancer experts and consultants and do all they could to save Liu Xiaobo. When the representatives of several Western governments expressed a desire to welcome Liu Xiaobo for cancer treatment, China's Ministry of Foreign Affairs asserted that the Lius would willingly remain in China to undergo treatment.

During this time, Herta and Harry Müller often came to my home. Our translator and good friend, Zuo Jing, was always together with us. In my home, Herta drafted the joint statement signed by over 130 Nobel laureates, and I remember Herta saying at the end: "We can't let Liu Xiaobo die like this in China, and we can't let Liu Xia live like this in China." Correspondence between the Biermanns and myself was frequent, sometimes several letters a day. On June 25, 2017, the day before Liu Xiaobo's critical illness was revealed to the world, Pamela wrote:

Dear Yiwu,

I talked to my friend today. She sends cordial greetings to you and says she will not forget you and your friends. She tried to make a difference the first time we brought her your message. Unfortunately, her counterpart was not very enthusiastic and rather hostile. That's probably because our case is pretty well-known. Therefore, I think, it is advisable to keep calm and to make as little kerfuffle as possible in order not to obstruct the way to a quiet solution.

My friend will take care of it again, even if she has the big meeting soon. It seems to be rather difficult. But she will do her best.

Please write me that you got this email.

Best regards, also from the Biermanns,

Pamela

I immediately responded:

Dear Pamela, Dear Wolf,

Many thanks for everything. I understand that this is not an easy thing to do. Nevertheless, I thank your friend from my heart and I trust in her wisdom. If there's a god in this world, may it also protect my friend and keep him from death.

Yiwu

A short while later, Pamela wrote back:

Dear Yiwu,

I thought it over again. Your friend is now a patient. He should undergo a special medical treatment that exists in Berlin, for example. Maybe it will work this way. I advised my friend in this sense; she found the idea a good one. Let's wait and hope together with you.

Greetings,
Pamela

And again I responded:

Dear Pamela,

Yes, that's a good idea. Your friend was on the phone with us. We had to be silent. We are waiting for more news in peace.

Best Regards,
Yiwu

In fact, I wasn't sure. During the subsequent G20 summit in Hamburg, Angela Merkel, the "friend" in Pamela's letter, repeatedly told Xi Jinping that there was a special treatment for Liu Xiaobo's condition that could only be implemented in Germany. Xi Jinping gave a perfunctory response, saying in effect: Wait until I understand more about the situation and then I'll decide. Then the German and American cancer experts arrived at Liu Xiaobo's bedside, listened to his wishes, and published a report and a statement, reiterating that Liu Xiaobo could travel long distances under the care of medical personnel. And the German embassy in Beijing issued a statement:

A certain authority released an audio-visual recording of a German doctor who consulted with Liu Xiaobo. This act violated the wishes of the German side and violated the written agreement between the two parties before the visit. These videos were selectively leaked to certain Chinese official media. It seems that security agencies are leading the process, not medical experts. This behavior undermines trust in the authorities handling Liu Xiaobo's case—which is crucial to ensure maximum treatment success.

On July 11, I wrote to the Biermanns, making a final appeal to Mrs. Merkel:

Dear Wolf, Dear Pamela,

My friend Liu Xiaobo fell unconscious two days ago. According to the official announcement, the hospital is trying to save him. I'm full of worries and I need to bother you again, which I apologize for now.

A segment of the video surveillance was officially released: a group of white-gowned puppets stood around Liu Xiaobo; only a view of Liu Xia's back was visible. She seemed to be sobbing, as when the German expert voiced his opinion, the American expert stroked her shoulder and suggested they bring some tissues. This scene seemed like a dream to me. After the German and American experts had left the room, the remaining ghost doctors stood expressionless around Liu Xiaobo and Liu Xia.

The German and American experts have heard Liu Xiaobo's repudiation with their own ears: "Germany is the first choice! I would go to the US too. I hope the Chinese government approves my departure." I would like to reiterate that Xiaobo wants to save Liu Xia and Liu Hui [Liu Xia's brother] by bringing them to Germany with his last remaining strength. On June 16, someone from his family called me and reported that Liu Xiaobo had called out in great pain: "It would be better to die in Germany if I have to die!"

Dear Wolf, dear Pamela, I have caused you many problems. Of course, through your letters and phone calls, I know that Mrs. Merkel has tried everything she can. However, I approach you with this question: Would it still be possible to ask them to talk with the highest level in China again, even Xi Jinping at the top? Many rumors and conjectures are circulating these days, and even the artist Ai Weiwei is heavily involved in the rumor mill. Since he is influential, the rumors spread even faster and further, so I had to denounce him with allegations against him on Facebook. However, I have not revealed anything not approved by you.

I have kept my promise. My friend A will be made known when this is over. The salvation of Liu Xiaobo and Liu Xia is a major historical event, almost a Chinese version of "Schindler's list." Every detail and every piece of writing will be archived and documented. Ai Weiwei's recent remarks, such as "Pandas and planes are more important than Liu Xiaobo," cause confusion and distrust, which weakens the rescue effort.

The story repeats itself. Schindler had to deal with the criminal Nazi regime to save as many Jews as he could. The Chinese regime today is not inferior to the Nazis in its malevolence. So I understand very well, as you repeatedly emphasize, how difficult Mrs. Merkel has it. However, I cannot hold back and have to write again for one reason: Liu Xia will die soon after if Liu Xiaobo dies in China and she is not allowed to leave. Depression, heart disease, and despair would kill her quickly. And this would cause an agony that would never leave me.

So I count on you again with this request: Please speak again with Mrs. Merkel. Will you do this for me?

Your loving Yiwu,
Berlin, 11.07.2017

On the morning of the twelfth, the German embassy in Beijing asked the Berlin-based reporter Su Yutong to contact me. He urgently asked for visa photos for Liu Xiaobo, Liu Xia, and Liu Hui. The diplomats spoke guardedly but confirmed that the German side was prepared to move ahead.

I stayed up all night and haunted the house like a ghost. I took out three bronze coins and made a divination with the *I-Ching*, or *Book of Changes*. I got 贲, with a change to 既濟. 贲 is a decorative motif, 既濟 is completion, meaning that to seek virtue is to attain virtue. A week ago, for the same reason, I obtained 明夷, without a change. The literal translation of 明夷 is "Light is injured, the sun sinks into the earth's core." Sure enough, at noon on July 13, 2017, I received a long letter from Biermann, which began:

Liu Xiaobo is Gone

Dear Liao Yiwu,

I just received the message: not "We did it . . ." but the pigs have unfortunately managed to let your heart's brother die in China. This long-suffering man went in his own way today: Liu Xiaobo is dead. I know it from Pamela, who just called me. And she is back to communicating with our friend in Berlin, as discreetly as the last time.

But now it's a new situation. Now, unfortunately, it can only be a question of saving at least the widow at the edge of the abyss.

As you know, our friend in Berlin has always tried hard to help Liu Xiaobo. Yes, my dear, next to the G-20 summit meeting, next to the idiotic excesses of inhuman violence in Hamburg, beside contracts on free trade, panda diplomacy and Erdoğan terror and Putin's heroic deeds for the dictator in Syria and for the annexation of Ukraine . . . in addition to dealing with the Chinese turbocharged concentration-camp capitalism, it is always about the most important thing: the individual in this bestiary of world politics . . .

Just two days later, Xiaobo's ashes were thrown into the Yellow Sea. The authorities stressed that these were Liu Xia's own wishes. Liu Xiaoguang, Liu Xiaobo's eldest brother, a retired cadre of the Communist Party who had severed relations with his brother after the June Fourth massacre, gave his "heartfelt thanks to the Party and the government" at the supposedly globally broadcast live press conference. Soon after, a distraught Liu Xia was hurried off to Dali, in Yunnan, escorted by a large number of officers of the secret police.

———

A Dirge for Liu Xiaobo

What difference will it make? He's dead.
Nailed to the cross by the Communist Party, he is now eternally
    there like Jesus
Who rose again after being tortured to death
I still wait to hear you have news of his takeoff
I wait for him to write that last love letter
For him to send his wife thousands of miles far away and later be
    buried in a foreign land
We will often go to visit him. As the nighttime darkness gathers
The past sweeps by like a river flood sweeping past tree branches.
But everything was shattered, he is not free
His life and his death, his cremated ashes, his love, none of them
    are free
The whole world watched helplessly as a man of integrity
Like an outstanding book, was torn apart bit by bit
Nobody can stop these ignorant atrocities

But everyone hoped that they could be stopped!
Nobody can do anything about that, dear God
He is dead.

What did I do wrong? I had been trying since 2014. If you believe the
official account, things moved too fast. They say they convened the
country's top experts and consultants to save him—when, in fact, following similar practice, even if there had been no treatment, he should
have survived another three to five months or more. After a sudden fire
in a sector of Jinzhou Prison where he had been incarcerated, all records
of prisoners' physical exams over the years were turned to ashes. No
country imposed even the slightest sanctions on China for any of this.
Not Germany, either, although no other country had done as much as
Germany to help Liu Xiaobo and his wife.

History has proven on countless occasions that rumors disguising
the truth spread faster than the truth. Some people say these days are
like the 1930s—that China, rising like some monster, is reminiscent
of the Nazis. On September 2, the German weekly magazine *Der Spie-
gel* published an interview with Ai Weiwei, an "exiled dissident" who
has repeatedly returned to China over the years. "Until his death, Liu
Xiaobo seems to have been well treated in the hospital," said Ai Weiwei. "Liu Xia, who'd been allowed to stay by his side, was also in a
good mood." Ai also said that Liu's detention conditions were obviously much better than that of others. This was of course a trick of the
Chinese authorities, meant to give the impression that they had been
treating Liu Xiaobo well all along.

On Chinese Twitter, Ai Weiwei posted several comments that
closely resembled pronouncements by Chinese officials. On July 16, he
wrote: "People deliberately ignore the fact that Liu Xiaobo and his wife
maintained communication with the outside world until the last days of

his life . . . From the look of it, the couple's last days were spent in good spirits, thank God. There are pictures, written words, and voice recordings of this. Liu Xia kept the funeral simple of her own free will, invited no friends, a quick burial at sea . . ."

But there is proof. On the afternoon of August 31, 2017, I called Liu Xia again. I understood that someone must be eavesdropping, but I also felt—in the face of these rumors—that indelible testimony must be left.

"On June 6, I received a message and immediately rushed to Jinzhou from Beijing," Liu Xia told me. "As always, we gazed at each other through glass. He was still in prison and not yet hospitalized, but feeling very sick. His high fever had not abated for half a month, and there was no strength in his entire body. He said he had never felt this way before."

"Still no outside medical treatment?" I asked.

"Not yet."

"Do you think this is a routine visit?"

"No. They phoned. I had a sense: they're letting me come when it isn't prison visit time, something that has never happened before.

"Then he was transferred from prison to Shenyang Hospital, several hundred miles away. We also went to Shenyang to stay; we couldn't leave. At this time there was still no medical parole. It was just like the visits in prison: each time you meet for twenty minutes, at most twenty-five, police all around, unblinking stares, no human feeling."

"Did he have trouble speaking?"

"He could speak very feebly. Later the doctors and I talked it over and decided to tell him about his illness, since it would be awkward to perform such a complicated treatment without informing the patient. So I told him. He said don't treat it. 'But if you don't treat it, you can't leave,' I coaxed him, saying that on returning to Beijing, before going abroad, it would be best to undergo treatment. He listened to me . . . but, really, I didn't want it treated, either! I was also naïve at the start. Even if it was incurable, they should have let us go, whatever stage the treatment was at; when it was over our friends would be with us. But there was no choice, no way, I felt I was useless, no use at all."

"Once in the hospital, there was no getting out . . ."

"Round the clock, intubation all over, but the cancer cells kept spreading . . ."

"I'll tell you one thing. During the day on the twelfth, the German embassy wanted passport photos of you, Liu Hui, and Xiaobo, to prepare visas in anticipation of you all being let go. I really believed you and Liu Hui would come with Xiaobo."

"At first they said they'd deal with it, then that there'd be a wait of two or three months, and then he died. Xiaobo never wanted treatment; he accepted it all for me and Liu Hui."

"Was it any use?"

"I have no idea. Anyway, each day was worse than the last. You're just watching a person waste away bit by bit."

"How long were you and Xiaobo allowed to be together?"

"Not long. After the medical parole paperwork was done, there wasn't even a month left. People were with us all the time."

"Space to move?"

"Just the ward."

"Like being in a cage."

"Not just the two of us. There were others around us continuously. I counted every day over a hundred doctors, nurses, all kinds of assistants. But still, in other words, no choice."

"You two were never alone together."

"Right. There was little time for us to really be able to speak a few words, even. Xiaobo said it was like we were living together. He kidded me, saying I should take him out to tea, take him to the countryside to play, but actually at the time he already couldn't get out of bed, couldn't eat anything. At the time he was always saying to people, 'This is my wife, this is my wife.' Of course, the whole room full of doctors and nurses knew I was his wife, but he'd still say it to everybody he saw. Too silly."

"There's a photo of him sitting, with you feeding him soup."

"One day good, one day bad; one day he could eat a little, the next he couldn't. When he was finished eating, he couldn't even piss; he had to do dialysis."

"There's another photo, of the two of you walking in the ward."

"While walking in the ward, he wouldn't allow anybody to support him; he wanted to walk on his own. Every morning he'd make a nurse wait as he washed himself in the bathroom, and he'd be as clean as a whistle, waiting for me there."

"Would he walk a bit after washing?"

"After washing, there were all sorts of IV bags to reattach. Most of the time he was lying in bed."

"He was able to write a foreword for your photo album. I read it and felt that if he could still write, he could still hold on."

"Later he couldn't write. He was done. Whatever he ate he vomited up."

"The day before yesterday you said, just before he died, that he told you 'Go out, go out.' I couldn't sleep that night because of that."

"That was on the twelfth, he tried to drive me away from his bedside. He knew he couldn't leave, so he pushed me to leave."

"Could he still get up from the bed then?"

"No, he couldn't any longer."

"That German expert said Xiaobo still particularly wanted to get out of China. We'd already talked this over."

"Right. Who knows. Anyway, I don't know."

"At the time, I still thought you and Liu Hui would be able to get out, carrying his ashes."

"He's at peace, waiting for me. I definitely want to die now."

"No matter what, you can't think this way. You are an extension of his life. You haven't left China yet. What sort of extension is that? You're wrong to think like that."

"Give me time. I can't leave now. You have to understand: it's not that I don't want to go; it's that I'm not allowed to. You have to understand this. You pressure me and pressure me, but it's useless: you'll pressure me to death. What can I do locked up alone at home? Think about it. I told you, and I also told them: in a few months, in a few months . . . Isn't this clear enough? I've fought for all I can fight for, and your pressuring me makes me even more anxious. No one would put themselves through days like these! Last night I came upstairs with a cigarette. I don't know how I did it, but I burned the quilt. I'm still in a daze, feel nothing."

"You have to be careful, alone at home."

"I won't take a cigarette upstairs in the future."

"Two days ago, you said his death was still . . ."

"He was unconscious for a few hours at the end. His life was entirely supported by drugs and a beating heart."

"I don't dare think about it."

"I feel like it wasn't real even now."

"So live a better life."

"I persevere, but he couldn't. I didn't want to see him plugged into machines, either, living as a vegetable."

"You didn't agree to the throat intubation?"

"If he had the tube in, he would never have woken up again. And it wouldn't have lasted long, because it all depended on drugs. As long as a tube was inserted, much of what we said to each other couldn't have been said. When it's inserted, there are a lot of anesthetics, then a coma, maintaining a heartbeat. I couldn't bear to watch him lying there like that, so I said to Xiaobo that he shouldn't agree to it. Xiaobo said: 'Oh, I understand.' As final discretionary power was given to me, if I'd wanted him to live with tubes, he'd be living, but I didn't want him lying in a bed like that, on the surface unconscious, but with the body still suffering."

"Would he still be able to speak with you?"

"Not in a coma."

"When did he go completely into a coma?"

"The afternoon of the thirteenth, he couldn't communicate with me; he was just lying there, talking especially fast; you couldn't hear clearly what he was saying. He continued speaking for over an hour, especially fast. Because he had a nose tube, his voice was changed. Once the speed at which he spoke increased, you couldn't understand what he was saying."

"You must have been able to make sense of a few sentences, no?"

"No. In the end he stopped speaking, just moved his legs. His legs were going nonstop, as if he were walking, continuous. More than an hour went by . . . Nonstop, nonstop . . ."

"After he died, how have you gotten by?"

"I don't know how I've done it. I have no idea even now. The time spent crying is more than the time I've spent sleeping."

"How was it that the sea burial happened so quickly?"

No response.

"Liu Xia. Liu Xia."

No response.

The line went dead, and I couldn't reconnect. On September 1 and again on September 4, I called Liu Xia again, and we were careful to avoid speaking of the sea burial, as if that windy and sun-drenched sea was Tiananmen Square itself, with Xiaobo standing between the sea of people, as he had twenty-eight years earlier, and the sea of waves. Liu Xia said she was just about to go to the hospital for a checkup, meaning she was going to "disappear" until the close of the Nineteenth Party Congress.

Having experienced all of what happened surrounding Liu Xiaobo, nothing in this world will ever shock me again.

August 28, 2018, in Charlottenburg [Berlin]

APPENDIX ONE

A Guide to What Really Happened

By Ding Zilin and Jiang Peikun

In 1989, Jiang Jielian—son of Professors Ding Zilin and Jiang Peikun— was only seventeen. A high school student swept up in the fervor of the patriotic student movement, he gave himself over to the street protests. On the night of June 3, he was shot in the chest and died before reaching the emergency room. His grieving parents decided to speak out and publicly accused the government of their son's murder. With Ding and Jiang in the lead, some of those who had lost loved ones in the massacre came forth one by one and formed the Tiananmen Mothers movement. The murderers still govern the country, while the parents who lost their children grow old and die under the gaze of the secret police. But the Tiananmen Mothers bear witness.

For many years, friends would ask us: "How many people were actually killed in the June Fourth massacre?" We cannot yet answer that question. At the time—according to the report that Chen Xitong, mayor of Beijing, gave the Standing Committee of the National People's Congress, for example—the government openly acknowledged that more than 200 people had been killed, including 36 university students and some soldiers. That figure clearly conceals a great deal. At the time of the massacre, the Chinese Red Cross Society announced that the real number of the dead was between 2,600 and 3,000. That figure was soon buried by official government figures and people never mentioned it again.

We believe even if the Red Cross number is not completely accurate, it is an important reference point. This view was verified in the course of our own work of searching for and interviewing victims' families. When the massacre occurred, we, the families of the victims, visiting hospitals throughout Beijing, saw with our own eyes the dead bodies of the victims and the lists of the dead posted by the various hospitals. (The majority of victims were quickly cremated, as is common practice today in China.) What we witnessed firsthand far, far exceeds the official numbers. When the family of the massacre victim Du Guangxue collected his remains from the Peking Union Medical College Hospital, the serial number on his body was "No. 30." Who, then, were numbers 1 through 29? How many more were there after number 30? We have recorded fewer than ten victims from Peking Union Medical College Hospital. How many more dead were "disposed of" and never sent to the hospital? How many so-called missing people were there? We know even less about those cases.

The following two lists are the names of 202 people killed and 49 wounded in the June Fourth massacres. They are the fruit of twenty-two years of perseverance by the Tiananmen Mothers group, which has conducted extensive interviews. The lists are soaked with the blood, tears, and suffering of these fellow victims. In an article written on the tenth anniversary of June Fourth, Ding Zilin wrote: "Over the past decade, I have been crawling in the pile of the victims' 'corpses' and floating on the deep sea of tears of the victims' families. The feelings of suffocation and the overwhelming grief I have felt these days and nights have made me understand what death is." These are not only the personal feelings of Ding Zilin, but of everyone who took part in the work of locating and interviewing the families of the victims of June Fourth.

Recording the names of the dead is a sacred and heavy responsibility. The process is not only about the lives and deaths of individuals but also about bearing witness to history. We are determined to avoid the slightest negligence or error. We remember how in 1996, the seventh anniversary of the massacre, a document from our group proclaimed,

"Up to this point, we have already found nearly 200 people killed in the June Fourth massacres." But in the months and year that followed, these numbers did not increase; on the contrary, they decreased. Twenty-two years after June 4, 1989, our list of the June Fourth dead has only 202 names. The reason for this is that the people who provided us with clues about the names of the dead gave us neither the names of eyewitnesses nor any other necessary evidence.

We put our best efforts into searching for evidence and confirming information about the victims, but until we have definite proof, there must be reservations. Following initial leads, we proceeded to confirm the information. For example, it took us a total of eight years to find the family of the June Fourth victim Wu Guofeng. Some leads about the June Fourth dead we were not able to verify, despite repeated investigation, and so we decided to remove those names from the list. In 1998 alone, we eliminated ten names.

Searching for families and interviewing them was a long process that advanced slowly as more information accumulated. Even with those killed or injured whose information was already on record, it was still a tedious process to verify such facts—from piecemeal to complete, from sketchy to precisely correct—as the place where they were killed or injured, where the bullets hit them, the hospital where they died, and the way in which their families are getting by in the aftermath. Regardless, this list will have gaps that need to be filled in and mistakes that need to be corrected. We earnestly hope that our readers will provide new evidence that will make the list more accurate.

Some of the families of the June Fourth victims (including the wounded and disabled), intimidated by pressure from the Chinese authorities, were afraid to provide relevant information. Some of the people with knowledge of the cases, from an instinct for self-preservation, would not cooperate and refused to provide information. The addresses of some of the people involved changed constantly over the months and years, so that some of the leads we originally had became useless.

At the same time, we have received tremendous sympathy and help, including from Chinese students overseas who have provided us with valuable leads. Here we express our profound gratitude to them and hope that they will continue to support us.

This list of names has been provided to the outside world five times over the years:

- In 1993, the United Nations World Conference on Human Rights was held in Vienna. Ding Zilin was invited but in the end was unable to attend because of obstacles set up by the Chinese authorities. Instead, she provided a written statement to the conference providing the names she had already found of sixteen massacre victims.
- In 1994, Ding Zilin published the "List of the June Fourth Victims" in Japanese, Chinese, and English. In those three editions, Ding Zilin in her personal capacity released the names of ninety-six dead and forty-nine wounded.
- In 1999, on the tenth anniversary of June Fourth, our group, with the assistance of the New York–based organization Human Rights in China, edited and published a booklet called *Witness to the Massacre—the Search for Justice*. In the booklet were the names of 155 of the dead who had been confirmed as June Fourth victims.
- In 2005, the Hong Kong magazine *Kaifang* (*Open*) published Ding Zilin's book *In Search of the Victims of June Fourth*. The number of names of the dead published in that book increased by 31 to 186.
- In 2010, a list was released that included 201 people killed in the June Fourth massacre, including some people whose full names or first names were not known. There are two reasons for this missing information. The first is that family members did not wish to publicize the names of the deceased. The second is that the whereabouts of the deceased's family members had not been found. In these cases, at least two eyewitness accounts were needed for them to be included. We obtained the names of many people rumored

to have been killed, but we did not include them without reliable eyewitness testimony. The last six names on the list were provided in the book *The Explosion of History* by the Xinhua Press Agency journalist Zhang Wanshu. Zhang listed the names of twenty-three dead in his book, seventeen of whom we had already found prior to the publishing of the book, but six of whom we had not found. We added those six names to the list. The names that Zhang provided are very credible. Zhang said that at five a.m. on June Fourth, the Beijing University of Posts and Telecommunications hospital listed twenty-nine dead. Jiang Peikun had gone to the hospital at almost the same time and got a number of twenty-eight, a difference of only one name.

We have published the "List of Victims of the June Fourth Massacre" several times so that the world will not forget those people who sacrificed themselves for Chinese democracy and freedom and those innocent people who were deprived of their right to live. We do this also so that the world will pay attention to the families of those killed in the massacre and those disabled people who were fortunate to have survived their injuries.

Ordinarily, the work of collecting and publishing the names of victims would be the job of the Chinese government. Indeed, some Chinese government leaders pledged to do so when they met some foreigners visiting China. However, that pledge has never been kept. Because of this, we, as members of a victims' group, and as mothers who have lost our sons and daughters, have dedicated our meager strength to collecting and preparing the names of the dead and disabled. Naturally, our strength is unequal to the task, and we hope that more people will participate in this work.

Judging from the information above, the 202 June Fourth victims that we are releasing today represent only a fraction of the total number of actual victims. We will keep up the search.

APPENDIX TWO

List of 202 People Killed in the Massacre

Collected by the Tiananmen Mothers (1989–2011)

Provided by Ding Zilin and Jiang Peikun

This marks the first time the full updated list of Tiananmen victims, edited and in some cases expanded here from the original, has been published in English.

1. Lü Peng, male, 9, third grader at Shunchenggen Elementary School in Beijing

On June 3, around midnight, this mischievous child, who had not gone to sleep at his bedtime, snuck out of the house without his parents' knowledge to join in the patriotic demonstrations of the grown-ups. Near the Fuxingmen Bridge intersection he was shot in the chest by martial law troops firing wildly. The angry crowd put Lü's body on the roof of a convertible, parading it up and down the street as a demonstration of how even small children were in danger during the Chinese military's murder of the innocents.

2. Xia Zhilei, female, 22, university student in southern China

A little past four a.m. on June 4, Xia followed other students as they retreated from Tiananmen. Reaching Dongdan, they were met by gunfire. Staggering and falling, Xia shouted, "Hurry! Hurry! Find a place to rest. I think I've been shot." She held her chest tightly as blood kept gushing out from between her fingers. In the confusion and darkness, martial law troops charged the group from all sides. People had no choice but to keep walking and carry the unconscious girl with them. A few minutes later, momentarily recovering consciousness before dying, Xia said to those around her: "Classmates! My blooming season is over." Xia Zhilei means "summertime flower bud," which withers and dies very quickly.

3. Liu Junhe, male, 56, small-business owner in Beijing, personal details unknown

"Fresh, thin-skinned, thick-fleshed watermelons!" Liu would shout again and again. "If they aren't sweet or crisp, you don't have to pay!" Early on the morning of June 4, he was at his vendor's stall as usual next to the watchtower on Qianmen Avenue. Suddenly a line of army trucks drove by. With a rat-a-tat, the streetlights were shot out and the slaughter reached its climax in the dark. One after another, demonstrators fell to the ground, while others scattered in all directions. As Liu rushed to pack up his cart, he was hit in the face by a random gunshot. Blood spurted from his neck. Shortly after, he died at the Beijing Friendship Hospital.

4. Jiang Jielian, male, 17, sophomore at the high school attached to Renmin University of China

Jiang left home at 10:30 p.m. on the night of June 3. About forty minutes later, while he was standing outside the building at Fuxingmenwai Dajie No. 29, he was hit by wild gunfire from the People's Liberation Army martial law troops. Bystanders immediately brought him to the nearby children's hospital. His death certificate stated that he was dead on arrival.

5. Wang Nan, male, 19, sophomore at Yuetan High School in Beijing

After going out with his camera to "record history," Wang was hit in the head by a stray bullet around midnight at the southern end of Nanchang Street. Those nearby shrieked and wanted to help him, but martial law troops fired shots in the air to stop them until he was dead.

As they did with many victims, soldiers carelessly buried Wang in a field in front of Beijing Middle School No. 28 on the western side of Tiananmen Square. Three days later the decaying bodies began to smell. After the school made a request to the authorities, all the bodies were allowed to be dug up and quickly cremated.

6. Xiao Jie, male, 21, journalism student at Renmin University of China

Xiao participated in the Tiananmen hunger strike and saw many of his fellow students injured in the bloodbath on the streets. With feelings of grief, indignation, and fear, he bought a train ticket home to Chengdu so that he could leave the Beijing nightmare as soon as possible.

However, at 2:10 a.m. on June 5, while he was about to cross the street at the Nanchizi Street intersection, Xiao accidentally stepped on a red warning line that the martial law troops had painted on the street. A soldier yelled "Halt!" but he continued, panic-stricken. Gunfire struck him from behind. He spun halfway around and fell. A red flower erupted on his chest. The crowd screamed and rushed forward. They laid him out on a three-wheeled flatbed cart and rushed him to Gong'an Hospital. At 2:55, emergency treatment having failed, he stopped breathing.

7. Xie Jingsuo, male, 21, sophomore in the light industry college of Beijing Lianhe University

As he was recording history with his camera at the Liubukou intersection in Xidan during the early morning of June 4, Xie was attacked by a ferocious band of martial law soldiers, who rained blows on him with their clubs. Lying there with an assault rifle pressing down on the left side of his chest, Xie screamed for mercy. Two shots were fired. The crowd took him to the emergency treatment center, but it was already too late.

8. Xiao Bo, male, 27, lecturer in chemistry at Peking University

Xiao Bo, a precocious student, tested into the Peking University technology and physics department at the age of sixteen

Late on the night of June 3, disregarding his own personal safety, Xiao passed through streets filled with heavy gunfire to Muxidi to help his students return to campus, when a stray bullet penetrated his chest. He was immediately carried to Fuxing Hospital for emergency treatment, which proved ineffective. He died soon after, on his birthday, leaving twin sons not quite three months old.

9. Jin Ying, male, 18, Beijing, occupation unknown

On the evening of June 5, Jin went out with a colleague and never returned home. His family visited all the major hospitals in Beijing, but they heard nothing about him until seven days later when someone found him by chance at the Erlong Road Hospital in the western district of Beijing. The mortuary personnel at the hospital explained to his family that he was so small and thin that they thought he was a child. His body was covered with small white flowers: after breathing his last, he had been dropped in a flower bed in Muxidi. Jin had been struck by three bullets. Judging from all the blood he had lost, he must have struggled for some time.

10. Lu Chunlin, male, 27, graduate student at Renmin University of China

Just before he died—late on the night of June 3, at Muxidi in the city center—Lu raised his blood-soaked body and asked passersby to send his ID card back to his school. University officials identified his body, and he was cremated. His relatives took his ashes back to his hometown in Jiangsu Province for burial.

11. Zhang Xianghong, female, 20, student in the Renmin University of China international politics department, specializing in the international Communist movement

Along with her elder brother, his wife, and several other people, Zhang left the home of relatives in Zhushikou at eleven p.m. on June 3, but martial law troops separated the group. The trailing light from flying bullets made webs of fire. Running hand in hand, Xiang and her sister-in-law hid in bushes to the west of Daqianmen. A bullet struck the main artery on the left side of Xiang's chest and went out through her back. The crowd carried her to a city emergency medical center, where she was treated. Early in the morning of June 4, after heartrending screams, she died.

12. Cheng Renxing, male, 25, English major in the foreign languages department of Central China Teacher's College in Wuhan; graduate student at Renmin University of China with a double major at the Soviet Union and Eastern Europe Studies Institute

Cheng and several classmates were battling the siege at the flagpole in Tiananmen Square on the morning of June 4. When the tanks rolled in, he was shot in the stomach. He screamed in pain and was taken to Beijing People's Hospital. There were too many people waiting, and he died from loss of blood. The family lost their only university student, an award winner and an excellent scholar, a good leader and a member in good standing of the Communist Youth League.

13. Wang Yifei, male, 31, employee of the Datong Company in Zhongguancun, Beijing

On the night of June 3, Wang was suddenly hit by a bullet at the entrance of the headquarters of Academia Sinica in Sanlihe. It went through his lung on the left side of his chest. He died on the spot.

14. Yang Yansheng, male, 30, employee at *Sports News* in Beijing

Yang was shot in his lower abdomen with a dumdum bullet (a bullet that expands more than usual upon hitting an object) while helping injured people at the Zhengyi Road intersection on the morning of June 4. He went down on his knees as his intestines splashed out. Like many other wounded, he was taken by the crowd to Beijing Hospital for emergency treatment, but he could not be helped.

15. Zhang Jin, female, 19, graduate of the Beijing Foreign Trade Center's foreign affairs service school and trainee at the International Trade Center

Zhang was caught in the crossfire around midnight on June 3; she was struck from behind as her boyfriend grabbed her and ran with her into a nearby alley. Her head instantly exploded. She was taken to the Beijing University of Posts and Telecommunications hospital, but she was already dead.

16. Duan Changlong, male, 24, graduate of the Tsinghua University chemical engineering department, specializing in applied chemistry; class section leader

Duan left home on his bicycle to "witness history" and came upon a confrontation between a large crowd of unarmed civilians and heavily armed soldiers. Amid a hail of bullets, people ran in all directions or were cut down. Just as Duan turned around, a bullet hit him on the left side of his chest. An examination revealed that he was shot with a small-caliber weapon at extremely close range. His ashes were interred at the Wan'an Public Cemetery in the western suburbs of Beijing.

17. Wang Weiping, female, 25, intern at Beijing People's Hospital department of gynecology and obstetrics; recent graduate of Beijing Medical University

On the night of June 3, Wang was hit in the neck by a bullet while bravely rushing to the front lines to rescue the injured. She was taken to one of the Beijing Medical University hospitals for emergency treatment, but died there. Her ashes were interred at the Wan'an Public Cemetery with the simple inscription on her headstone "Born December 21, 1964. Killed in an accident June 3."

18. Wang Jianping, male, 27, driver for the Beijing Gas Company

Wang joined the blockade of military vehicles on the night of June 3. He was shot on the left side of his chest at the Xidan intersection. He died the following morning from loss of blood. After his cremation, Wang was carelessly buried for some unknown reason in a deserted field in the suburbs of Beijing.

When he was killed, he left behind twin girls, only eight months old.

19. Wang Peiwen, male, 21, student in the youth work department of the China Youth College for Political Sciences

Wang was a demonstrator retreating from Tiananmen Square early on the morning of June 4. He was in the first row of a long column of students, passing through a human wall of troops and their dark gun barrels. Feeling lucky to have escaped danger, he was knocked down and crushed by a tank charging into the Liubukou intersection. His so-called remains were a mash of human flesh and blood pressed into the pavement at the intersection.

20. Dong Xiaojun, male, 20, student in the youth work department of the China Youth University of Political Studies

Dong was a demonstrator retreating from Tiananmen Square at the tail end of a long column of students early on the morning of June 4. A tank came up behind him. Dong was knocked down and crushed. His remains were scraped together bit by bit and, after cremation, were laid to rest at his family home in Yancheng, Jiangsu Province.

21. Yuan Li, male, 29, engineer at the Beijing National Electronic Industry Automation Research Center

Yuan had traveled to Germany as an engineering expert and was preparing to make a trip to the United States. A little past eleven p.m. on the night of June 3, he left his house and walked to Muxidi. Troops attacked the crowd. Amid the wild shooting, a bullet hit Yuan in the throat and came out the back of his neck.

With no identification on him, he was pronounced dead at the Navy General Hospital and listed as "Anonymous Corpse no. 2." For more than ten days, Yuan's family looked for him everywhere, visiting forty-four hospitals all over Beijing. Eventually they found out the circumstances of his disappearance. They brought his body home on June 19.

22. Ye Weihang, male, 19, junior at Beijing No. 57 High School; class leader; student association cadre

Ye was shot at Muxidi in the early morning. He was listed as "Anonymous Corpse No. 1" after the Navy General Hospital determined he was dead. He was found to have three bullet wounds: an open wound in his left arm, a closed wound in his right chest, and a closed wound at the right rear side of his head. On June 5, Ye's family learned the reason for his disappearance. They recovered his remains and had them cremated, and his ashes rest at home.

23. Wu Guofeng, male, 21, student in the industrial economics department of Renmin University of China

During the 1989 student movement Wu was elected a member of his university's Capital Autonomous Federation of University Students preparatory committee. He participated in the five days and nights of the Tiananmen hunger strike.

On the evening of June 3, disregarding repeated warnings from the school, Wu grabbed his camera and rode his bike to the scene to record history. The army butchered him, although it is not known exactly where. According to forensic evidence, after he fell to the ground with a gunshot wound, he was shot again at close range and, lying face up, stabbed with a bayonet. He had grabbed the bayonet in his death throes, enraging his executioner.

24. Wang Chao, male, 30, an employee of the Beijing Zhongguancun Sitong Company

Wang was killed the night of June 3. The place and details are not known. He was at first listed as "Anonymous Corpse No. 3" by the Navy General Hospital.

25. An Ji, male, 31, editor of *Township Construction*, a magazine of the Ministry of Construction's construction technologies research center in Beijing

On June 6 at midnight, seven young people were going home after a meeting. When they passed through the Nanlishi intersection, they were attacked by troops. All five of the young men were shot down amid heavy gunfire. The two frightened young women knelt and begged loudly for mercy over and over, and their lives were spared. Besides An Ji, the names of the other three murdered men were Wang Zhengqiang, Wang Zhengsheng, and Yang Ziping. Yang Ziming survived, as did the two women, Yang Yuemei and Zhang Xuemei.

26. Wang Zhengsheng, male, 20, employee at the Beijing North China Material Supply Station

Wang was killed at the same time as An Ji. (See entry no. 25.) He was shot in the back and sent to the hospital along with his elder brother Wang Zhengqiang, who, though seriously wounded, recovered from his wounds.

27. Yang Ziping, male, 26, worker at Beijing Machinery Factory No. 1

Yang was also killed at the same time as An Ji. (See entry no. 25.) He was shot in the back. Yang was sent with his elder brother Yang Ziming to Fuxing Hospital. Yang Ziming was seriously wounded but recovered from his near-fatal wounds.

28. Qian Jin, male, 21, student at the University of International Business and Economics in Beijing

On June 3 at about ten p.m., Qian was riding a bicycle with a classmate surnamed Yuan at the Beifengwo intersection, heading in the direction of Muxidi. While turning toward home, Qian ran into a barrage of gunfire sweeping across the street like a fan. He and Yuan were shot along with others in flight around them. The crowd took them to the Beijing Railway General Hospital for emergency treatment. Qian was wounded in several places, and an artery had been severed. He died on the morning of June 5 from loss of blood.

29. Liu Hong, male, 24, graduate student in environmental science at Tsinghua University

Liu was in the long column of students retreating from Tiananmen to Qianmen early in the morning of June 4, when soldiers shot him in the abdomen. He fell to his knees and his intestines spilled out. His classmates tried to stuff his viscera back inside him, but they fell out again; this happened several times. Liu's classmates could only press a small washbasin upside down on his wound. He died in their arms as they carried him to the hospital.

30. Zhong Qing, male, 21, student in the precision machinery department at Tsinghua University

On the night of June 3 in Muxidi, Zhong ran back and forth as gunfire swept the area. When he was finally hit, half of his face was blown off. Many of his classmates could no longer recognize him. A little later, after searching the pockets of his trousers, they were able to determine his identity.

31. Zhou Deshi, male, 20, recent graduate of the Chinese Academy of Sciences Biophysics Research Institute; already assigned to Nanjing University

Zhou was shot and killed on the night of June 3. No details are known.

32. Name unknown, male, age unknown, ticket seller on Beijing bus route 101

At five a.m. on June 4, this man's dead body lay to the north of the Hongmiao intersection in the eastern suburbs of Beijing. The information was provided by several eyewitnesses.

33. Zhang XX, male, 53, section chief in the infrastructure department of the thermoelectric plant in the eastern suburbs of Beijing

On June 4 at five a.m., Zhang's dead body lay to the north of the Hongmiao intersection in the eastern suburbs of Beijing. This information was provided by several eyewitnesses.

34. Yang Minghu, male, 42, employee of the China Council for the Promotion of Foreign Trade patent section legal office

On the morning of June 4, Yang suddenly came under fire while standing in front of the main gate of the Ministry of Public Security on Chang'an Avenue. He was hit in the abdomen by dumdum bullets, which are forbidden by international treaty, smashing his bladder and pelvis. He died two days later in great pain at the hospital, his eyes wide open.

35. Zhuang Jiesheng, male, 27, salesperson at the Wudaokou Department Store in Beijing

Zhuang left home during the afternoon of June 3 but never returned. His family searched for him far and wide until June 11, when they saw the photographs of a series of "anonymous corpses that have not been claimed," provided to the public by Tongren Hospital in Beijing. They had found him.

36. Yuan Minyu, male, 35, electric welder at the Beijing Geological Instrumentation Factory

At midnight on June 3, Yuan was somewhere between Sanlihe and Muxidi, when he was struck in the heart and throat by two bullets. Emergency treatment proved ineffective and he died on the afternoon of June 4 at Beijing Children's Hospital.

37. Du Yanying, male, 29, worker at a company subordinate to the Beijing reform-through-labor bureau

Du was hit in the waist by a dumdum bullet at two a.m. near the Dabei Photography Studio at Qianmen. His heart and liver were blown apart. He died on the morning of June 5.

38. Lu Jianguo, male, 40, driver for the Beijing Travel Bureau

Lu was struck in the chest by dumdum bullets around eleven p.m. on June 3 at No. 27 Juchang Road near the Sanlihe market. He died where he fell.

39. Yu Di, male, 32, engineer at the Solar Power Research Institute in Beijing, who, working together with colleagues, had invented a thermoelectric membrane and won a prize for this work

During the standoff between martial law troops and tens of thousands of Beijingers along the stretch of road between Nanchizi and the National Museum of China, at around two a.m. on the morning of June 4, gunfire and explosions lit up the night in four furious waves of assault. Yu fell, completely covered in blood. He was taken by others in the crowd to Peking Union Medical College Hospital. A bullet that had entered at his lower left rib and exited by the upper right rib damaged eight of his organs, including his liver, kidneys, and lungs, as well as injuring his backbone. Physicians spared no effort, working on him for more than twenty days. Yu underwent four major operations and the removal of a kidney. However, his high fever did not go down. On the night of June 30, he died in pain.

40. Li Changsheng, male, age unknown, custodian at the Beijing Lianhe University automation engineering department library

Li left home at dawn on June 4 and went to Tiananmen Square to support the patriotic students. He was never seen again. His body was never found.

41. Xi Guiru, female, 24, employee of the Beijing Exhibition Center Labor Services Company

Xi was struck by a bullet in her left shoulder at dawn on June 4, at the north entrance of February 7 Theater Road. She died at Beijing People's Hospital.

42. Dai Wei, male, 20, cook at Hepingmen Roast Duck Restaurant in Beijing

On the evening of June 3, Dai went to work at the usual time. When he reached the entrance of the Beijing Minzu Hotel, he was dragged along by a panicked crowd fleeing troops. Dai was hit in the back, lost too much blood, and died in the hospital.

43. Wu Xiangdong, male, 21, employee of the Beijing Dongfeng Television Factory

Wu ran into troops at the end of Muxidi Bridge at a little past eleven p.m. on the night of June 3. He was hit in the neck by a dumdum bullet. He was sent to Fuxing Hospital for emergency treatment but had lost too much blood. Before he died, he wrote the address of his work unit on a piece of paper currency and asked a university student to notify his company of his death.

44. Liu Jianguo, male, 35, salesperson at the Beijing Great Wall Trench Coat Company

Liu was shot in the chest around midnight on June 3 at the Xidan Road intersection. He was sent to the Erlong Road Hospital for emergency treatment but could not be saved.

45. Lai Bi, male, 21, of the Zhuang ethnic minority; student at Beijing Medical University

Lai was struck by a 10mm bullet at the intersection of West Chang'an Avenue and South Chang'an Avenue around two a.m. on June 4. The bullet struck his forehead and exited the back of his head. On the morning of June 6, the hospital, under political pressure, made out a death certificate stating that Lai had been "accidentally injured."

46. Dong Lin, male, 24, employee at the Beijing Eastern District People's Court

Dong was hit in the ribs on the right side of his chest by a dumdum bullet around eleven p.m. on the night of June 3, on the eastern bank of Muxidi and died. According to several eyewitnesses, four other people were also hit in the fusillade that struck him. One was hit in an artery in his thigh; his whole body twitched for a while and then he died. The crowd took the other three to the Fuxing Hospital for emergency treatment. Physicians there worked day and night but could save only one of them.

47. Guo Anmin, male, 23, recent graduate in jet propulsion at Beihang University; had just passed the entrance exam to study for his master's degree

Guo died a violent death early on the morning of June 4 at an unknown location. He was shot in the forehead; half of his face was blown away. Nobody knows just who, in the confusion that followed, took his body and put it in the hall of the main building of China University of Political Science and Law. Several days later his school retrieved his body.

48. Lin Renfu, male, 30, recent PhD in materials science at the University of Science and Technology Beijing; had just obtained his passport and was about to go to Japan in October for further study

Together with his classmate Wang Kuanbao, Lin retreated from Tiananmen Square early on the morning of June 4. He had just reached the Liubukou intersection, when he was knocked down and crushed beneath a pursuing tank.

49. Sun Yanchang, male, 24, driver at the Beijing Construction and Furnace Building Company

Sun went out on the night of June 3 to look for his younger brother, who had not yet come home. When he got to the south side of the main station for the Hongmiao 110 bus, in the eastern suburbs of Beijing, a spray of gunfire hit him. The crowd brought him to the Chaoyang Hospital for emergency treatment. After six months of treatment, he died.

50. Qian Hui, male, 21, recent graduate specializing in news collection and editing at the Beijing Broadcasting Institute

On the morning of June 5, as Qian walked out the main gate of his school to take stock of the situation, he was shot in a hail of fire from a tank. An artery in his thigh was pierced and a jet of blood spurted from his body. His bladder was damaged. His mind was still clear, so he warned the students coming to help him, "Watch out! The military vehicles aren't gone yet!" Everybody helped to carry him back into the school, with the trail of his blood stretching over 300 feet. Qian stopped breathing before he reached the hospital.

51. Zou Bing, female, 19, student at the Beijing Broadcasting Institute

Zou escaped the slaughter of June 4 but was interrogated because of her active participation in the student movement. She was unable to avoid the roadblocks and had no way to escape. In the middle of September, she climbed to the roof of a thirteen-story tower on her campus and jumped. Her suicide caused a sensation; the school, under considerable political pressure, was forced to slander her as having had mental health problems. In fact, she was a healthy, optimistic girl who, several days before she died, had mailed a note to her parents apologizing that she had not lived up to the love and care they had given her since her childhood.

52. Pu Changkui, male, 47, of the Korean ethnic minority, performer in the China National Ethnic Song and Dance Ensemble

Somewhere on the road between Xidan and Fuxingmen on the night of June 3, Pu was shot in the back left part of his head by a bullet that emerged from the right side of his neck. He died on the spot. His ashes were interred at Jinshan Cemetery without any grave marker or inscription.

53. Bian Zongxu, male, 40, manager at the Xinjiekou Mechanical and Electronic Products Supply and Sales Company in Beijing

On the morning of June 4, Bian was standing in front of a furniture shop in Xidan, when a stray bullet went through his head. He died there. His ashes were interred in the Taiziyu Public Cemetery, where a headstone was erected in his name. He left behind twins, a boy and a girl.

54. Tian Daomin, male, 22, student in the management department of the University of Science and Technology Beijing

Tian followed the advice of his school and stayed in his dormitory room all night to write his graduation thesis, but on the morning of June 4, he went out the main gate of his school and ran to Liubukou to see what was happening. A tank barging through the intersection flattened him.

55. He Jie, male, 23, graduate student at the Institute of Computing Technology at the Chinese Academy of Sciences

He, together with many classmates, went to Tiananmen on the evening of June 3 to support the student protest. He had just arrived at Nanchizi when he was shot and killed.

When he started high school at the age of fifteen, He impressed Tsinghua University so much that the usual rules were waived to admit him as an underage university student. Later he advanced rapidly, again contary to standard procedure, to become a master's student at the Chinese Academy of Sciences, where he was called a boy wonder.

56. Song Xiaoming, male, 32, technician at Factory 283 of the Second Academy of China Aerospace in Beijing

On the evening of June 3, Song was on the sidewalk on the southwestern side of the Wukesong intersection in a big crowd, yelling slogans of protest that drew gunfire from soldiers on army trucks. Several people fell; Song was among those hit. The major artery in his thigh was severed and he bled heavily. He was taken to the emergency room of the nearby 301 Hospital (People's Liberation Army General Hospital). A soldier who followed him gave orders to the hospital, "Don't treat him! Don't give him blood transfusions." The physicians and nurses who stood ready to save him could only watch as he died before dawn. His mother could not bear what had happened to her son. Her kidneys failed and she soon followed him in death.

57. Liu Yansheng, male, 37, worker at the Beijing Household Electric Appliances Research Center

A stray bullet pierced Liu's abdomen on the night of June 3 when he was at the Palace of Nationalities intersection on Chang'an Avenue. He was sent to the

Beijing University of Posts and Telecommunications hospital but could not be saved. He bled to death.

58. Wen Jie, male, 26, master of arts from the Chinese literature department at Peking University; teacher at the Beijing Institute of Fashion Technology

Wen was arrested by the authorities after the June Fourth massacre because he had actively participated in the student movement. He suffered from acute abdominal pain while in prison and was diagnosed with late-stage intestinal cancer. He passed away shortly after being released on bail.

59. Li Huiquan, male, 35, journalist at *China Metallurgy News* in Beijing

Li was killed at dawn on June 4 while passing through the south side of Liubukou. No details are known. On June 11, following leads, his parents found his corpse at the Beijing University of Posts and Telecommunications hospital. It was headless.

60. Zhang Runing, male, 32, deputy director of the Russian-language service at China Radio International in Beijing

At about ten p.m. on the night of June 3, while walking from his home to his work unit, Zhang was shot as he crossed the street near the Muxidi Bridge. A dumdum bullet blew a hole in his abdomen. The crowd rushed him to the Fuxing University Hospital, where treatment proved ineffective. His remains were interred in the Futian Public Cemetery in the western suburb of Beijing.

61. Liu Fenggen, male, 40, worker at the drilling equipment factory of the Ministry of Geology

Liu's sense of morality and justice led him to leave his home at around ten p.m. on the night of June 3 to rescue injured people in the Xidan area. Amid intense gunfire, he was struck three times—in his back, his arm, and his heart. He died at the Beijing Erlong Road Hospital.

62. Li Meng, female, 32, assistant researcher at the State Language and Writing Reform Commission

At dawn on June 4, Li found her husband, who had been seriously wounded by a dumdum bullet, in a pile of dead bodies. She took him to a hospital for emergency treatment; he survived. However, she suffered a mental breakdown because of all the bloodshed. In late 1990, Li went missing near her home. Her family looked for her for many years, but they didn't see her alive or find her dead body. Because of this, the Ministry of Public Security issued a death notice and canceled her household registration.

63. Bi Yunhai, male, 22, worker at the street committee office at Guang'anmennei in Beijing

Bi left home on the night of June 3 and did not return. His family found his body the next day at Fuxing Hospital. His abdomen had been torn open by dumdum bullets. His ashes were interred at the Jinshan Public Cemetery in the western suburbs of Beijing.

64. Liu Hongtao, male, 18, student in the optical engineering department at the Beijing Institute of Technology

Liu was killed near the Cultural Palace of the Nationalities at one a.m. on June 4. His school retrieved his body from the Beijing University of Posts and Telecommunications hospital.

65. Zhou Xinming, male, 16, high school student in Beijing

Zhou was killed early in the morning of June 4. There is little personal information available about him. He is buried in the Jinshan Public Cemetery in the western suburbs of Beijing.

66. Wang Gang, male, 20, technician at the Beijing Coking Plant

On the afternoon of June 3, Wang left home to work the night shift. At seven a.m. the next morning, June 4, while he was buying breakfast in front of the main gate of the factory, a long line of army trucks screamed by at high speed. Hundreds of people waited on the side for a chance to cross. At that moment an army truck crashed into the crowd. People screamed and ran off in every direction. Three were unable to escape and were crushed to death. The young technician Wang was one of them.

Following the tragedy, the soldiers boarded the vehicle that followed and left. To vent their anger, the frustrated crowd shouted slogans and set the deserted bloodstained military truck on fire.

67. Zhang Lin, male, 37, Beijing resident, personal information unknown

Zhang was killed on June 4. No details are available. His remains were buried in Jinshan Public Cemetery in the western suburbs of Beijing.

68. Han Ziquan, male, 38, electrician at the University of Technology in Beijing

Han was accompanying a relative to work at a little after five a.m. on June 4. Less than half an hour later, he was shot in the neck and died near the Agricultural Exhibition Center.

69. Li Dezhi, male, 25, graduate student in the department of applied physics at the Beijing University of Posts and Telecommunications

Li was killed early on the morning of June 4. No details are available. His relatives retrieved his remains from Fuxing Hospital.

70. Zhou Yongqi, male, 32, head of the motor group at the Beijing Spring Plant

Zhou was shot near the Beijing Union building at a little past eleven p.m. on June 3. The bullet entered the left side of his chest and exited his right lung. He was sent to Fuxing Hospital for treatment, but it was too late.

71. Nan Huatong, male, 31, driver at the Beijing Wallboard Factory

Nan left home and took a walk down Chang'an Avenue to see what was happening in the square at around five a.m. on June 4. He never returned. Two days later his family recognized a photo of his remains at Peking Union Medical College Hospital. A dumdum bullet had entered his left rear shoulder blade and blown out his entire chest cavity.

72. He Anbin, male, 32, Beijing resident; personal information unknown

He was killed on June 4; no other details are known. His remains were interred at the Taiziyu Public Cemetery in suburban Beijing.

73. Zhong Guiqing, female, 31, Beijing resident; personal information unknown

Zhong was killed on June 4; no other details of her death are known. Her remains were interred at the Taiziyu Public Cemetery in suburban Beijing.

74. Mu Guilan, male, 48, finishing department worker at State Textile Plant No. 3 in Beijing

While going out to buy breakfast at around 6:30 a.m. on June 4, Mu walked by the Chaoyangmen overpass, where he ran into a long column of tanks and combat vehicles coming from Tong County at high speed. Flaunting their strength, they randomly took shots at pedestrians streaming by. A slug coming in from an angle struck Mu's head, killing him instantly. After the scene calmed down, a pedestrian took his picture and mailed it to his family.

75. Xiong Zhiming, male, 20, student in the economics department of Beijing Normal University

According to several eyewitnesses, on the night of June 3, Xiong and a female classmate had taken refuge in an alley, but a group of soldiers pursued them and shot at them. Xiong turned around to help his classmate, who had been hit, when he, too, was shot. He was subject to a bloody and brutal attack that spared no part of his body. His classmates recognized him only by his clothing.

76. Zhang Weihua, male, 24, master's student at the National Marine Environmental Forecasting Center in Beijing

Zhang was shot in the abdomen early on the morning of June 4 on Lishi Road. He died on the spot.

77. Zhang XX, male, 19, student in business management at the College of Commerce

Soldiers with clubs attacked Zhang and others in a long line of students retreating from Tiananmen to Liubukou early on the morning of June 4. Zhang turned and ran but received a blow to the top of his head. He fell to the ground. A gun was aimed at his throat and fired. Zhang stopped breathing while being carried to the Beijing Emergency Medical Center.

78. Gong Jifang, female, 19, student in business management at the College of Commerce

Gong was one in a long line of students retreating from Tiananmen to Liubukou on the morning of June 4, when they ran into a fierce attack. A dumdum bullet hit and severed Gong's left arm. She fell down, was overcome by a cloud of poison gas, and lost consciousness. The cause of death, given on her death certificate, was lung erosion caused by poison gas.

79. Jiang XX, male, 26, master's student at the China School of Journalism

Jiang was shot and killed in the area of Jianguomenwai Avenue on the evening of June 3.

80. Liu Chunyong, male, 24, bath attendant at the Nantong Service Complex in the Tianqiao District of Beijing

On the evening of June 3, Liu was at the main terminal for the No. 15 bus line, near the Tianqiao District, when a volley of bullets from People's Liberation Army troops advancing from the south hit him. His head was blown open.

81. Chen Laishun, male, 23, photography student in the journalism department at Renmin University of China

On the evening of June 3, on the roof of an apartment on the western side of the Great Hall of the People, Chen raised his camera to record the bloodbath, when he was shot in the head by a marksman's bullet. He died instantly.

82. Liang Baoxing, male, 25, driver for the Huafeng Sewing Machine Factory in Beijing

A bullet went through Liang's cheeks on the evening of June 3, near the terminal for the No. 15 bus, close to the Tianqiao District. He died on June 5.

83. Luan Yiwei, male, 35, engineer at the Steel Design Research Institute in Baotou, Inner Mongolia Autonomous Region

Luan, who had come to Beijing on a business trip, went to the Nanchizi area in the predawn hours of June 4 to see the street scene amid clouds of gun smoke. He was hit in the waist by a stray bullet. He died at Beijing Tongren Hospital after emergency treatment failed.

84. Su Jinjian, male, 25, graduate in electronics from the Beijing Vocational High School; self-employed clothing entrepreneur

Under circumstances still unknown, Su was hit in the head by a bullet on the night of June 3 and taken to Beijing Friendship Hospital, where he soon died. The hospital labeled him "Anonymous Corpse No. 1." His father spent two weeks searching for him at dozens of hospitals.

85. Zhang Luohong, female, 30, employee at the Beijing General Political Department Sanatorium for Retired Cadres

Zhang was killed on the night of June 3 in Muxidi. The details of her death are unknown.

86. Wang Zhiying, male, 35, lathe operator and well-known as a "model worker" at the Beijing Third General Machinery Factory

Wang and his wife were on their way from his mother-in-law's home in the Xuanwumen area back to their own house on the east side of Zhushikou at midnight on June 3. They had almost arrived, when they ran into martial law troops heading north and sweeping the streets with gunfire. Although the couple tried to dodge the bullets and hid behind a van, a bullet drilled into Wang from the side, hitting his carotid artery.

Wang was initially taken to the Qianmen Hospital but could not be helped because of all the people who were being treated. He was then taken to Beijing Tongren Hospital, where he died due to massive blood loss, the first victim to die at that hospital that night.

87. Wang Hongqi, male, 21, worker at the Leather Research Institute in the Haidian District of Beijing

Wang finished his shift at midnight on June 3 and was returning home, when a bullet went through his chest. The next day the family received a phone call from an eyewitness and went to the Navy Hospital to identify and recover his remains.

88. Li Shuzhen, female, 51, cafeteria worker at a unit of the Beijing Water Supply Company

Li and her husband went out on their bicycles on the night of June 3. Near the Military Museum of the Chinese People's Revolution they were attacked by martial law snipers. Three bullets struck her. On the way to emergency treatment at the Beijing University of Posts and Telecommunications hospital, she stopped breathing.

89. Ma Chengfen, female, 55, retired cadre of the People's Liberation Army general political department in Beijing

Ma joined the PLA in 1949, crossing the Yalu River while fighting in the Korean War. In 1953, after the cease-fire, she returned to China and became a PLA railroad engineer corps soldier.

As was her habit during the summertime, Ma went out with neighbors on the night of June 3 to relax in the cool courtyard of the compound where she lived. She was in high spirits, when disaster struck. Bullets from a passing convoy struck her in the abdomen. Her intestines spilled out on the ground. Ma's murder deeply shocked her husband. Several times he wrote letters to higher authorities, in accordance with military regulations, to report on this outrage. He wanted the matter to be investigated, but it was like throwing a rock into the ocean. There were no two ways about it. In an instant, this outstanding servant of the People's Republic had become a disgrace. In 1992 the family had Ma buried at their own expense in the Jinshan Public Cemetery in Beijing.

90. Guo XX, male, 22, Beijing resident; personal details unknown

Guo was shot and killed at the intersection of Fuxing Road and Yongding Road at a little past nine p.m. on June 3. The details are unclear.

91. Yang Zhenjiang, male, 32, service worker at the Huaiyangchun Restaurant in Beijing

Yang and some colleagues ran into barrages of bullets from army trucks passing through Muxidi early on the morning of June 4. A bullet hit Yang in his left thigh, piercing an artery. He was sent to the Navy General Hospital for emergency treatment, which proved ineffective. On June 6 Yang's family found his body. His cremated remains were stored in the columbarium at the Wan'an Public Cemetery.

92. Li Li, female, 20, student at the Chengdu Electronics and Communications Engineering Institute in Sichuan

Li went with her boyfriend on the morning of June 4 to the square by South Renmin Road in Chengdu. Suddenly a conflict broke out between the People's Armed Police anti-riot squad and a large crowd of demonstrators. The police threw several tear gas grenades to disperse the crowd. Li was caught by the police as she fled the plaza, then she was beaten and fainted. Soon the crowd took her to the hospital for emergency treatment, but her wounds were too serious, and she died that night. Her school held a memorial meeting for her. Her parents came from Guizhou Province to retrieve her ashes so they could be buried in her hometown.

93. Kou Xia, female, 31, teacher at the Xisibei Nursery School, Beijing

On the night of June 3, while Kou was walking on the sidewalk across the street from the Military Museum of the Chinese People's Revolution, a bullet tore through her abdomen. She was immediately taken to the Beijing Railway General Hospital for emergency treatment but could not be saved. She died at five p.m. on June 4.

94. Han Qiu, male, 25, salesperson at the Jiamusi City Nailery in Heilongjiang Province

Han came to Beijing on business late in the student strike. Early on the morning of June 4, he was shot in the head at an unknown location.

95. Liu Jinhua, female, 34, employee at the Third Cadre Retirement Home of the People's Liberation Army general political department in Baishiqiao, Beijing

Liu went with her husband from their home in Balizhuang to her aunt's home in Yongdingmenwai at nine p.m. on June 3 to get medicine for their child. While passing through Xidan, the couple ran into martial law troops, who were slaughtering innocent people. The couple returned home. They waited until eleven p.m. and went out again, and again ran into gunfire from martial law troops, this time near the Yanjing Hotel in Muxidi. Pedestrians fell one by one. The couple fled into a small alley next to Building no. 21 in Muxidi. The soldiers chased them, still shooting. Liu was shot in the forehead and died instantly. Her husband, hit by several bullets, was seriously wounded. He was taken to a hospital and saved.

96. Wang Tiejun, male, age unknown, employee in the Muxidi passenger office of the Beijing Railway Bureau

Wang was working the night shift at his unit on June 3. Out of curiosity, he went up to the roof with a telescope to watch the martial law troops enter the city. A sharpshooter saw him and killed him with one shot.

97. Huang Tao, male, age unknown, a university student in Beijing from Zhangjiagang, Jiangsu Province

Huang was killed in the early morning hours of June 4. The details of his death are unknown.

98. Tao Zhigan, male, 24, a university student in Beijing from Tiantai County, Zhejiang Province

Tao was killed in the early morning hours of June 4. The details of his death are not known.

99. Xu Jianping, male, 19, a university student in Beijing; personal details unknown.

Xu was killed during the predawn hours of June 4. Bullets blew away half his face and then he was flattened by a tank. His flesh and bones were embedded in the street.

100. He Guo, male, 27, worker at a grain shop in the Yuetan neighborhood of Beijing

Guo was killed at midnight on June 3 or early on June 4, when he was shot as he passed through Muxidi. His remains were found at Fuxing Hospital.

101. Li Hui, male, 19, recent graduate from a law school in Beijing

At eleven p.m. on June 4, Li suddenly heard gunfire. He asked his brother Li Ming to go out with him, and they left their parents' home in the dormitory of the People's Public Security University of China, in Muxidi, to find out what was going on. Soon afterward a stray bullet entered his left cheek and exited his ear. His brother was shot in the left leg at the same time. More than an hour later, the family found Li's body at Fuxing Hospital.

102. Luo Wei, male, 30, assistant engineer at the Beijing Semiconductor Materials Factory

Luo was shot on the night of June 4 while riding a bicycle along the western side of Chang'an Avenue. The Guang'anmen Hospital issued a relatively detailed death certificate: "Gunshot to the abdomen, not immediately fatal; two bullets removed from the abdomen; one was a dumdum bullet that exploded in the abdomen, damaging the liver, kidneys, gallbladder, stomach, and digestive tract. An operation was performed to treat his liver and stomach, but he could not be saved. He died of acute kidney failure."

103. Qi Wen, male, 16, student at Beijing Railroad Middle School No. 3

Qi was killed on the night of June 3 by a bullet that struck him as he passed through Muxidi. His remains were found at Fuxing Hospital.

104. Liu Zhanmin, male, 38, employee of the China National Metals and Minerals Import and Export Corporation in Beijing

Between three and four a.m. on June 4, Liu got a call from his wife, who had just given birth. Excited, he rushed from his home at No. 44 Dongsi Liutiao to his mother-in-law's home on the southern end of Dong Si Liu Tiao. Nothing was heard from him after that. Three days later his family found his body at Peking Union Medical College Hospital labeled "No. 21." The cause of death was a bullet to the right side of Liu's jaw. Those who were there remember seeing that the hospital had put on display more than forty photographs of corpses with such serial numbers.

105. Shi Yan, male, 27, musician in the song-and-dance ensemble of the People's Liberation Army Air Force political work department

During the early hours of June 4, Shi was shot in the head at an unknown location. A Red Cross ambulance took him to Beijing People's Hospital for emergency treatment. He could not be saved. Later he was cremated at Babaoshan Revolutionary Cemetery in Beijing.

106. Ren Jianmin, male, 30, peasant from Chenzhuangzi Village, Dingzhou, Hebei Province

Ren was traveling in Inner Mongolia during the student strike, visiting his ethnically Mongolian wife, who had just given birth to their child. Just after enjoying his first taste of fatherhood, he was returning to his hometown in Hebei Province during the early morning hours. Passing through Beijing to change buses, he ran into martial law troops, who shot him in the abdomen, causing his intestines to erupt. He was sent to Peking Union Medical College Hospital. The examining physician pronounced him dead on arrival and sent him to the morgue. Then suddenly he "came to life."

When Ren's family heard the news, they rushed to the hospital—but since they had no money, they could not afford to keep him there for further treatment. Ren's brother-in-law took him back home to Hebei. During this so-called period of convalescence at home, the bullet hole in his abdomen continued to fester. He couldn't stand the endless pain, and so, after the Mid-Autumn Festival that year, he hung himself.

107. Sun Tie, male, 26, employee of the headquarters office of the Bank of China in Beijing; People's Liberation Army veteran

On the evening of June 3, Sun came across troops killing people in front of the Military Museum of the Chinese People's Revolution. With a friend, he fled into the nearby Beijing General Research Institute for Nonferrous Metals, but before they had a chance to catch their breath, the soldiers caught up with them and attacked. No other details are known.

108. XX, male, age and other details not disclosed by the family, high school student at Beijing High School No. 190

This boy was the son of the captain at a Beijing police precinct station. During the night of June 3, out of his deep love for his father, he disregarded the martial law order and went out to look for his parent, who sternly reproved him and kept him in the station until early the next day. The father thought that calm had been restored and ordered one of his policemen to escort his son home. Walking in the area of Nanheyan Street, the boy was shot and killed.

109. Su Shengji, male, 43, a journalist who worked at the *Residential Construction News* in the Asian Games Village, Beijing

Su was discussing work at a friend's house on Songshu Street in Xinjiekou late in the day on June 3. When night fell, the emergency martial law notice was announced on television, so Su headed back home. That was the last anyone heard of him. Su's family searched for him for many years, but they never saw him again, either alive or dead.

110. Ren Wenlian, male, 19, freshman in the mining department of the University of Science and Technology Beijing

Ren was killed early in the morning on June 4. The details of his death are unknown.

111. Huang Peipu, male, age unknown, living in Huang Zhuang in Dongran Village, Sijiqing Gongshe, in the Haidian District of Beijing

Huang was killed before dawn on June 4. The details of his death are unknown.

112. Zheng Chunfu, male, 37, squad leader of the Old Buildings Construction Brigade at the former imperial palace in Beijing

Zheng left his home on Yanyue Lane in the eastern district of Beijing after eleven p.m. on June 3 and was never seen again. For years his family looked for him in the hospitals and crematoria of the Beijing region but never found him.

113. Name unknown, male, 16, student at the Beijing Construction Industry School

This boy was shot at an unknown location on the night of June 3. With two bullets in his body, he was sent to the People's Liberation Army Air Force General Hospital for emergency treatment, which proved ineffective.

114. Cao Zhenping, male, 29, employee at the computer center of the Beijing College of Agricultural Machinery Engineering; People's Liberation Army veteran

During the night of June 3, just as Cao was bending over to support the neck of a female journalist who had been shot, he himself was shot in the back. Immediately after, his lower abdomen was blown apart by a dumdum bullet.

115. Li Zhenying, male, 45, technician at the instrumentation factory at the People's Liberation Army's Academy of Military Medical Sciences in Beijing

Li went to the hospital on the night of June 3 to get medicine for his child. At around ten p.m. he was seen standing at the northern entrance of the 301 Hospital (People's Liberation Army General Hospital). As he chatted with a guard, a martial law convoy came from the west and fired indiscriminately. Struck, the guard staggered like a drunk, and Li quickly steadied him. He had just barely managed to say, "What's going on?" when the two men fell to the ground dead simultaneously, looking as if they had been fighting.

116. Yang Ruting, male, 41, administrative section chief at the Beijing No. 1 Machine Tool Electrical Apparatus Factory Limited Company

Yang went outside for a walk at eleven p.m. on June 3 because he was curious about what was happening. When he had reached the Fuxingmen overpass, two bullets struck him; one went through his lungs and the other broke an arm. When his remains were discovered, there was a large hole straight through his chest to his back.

117. Wang Qingzeng, male, 34, driver for the Tiantan Staple Food Control Office

Wang rode his bicycle from his home in the Zhushikou district at eleven p.m. on June 3 to report for the night shift. When he passed along the section of road facing Rubber Factory No. 8, wild gunfire was coming from the south. Wang was shot through the stomach.

118. Zhou Deping, male, age unknown, master's student in the Radio Electronics Department at Tsinghua University

On the night of June 3, Zhou ignored warnings from his school and went out by himself. He was killed by a shot to the head at an unknown location.

119. Wang Wenming, male, 35, mold fitter at the Beijing Qianjin Shoe Factory

When the sound of gunfire reached his home at midnight on June 3, Wang, who had never been in a war, invited a neighbor to go with him to Zhushikou to see the real thing. They were hit by gunfire. A bullet went through the ribs on

Wang's left side and out the right side. A physician removed over six feet of his intestine but couldn't go any further. Wang's high fever would not go down. He died the following night. After Wang was cremated, his ashes were returned for burial to his home area of Wen'an County in Hebei Province.

120. Yin Jing, male, 36, employee at the Ministry of Metallurgical Industry in Beijing; son-in-law of the deputy chief prosecutor of the Supreme People's Procuratorate

On the night of June 3, Yin was in his home on the eighth floor of building no. 22 in the Muxidi District, when he turned on his light and went into the kitchen. A sharpshooter shot him in the head, killing him.

121. Name unknown, female, over 60, a housekeeper from Wan County, Sichuan Province, who was serving in building no. 22 in Muxidi in the home of a vice minister

According to the testimony of the son of the deceased, on the night of June 3, the sound of gunfire in the street sparked the woman's curiosity. She leaned out from the fourteenth-floor balcony of the vice minister's home and looked down. She was noticed by an army sharpshooter, who shot her in the stomach. She was killed.

122. Zhao Long, male, 21, Beijing resident and high school graduate

Zhao left home at one a.m. on June 4 and was shot three times on the left side of his chest while passing through a street in Xidan. He fell over dead. On June 7 his family found his remains at the Beijing No. 2 Hospital.

123. Lei Guangtai, male, 33, driver for the Xitaishang Village production brigade in Miaocheng rural district in Huairou County, Beijing

In June 1989, the motor transport brigade was undertaking an earth-moving project for the customs building under construction at Jianguomen. There was some free time on the evening of June 3, so two of Lei's colleagues invited him to go along to Tiananmen Square to see the *Goddess of Liberty* statue. They reached the Nanchizi area around eleven p.m. and were squatting down at the base of the red wall there to smoke cigarettes, when army vehicles arrived from the direction of East Chang'an Avenue, accompanied by the sounds of random gunfire. Lei and his coworkers hurriedly put out their cigarettes. No sooner had

Lei stood up than he was hit by a bullet. People ran in a panic. Many fell to gunshots and blood flowed in the streets. Some people saw Lei taken away by local residents in a three-wheeled cart. But where did he go? Nobody knows.

124. Zhong Junjun, male, 22, third-year student at the Beijing University of Agriculture

On the night of June 3, Zhong rode his bicycle to Tiananmen with classmates to support the students. He was hit by bullets on the way and taken to the Beijing Emergency Medical Center, but he could not be helped.

125. Gao Yuan, male, 24, a physician in the department of traditional Chinese medicine at the Shijingshan Hospital in Beijing

Late on the night of June 3, while in front of the Fuxingmen subway station, Gao was hit in the chest by two dumdum bullets that went right through him, front to back, ripping open a hole the size of a soup bowl. An elderly man braved the gunfire to take him to Children's Hospital in a three-wheeled cart. Gao moaned all the way and was still breathing when he arrived, but the hospital was full. He died from blood loss. On June 9, his remains were transferred to Fuxing Hospital. The mountain of corpses stacked up in the hospital was too much for the morgue, so the bicycle shed became a temporary one. Finally, on June 11, Gao's family, after searching for him everywhere, found him in a stack of corpses and pulled him out. His body had decomposed and changed shape. In order to hold a memorial ceremony for him, his work unit was compelled to state in written form that Gao had been accidentally injured.

126. Ni Shilian, male, 24, employee at the China Petroleum & Chemical Corporation's Beijing design institute

Seven young people got together on the night of June 3 to go on a bicycle ride. Ni was one of them. When the group got to Xidan at around eleven p.m., they came under fire from martial law troops. Bullets hit Ni in the chest and abdomen and he fell to the ground. The others scattered. The crowd took him to the Xuanwu Hospital, where treatment proved ineffective. His work unit did not issue a death certificate until 1990. Their conclusion was that he had violated the martial law order and so was responsible for the consequences. A so-called consolation fund of 835 yuan, a sum equal to about ten months of Ni's salary, was sent to his family.

127. Kuang Min, male, 27, engineer at the Beijing Forklift General Factory

On the night of June 3, in Muxidi, a stray bullet struck Kuang in the small of his back and exited the right side of his abdomen. He died soon after arriving at the hospital.

128. Duan Shunqing, male, 30, worker at the Beijing Fangxiuyi Construction Engineering Company

Duan left home on his bicycle at seven p.m. on June 3. A few acquaintances saw him near the Beijing Telegraph Building after ten p.m. Others reported seeing him at Liubukou, but by then he had been hit in the streets. His family never recovered his body.

129. He Shitai, male, 31, worker in the foundry workshop at the Beijing No. 1 Machine Tool Plant

At midnight on June 3, after getting off the night shift, He rode off on his bicycle to visit his father-in-law, who lived in Puhuangyu. He soon reached the south end of Nanheyan Road, when martial law troops suddenly attacked. A bullet hit him in the temple. Surprisingly, he did not fall right away. Instead, he willed himself to get off the bicycle while still holding on to it. Soon the crowd proceeded to take him to the Peking Union Medical College Hospital. However, He stopped breathing en route and died before reaching the hospital.

130. Zhou Yuzhen, female, 36, confidential secretary in structural reform department of the National Planning Commission in Beijing

On the evening of June 3, Zhou was at home when she heard intermittent gunfire and went to the window with her husband and child to take a look. Soldiers sprayed the residential housing with gunfire. Zhou's husband reacted quickly and pushed their child down as a bullet whizzed past his ear. A bullet exploded in Zhou's head and she died on the spot. The child screamed when she saw her, which drew more bursts of gunfire.

131. Ya Aiguo, male, 22, Beijing resident, temporarily unemployed

As he was passing through Gongzhufen at about ten p.m. on June 3, Ya's head was half blown off by a blast of gunfire from an army truck on the street. The People's Liberation Army's 301 Hospital diagnosed the fatal blow as an injury through the brain stem.

132. Song Baosheng, male, 39, employee at the Beijing Glass Factory No. 4; member of the Beijing People's Congress; a "city-wide class shock worker" and "model worker"

On the evening of June 3, Song obeyed the martial law order and stayed at home in Muxidi. He went to bed early, but wild bursts of gunfire startled him and kept him awake. When he got up to shut the windows, a bullet hit him in the stomach, ripping into his intestines. He was taken to the hospital, but entry was prevented by the military, which controlled many hospitals and ordered that rioters not be treated. The hospital physicians and nurses could only watch as Song bled out, crying piteously until he died. The hospital was not permitted to list "gunshot wound" on his death certificate. They were allowed only to write that he had lost too much blood. Song's father wrote many letters to the Beijing Western District public security bureau and Prime Minister Li Peng to complain about the injustice his son had suffered. He received no answer.

133. Chen Senlin, male, 36, worker at Factory 707 in Beijing

On the evening of June 3, Chen was shot and killed by martial law troops while riding his bicycle to Xidan. His family, beside themselves with worry, searched all the Beijing hospitals but didn't find him. More than a month later they narrowed it down to the Beijing No. 2 Hospital. Chen's remains in cold storage had long since decomposed and changed shape. His family was able to recognize him only by his clothing and old scars.

134. Shi Haiwen, male, 20, recent graduate of Shenyang Pharmaceutical College who had come for training as a graduate student at the Beijing Yingyangyuan Institute

Shi was hit by a bullet in the neck on the night of June 4 and died. His remains were discovered at the Beijing Jishuitan Hospital.

135. Yang Hanlei, male, 19, student in the chef training class at the Liufang Hotel, Beijing

When Yang was walking with his classmates before dawn on June 4 by the south end of Nanchizi Avenue, he was hit in the spleen by a stray bullet. He died from blood loss. Surviving classmates notified his family.

136. Name and age not disclosed, male, journalist on the *Kailuan Miners News* who had been transferred at the time to the New China News Agency

He was killed on June 4. The details of his death are unknown.

137. Wang Yaohe, male, 40, chef at a restaurant in Chaoyangmenwai in Beijing

Wang was murdered in the early morning hours of June 4. The details of his death are unknown.

138. Peng Jun, male, 30, staff member at the Beijing representative office of the Xinjiang Production and Construction Corps

Peng left his work unit at Dongdaqiao in the Chaoyang District at about 6:40 a.m. on the morning of June 5 to buy breakfast. On the way, he was attacked by troops. Two bullets hit him, one in the ankle and the other in the right side of his back.

139. Liu Qiang, male, age unknown, student at Hebei Normal University

During the student strike, Liu went to Beijing to take part in the patriotic movement. He was lost without a trace during the great massacre in the early morning of June 4. To this day nobody knows what had happened to him.

140. Su Xin, female, 29, office worker at the China National Nonferrous Metals Import & Export Corp. in Beijing

Su left her mother's house in Fuchengmenwai Street at midnight on June 3, heading home, when she heard waves of rifle shots. Worried about her mother at home alone, she turned back. She was blocked when she reached the southern end of Lishi Road. Martial law troops came through like a tidal wave, laying down a carpet of fire. People in the crowd fell one after another. According to an eyewitness, six people were hit by bullets at the same moment. Su was one of them, with a hole drilled through her chest. She was an only daughter.

141. Bao Xiudong, male, 41, manager at a printing plant on Guloudong Dajie in Beijing

At midnight on June 3, Bao was shot and killed near the Western Returned Scholars Association by the Beijing Hotel.

142. Zhao Dejiang, male, 27, driver at the All-China Federation of Trade Unions and a People's Liberation Army veteran

Zhao was at the main gate of the All-China Federation of Trade Unions early on the morning of June 4, when he saw an old man shot in the street. He hurried forward to help the man but was shot and killed himself.

143. Name unknown, male, age and occupation unknown

According to multiple eyewitnesses, on the morning of June 4, this man was shot and killed in front of the main gate of the All-China Federation of Trade Unions. Zhao Dejiang (see entry no. 142) went to rescue him and was also shot and killed.

144. Cao XX, male, 21, draftsman at the Beijing Institute of Surveying and Mapping's design office

Not long after leaving home on the night of June 3, Cao was shot and killed in the Xidan District. The Beijing University of Posts and Telecommunications hospital notified his family on June 6. They hurried to identify and retrieve his already decomposing remains.

145. Cui Linfeng, male, 29, worker at the Sanlihe Clothing Factory in Beijing and member of the Joint Defense Command police auxiliary branch office in Beijing's Xicheng District

Cui left home for work at seven p.m. on June 3. Normally he would have returned at two a.m. Nothing was seen of him for two days. Cui's family went to the factory to search for him and learned that shortly after going on duty, he invited two of his coworkers to ride their bicycles with him over to Chang'an Avenue to look around. On the way, the three separated. Cui continued riding west, where he ran into tanks. Amid the bullets, he mysteriously disappeared. Cui's family has searched for him for years, checking all the Beijing hospitals, but they have found nothing.

146. Wang Fang, male, 50, employee at Beijing Coal Mining Machinery Factory

On the night of June 3 in Muxidi, Wang was hit in the head by a stray bullet. His skull was shattered. He died on the way to the Navy General Hospital.

147. Liu Jingsheng, male, 40, employee of the Beijing Railway Bureau

On June 4, Liu was killed near the Yangfangdian District. The details are unknown.

148. Zhang Jiamei, female, 61, retired former head of the personnel office at the administration and management bureau of the Ministry of Chemical Industry

While at home in Hepingli on the night of June 3, Zhang heard a disturbance on a nearby street. She pushed the window open and poked her head out. She was shot through the heart by a stray bullet and died.

149. Name unknown, male, age unknown, engineering student in the department of electro-mechanical at Jiangnan University in Wuxi City, Jiangsu Province

During the student strike, patriotic teachers and students sent this student to Beijing along with several other classmates to present their donations to the hunger-strikers in Tiananmen Square. He never returned.

150. Name unknown, male, 20, People's Armed Police guard at the north gate of the People's Liberation Army's 301 Hospital in Beijing

At around eleven p.m. on the night of June 3, martial law troops used gunfire and explosions to force their way in the direction of Muxidi. The crowd of demonstrators scattered in all directions. The armed policeman, watching people being mowed down like grass, took pity and opened the gate to the hospital to let the crowd take shelter inside. This infuriated the troops, so they sprayed him with gunfire. Bullets hit him in his head and his chest. He died at the scene.

151. Name unknown, male, age and occupation unknown

According to multiple eyewitnesses, this man was hit by an army truck while crossing the street and then flattened by an armored car into a bloody mass of flesh. All that was left of him was a disembodied hand. He seemed to have a flowery shirt on. His scattered remains were not removed until the afternoon of June 5, when they were shoveled up, put into plastic bags, and taken away.

152. Name unknown, male, age unknown, cook at the Great Hall of the People

This man left his home at Qianmen Alley early in the morning on June 4 to go to work at the Great Hall of the People. He was shot and killed on the way. His family received 10,000 yuan in compensation from the government.

153. Yen Wen, male, 22, sophomore in the Peking University mathematics department

Yan was in a crowd of people who were blocking trucks full of troops in Muxidi at around one a.m. on June 4. Just as Yen was helping a journalist set up a camcorder to record these events, he was hit by a spray of bullets in his right thigh, smashing his femoral artery. He died of his wounds.

154. Li Chun, male, 20, chef at the Minzu Hotel in the Xidan District of Beijing

Late in the night on June 3, after getting off the night shift, Li encountered the rampaging martial law troops. He pushed his bicycle along, unable to ride amid the barrage of bullets. While walking past the south side of the All-China Federation of Trade Unions building, he was shot in the ribs.

155. Name unknown, female, 31, employee at a factory in Beijing

This woman left work to go home early on June 5 after the night shift. While crossing the road near Wukesong, she was flattened by an armored car. Since she was the sister-in-law of a squad leader in the Beijing People's Armed Police and had died a violent death, her death was declared to be accidental, and a small pension was given to her family after much negotiation between the People's Armed Police and the martial law troops. This was confirmed by a former member of the Beijing People's Armed Police.

156. Du Guangxue, male, 24, printing plant worker at the People's Health Publishing House

At midnight on June 3, Du went on a bicycle ride with friends from Chang'an Avenue down to the Xinhuamen area, where there was a stream of shots and explosions and tank after tank charging east. They quickly turned around, and Du was shot through the temple. Du and his bicycle fell together in the road, with one of his legs still hanging from his bicycle.

According to multiple eyewitnesses, five others were shot at the same time. The crowd loaded them on a bus that had been used as a roadblock and rushed them to the Peking Union Medical College Hospital. Four of them died on the way, including Du. The remaining victim was seriously wounded and probably did not survive. When Du's family got the news, they hurried to Peking Union Medical College Hospital. Bodies were piled there in a mountain, and they couldn't check them one by one. They returned another day and were able to claim his body. His serial number was 30.

157. Sun Xiaofeng, age unknown, student at Beijing Sport University

Sun was killed in the early morning of June 4. The details of the incident are unknown.

158. Zhao Tianchou, male, 47, repair technician at the Beijing Research Institute of Mechanical and Electrical Technology

Zhao was shot four times at an unknown location—three times in the chest and once in the abdomen—early in the morning of June 4.

159. Hu Xingyun, male, age unknown, a student from Sichuan in the 1985 entering class at a university in Beijing

Hu has been missing for twenty years without a trace.

160. Zhai Shun, male, 30, Beijing resident, occupation unknown

Zhai was crushed by a police car at Muxidi on the morning of June 4. This was handled as a traffic accident at the time. Zhai's mother, deeply traumatized, became schizophrenic.

161. Chen Ziqi, male, 31, bus driver on the No. 339 route bus of the Beijing Capital Bus Company

As the driver of the first bus service of the day, Chen left his home to go to work at Liuliqiao on the night of June 3. He did not come home for three days. His family went to all the major hospitals in Beijing looking for him. They finally found his body at Beijing Children's Hospital. His head was distorted and there was a big hole in his chest. His family was finally able to identify him by his bicycle key and clothing. The bus company gave them 800 yuan in compensation, saying that if after some years the government should handle these events differently, then they should apply again according to any new regulations on compensation.

162. Qi Li, male, 22, student specializing in stage design at the Central Academy of Drama

Because Qi had enthusiastically participated in the student strike, it was not until the early morning of June 4 that he retreated from Tiananmen Square. He was sternly interrogated and, knowing that he could not pass the investigation, hung himself in despair.

163. Wei Wumin, female, age unknown, student in the theater arts department of the Central Academy of Drama

Wei actively participated in the student strike and was one of the Tiananmen Square hunger strikers. She witnessed the slaughter on the morning of June 4. Deep in anger and despair, she jumped in front of a train.

164. Zhu XX, male, age unknown, student in the physics department of Beijing Normal University

Zhu was killed in the early morning of June 4. The details of his death are unknown.

165. Dai Jinping, male, 27, master's student at Beijing University of Agriculture

Dai was shot and killed on Tiananmen Square near the Chairman Mao Memorial Hall at about eleven p.m. on the night of June 3. On June 10, Dai's family retrieved his body from the Beijing Friendship Hospital morgue.

166. Zhang Fuyuan, male, 66, Beijing resident, former People's Liberation Army 302 Military Hospital of China worker; Communist Party member

On the evening of June 3, after finishing his night shift, Zhang dropped in at the home of a relative in an alley that ran along the eastern wall of the Beijing Long Distance Telephone Building. Around midnight he heard the popping of tear gas canisters. Gas seeped into the room. Everybody ran to the front door to see what was going on, and were met by a hail of fire from martial law troops. As the crowd scattered, a bullet penetrated the right side of Zhang's waist, but he forced himself to run away with the others. Soldiers kept chasing them. He fell when he reached the gate to the courtyard of his relatives' home. Later, an ambulance took him to Jishuitan Hospital, but he had already stopped breathing. His children claimed his body the next day.

167. Li Haocheng, male, 20, student in the Chinese department specializing in ancient Chinese literature at Tianjin Normal University and secretary of the Communist Youth League branch committee

During the student strike, Li went with over 5,000 students and teachers from his school to Beijing to lend their support. According to eyewitnesses, early on the morning of June 4, when troops burst into Tiananmen Square, Li stood in the southeast corner of the square photographing the last retreating students. Enraged, soldiers shot him twice. His school gave his family 2,000 yuan in compensation.

168. Chen Zhongjie, male, 31, former employee of a subordinate unit of the former Third Ministry of Machine Building in Beijing

Chen was shot at the southern end of Fuyou Street at midnight on June 3. The bullet entered through his forehead and exploded out the back of his head. He stopped breathing while being taken to Peking University First Hospital.

169. Wang Dongxi, male, age and occupation unknown, Shanghai resident

Wang was killed in the early morning hours of June 4, 1989. Details are not known.

170. Guo Chunmin, male, 23, teacher at Beijing High School No. 61, at the time studying at the biology department of the Shijingshan campus of the Beijing Institute of Education, where he was class leader

Guo left home at eight p.m. on June 3 to go to Muxidi to visit a classmate and did not return. His family went to the Fuxing Hospital and saw his name on a list of the dead posted at the hospital entrance. Squeezing into the bicycle shed where they rummaged through several dozen bodies, his family was finally able to locate him. He had been shot twice. He was still breathing when he reached the hospital, but died shortly after from blood loss.

171. Han Junyou, male, 25, former worker at Beijing Leather Shoe Factory No. 1 and later a guard in that factory's security department

A bullet struck Han in the head on the night of June 3 in Muxidi. He died on the way to Fuxing Hospital. His family later found his remains in the hospital's bicycle shed.

172. Li Tiegang, male, 22, worker in the water supply workshop in the power plant at the Capital Steel Company in Beijing

On the night of June 3, Li left his home and encountered the large massacre being committed by martial law troops near Fuxingmen. He died after he was shot several times in the shoulder and in the liver.

173. Wang Ying, male, 30, employee at the Beijing Transformer Factory Company

Wang was killed on June 4. The details of his death are unknown.

174. Cai XX, male, age unknown, employee at the Commercial Press

Cai has been missing since the morning of June 4. There has been no news of him since.

175. Wang Junjing, male, over 30, technician at a factory subordinate to the Beijing Instrumentation Bureau near the Baita Temple

While on the way to work at about ten a.m. on the morning of June 4, Wang was shot by martial law troops. A dumdum bullet in the kidney resulted in damage to his heart as well. Wang was sent to Peking Union Medical College Hospital. When his relatives came to identify and take away his remains, there were already more than forty bodies piled up at the hospital.

176. Name unknown, male, under 20, occupation unknown

During the night of June 3, this male was killed east of Muxidi at the intersection of Fuxingmenwai Avenue and Sanlihe Road. The bleeding from a bullet wound to the chest would not stop. He was sent to the Beijing Children's Hospital for emergency treatment, which proved ineffective, and he died. According to eyewitnesses, he was wearing brown-and-green shorts and a white short-sleeved T-shirt, his sockless feet in sandals, and he had a wristwatch on. He had no identification on him, so the person in charge at the hospital said that if nobody identified him in four or five days, his remains would be turned over to the anti-epidemic station for cremation, along with fourteen other unidentified corpses.

177. Hu XX, male, age unknown, university student in Beijing

This student's family didn't hear about his fate until two weeks after the massacre. They were sad beyond description, but because they were poor and under pressure from the local government, they did not dare to identify his body.

178. Hao Zhijing, male, 30, research assistant at the Science and Technology Policy and Management Research Institute of the Chinese Academy of Sciences; had visited the United States in 1988

While passing through Muxidi at eleven a.m. on June 3, a stray bullet went through the left side of Hao's chest, killing him immediately. His relatives went to all the Beijing hospitals looking for him. A month later they discovered his body by chance at Fuxing Hospital.

179. Lin Tao, male, 24, a former People's Liberation Army scout who had worked at the Kunlun Beijing hotel

On the night of June 3, after finishing dinner, Lin was preparing lunch to bring to work the next day, when he heard that martial law troops had entered the city. He left home on his bicycle to go out on the streets and never returned.

180. Li XX, male, about 30, driver for the Beijing Municipal Urban Appearance Enforcement Team

From the night of June 3 into the early morning of June 4, Li was working on the second floor of the Beijing Municipal Urban Appearance Enforcement Team headquarters on the western side of the Great Hall of the People. He was hit by gunfire from martial law troops, fell backward into the arms of his office colleagues, and died.

181. Zhang Jian, male, 17, sophomore at High School No. 95 in the Xuanwu District of Beijing

On June 4, Zhang left home to visit his uncle and aunt who lived in Qianmen. On the way, he was murdered by martial law troops, who shot him through the heart. Zhang's body was sent directly to the morgue at Peking Union Medical College Hospital. At noon his parents discovered that their son had not visited his uncle's home and went to look for him. Finally, after searching through three large volumes of albums with photographs of about sixty of the dead, they identified his body.

182. Li Ping, male, age unknown, student in the political education department of Beijing Normal University

On the night of June 3, Li was shot and killed near the Military Museum of the Chinese People's Revolution, west of the Muxidi Bridge.

183. Ma Jianwu, male, age unknown, student at the Beijing University of Chinese Medicine

Ma was killed on the morning of June 4. The details of his death are unknown.

184. Huang Xinhua, male, 25, graduate student at the Chinese Academy of Sciences who had passed the entrance examination in 1988

Huang was killed in Tiananmen Square on the morning of June 4. After cremation, his elder brother Huang Linqiang took his ashes back to their home in Shaodong County, Hunan Province, for burial. The state paid compensation of 200 yuan and issued a certificate stating that he had been accidentally wounded.

185. Tao Maoxian, male, age unknown, employee at the Beijing City Factory No. 811

On the morning of June 4, while rescuing an injured person, Tao was shot in the small of the back and died immediately. The place where he was killed is not known.

186. Zou Zuowu, male, age and occupation unknown

Zou was shot and seriously wounded on the morning of June 4. He was sent to the hospital and both his legs were amputated. He died six months later.

187. Bai Jingchuan, male, 21, a student specializing in home appliance maintenance at Beijing Lianhe University

Bai was shot and killed on the morning of June 4. His remains were discovered at Beijing Tongren Hospital.

188. Jiang Jiaxing, male, age and occupation unknown, Beijing resident

Jiang was killed on the morning of June 4. The details of his death are unknown.

189. Sun Hui, male, 19, student in the chemistry department at Peking University

On the morning of June 4, wearing a Peking University T-shirt, Sun rode a bicycle in search of his classmates. When he passed through Xidan, he was shot and killed, and his corpse fell in the street. Three years after cremation, his ashes were returned to his ancestral home in Ningxia.

190. Liang Jianbo, male, 18, student at the Beijing University of Chemical Technology

Liang went to the police academy on the afternoon of June 3 to visit his elder sister. The guard would not let him in and would not let anyone inside go out. He had no choice but to leave. Nothing is known about where he went after that. More than ten days later, his family identified his body at the Jishuitan Hospital.

191. Wang Yongzhen, female, age unknown, student at China Agricultural University

Wang was killed on the morning of June 4. The details of her death are unknown. Her family sprinkled her ashes in the Hun River in Liaoning Province.

192. Zhang Jie, male, 16, Beijing resident, school unknown

Around five a.m. on the morning of June 4, Zhang rode his bicycle home from his elder sister's place. He was passing through Jinshui Bridge, when he ran into soldiers in a murderous rage. Unprovoked, they showered his head with blows, using their clubs. His sister was a manager at the Tiananmen Gate Tower. When she saw what was happening, she yelled, "He is one of our own!" but the soldiers refused to listen. They dragged him into the Beijing Working People's Cultural Palace and continued beating him to death.

193. XX, male, about 15, student at a junior high school in Beijing

This student was spending the summer at the Beijing representative office of the Qinghe Farm. On June 29 he finished his homework and went with his classmates to the roundabout near the Yuquanying intersection, where they ran into a peasant selling watermelons from his truck. The mischievous teenagers knocked a watermelon off the cart. The watermelon seller yelled, "What are you doing, stealing my watermelons?" Just then a patrol car passed by and sprayed them with gunfire. The other children scattered, but this boy was hit and instantly fell to the ground, dead.

194. XX, male, 36, cadre at a Beijing juvenile detention center

On the night of June 3, hearing sporadic gunfire, this man went outside to look. He was shot and killed near Jiaodaokou.

195. Liu Yongliang, male, 26, worker at the Beijing Internal Combustion Engine Factory

A bullet hit Liu in the head late on the night of June 3. He died at Beijing Hospital.

196. Liu Zhong, male, 19, student at China University of Political Science and Law

Liu was killed late on the night of June 3. The details of his death are unknown.

197. Fu Erke, male, 19, student at Minzu University of China in Beijing

Fu was killed in the early morning of June 4. The details of his death are unknown.

198. Gu Lifen, female, 19, student in the education department at Beijing Normal University

Gu was killed in the early morning of June 4. The details of her death are unknown.

199. Ma Fenglong, male, 27, a member of a work unit in Beijing

Ma was killed in the early morning of June 4. The details of his death are unknown.

200. Ma Junfei, male, age unknown, Beijing resident

Ma Junfei, the son of Ma Fenglong (see entry no. 199), was killed in the early morning of June 4. The details of his death are unknown.

201. Xu Ruihe, male, age unknown, Beijing resident, People's Liberation Army veteran

Xu was killed on the morning of June 4. The details of his death are unknown.

202. Chen Yongting, male, 21, of the Tujia ethnic minority; student specializing in political economy in the economics department of Minzu University of China in Beijing

On the evening of June 3, Chen was shot somewhere in the area around Tiananmen Square. Other details of his death are unknown. After cremation, his ashes were brought back to his home in the Youyang Tujia and Miao Autonomous County in Chongqing for burial.

APPENDIX THREE

List of 49 People Wounded or Disabled in the Massacre

Collected by the Tiananmen Mothers (1989–2011)
Provided by Ding Zilin and Jiang Peikun

Continual repression by the Chinese government and the lingering fears of those interviewed have hindered much of the Tiananmen Mothers group's efforts. Many of the injured and disabled are unwilling to reveal their personal information.

1. Fang Zheng, male, 22 (when he was wounded), student in the biomechanics department of the Beijing Sports College

Following the long line of students retreating from Tiananmen Square around six a.m. on the morning of June 4, Fang was passing through the Liubukou intersection, when a tank abruptly changed direction and headed straight at the students. They scattered immediately, but the tank kept chasing them, firing off a series of poison gas bombs. A student from the same school fainted beside Fang; she was about to be flattened by the tank, but Fang grabbed her and quickly dodged to the side. She was saved, but he was caught under the tank tread and dragged along for a considerable distance. He screamed in anguish and somehow managed to free the top half of his body, but both of his legs were torn off.

After emergency treatment at the hospital, Fang was finally revived. He stubbornly lived on. With the help of the organization Humanitarian China, he now lives in San Francisco.

2. Su Wenkui, male, 22, student at the China Youth College for Political Sciences

Following the long line of students retreating from Tiananmen Square around six a.m. on the morning of June 4, Su was passing through the Liubukou intersection, when he fainted from the poison gas fumes and was seriously injured by the same tank that severed Fang Zheng's legs (see entry no. 1). Shots were fired at him. Emergency treatment at the hospital pulled him through, but he was left disabled for life.

3. Liu Gang, male, 36, business manager at the Beijing Machinery Import and Export Company

On the night of June 3, a bullet hit Liu in the spine, leaving him a paraplegic. His mind remains clear, but he lost all functions of his limbs. Life now seems worse than death. His company pays his continuing medical expenses.

4. Song Qiujian, male, 17, student at a middle school

During the day on June 7, while riding his bicycle to school near the Beijing Train Station, Song encountered a martial law tank. Flaunting their force, the soldiers ordered everyone to lie down and then strafed both sides of the street with gunfire. Amid flying dirt and sand, innocent people were hit by gunfire and lay bleeding in the street. After the tanks had roared by, people finally dared to get up and help five injured bystanders, putting them in a three-wheeled cart and leading them to the hospital. Song was one of them. He had been hit by a cluster bomb, which are forbidden by international treaty. The bullet shattered when it punctured his skin, but the main fragment of the bullet drilled into his liver and bruised his backbone. After emergency care at Peking Union Medical College Hospital, he was left permanently disabled. Today he still walks with a limp.

5. Tian XX, male, 16, student in the middle school attached to Renmin University of China

During daylight on June 4, Tian was riding with his classmates on bicycles through the Nanchizi area of Wangfujing, when they ran into soldiers shooting indiscriminately. A bullet came flying by and he instinctively turned; the bullet furrowed his forehead. Severely traumatized, Tian developed a chronic mental illness. He was hospitalized at the department of neurology of the Peking University Third Hospital, where he underwent extensive therapy. He was never able to return to school and now is only capable of doing basic jobs.

6. Chu Manqing, female, 20, student in the Geology Department of Peking University

Chu joined a medical team on the night of June 3. An armored car rammed into her and crushed her leg while she was helping a person with a gunshot wound near Tiananmen. After round-the-clock hospital treatment, stainless steel rods were used to stabilize her legs. She battled a long period of intense suffering but recovered, graduated, and went overseas for advanced study.

7. Wang Yan, male, 20, employee at the Ministry of Aerospace and Aeronautical Industry 502 Institute

Early on the morning of June 4, at an unknown location, Wang was disabled by a bullet. In 1993, because he could no longer stand the physical torture, he swallowed more than seventy sleeping pills in a suicide attempt. His family found him and he was saved, but for years he had to remain under the care of his aging parents.

8. Chen Ning, male, 30, employed at the Cadre Training School in the China Geology Management Institute

As Chen hid behind the flower bed of building no. 29 in Muxidi on the night of June 3, both of his knees were shattered by stray bullets. During emergency treatment at Beijing Jishuitan Hospital, he underwent two operations. After two years he was finally able to walk a little. Chen was investigated at work, suspended from his job, and punished according to Communist Party discipline.

9. Li Lanfu, female, 30, office director at the Great Wall Group Corporation

Li was shot in both legs on the same night, in the same place, as Chen Ning. (See entry no. 8.)

10. Wang Tianjun, male, 28, occupation unknown

On the day of June 4, Wang was shot in the left arm near Wangfujing, and his motor nerves were severed. After emergency treatment at Peking Union Medical College Hospital, he was transferred to Beijing Jishuitan Hospital, where his left arm had to be amputated.

11. Yu Zhihan, male, 30, employee at the Policy Research Department of the State Environmental Protection Bureau

On the evening of June 3, Yu was hit by a bullet while in Muxidi, injuring his hip and leaving him disabled. Unable to stand the investigation and harassment that his workplace subjected him to, Yu soon resigned and later found employment in Shenzhen.

12. Xu Yangcheng, male, 40, employment unknown; had already left work at the time of his injury

Xu's leg was hit with a bullet on the night of June 3, resulting in poliomyelitis and requiring hours of bathing in a medicinal tank every day. For years he was not able to free himself of pain and poverty. He depends on the meager incomes of his mother and wife to get by.

13. Li Keqin, male, 20, trainee on contract in the photography section of the Journalism Department of Renmin University

He was hit by two bullets at an unknown location on the night of June 3. He suffered from those wounds for many years but is completely recovered today.

14. Kong Lixin, male, age unknown, teacher in the Mechanical Engineering Department of the Beijing Institute of Technology

During the night of June 3, Kong was shot in the calf in Muxidi. After treatment he was left with a conspicuous six-inch-long scar.

15. Chen Jun, male, 19, personal information unknown

Chen was shot in his left leg early on the morning of June 4 near the State Council National Economic Committee. After emergency treatment, he completely recovered.

16. Wang Kuanbao, male, 19, doctoral student at the Beijing Steel and Iron Institute

Wang retreated from Tiananmen with the student demonstrators around six a.m. on June 4. When they passed through Liubukou, he met another doctoral student also pushing a bicycle. As they walked and talked, a tank suddenly swerved and charged toward them, knocking both men over. Wang's pelvis was crushed, his flesh and blood mixed into a muddy, pulpy pool of human grime, but he survived. His companion was killed on the spot.

17. Cheng Chunzheng, male, 20, student at the Taiyuan College of Finance and Economics in Shanxi

On the night of June 3, Chen was shot in the thigh while in Xidan and sent to Jishuitan Hospital. He was stuck in the hospital for eleven months, and his school refused to pay his medical bills. Soon afterward his school expelled him.

18. Liu Baodong, male, 20, student in the Chinese literature department at the Baoding Teachers College in Hebei

On the night of June 3 in Nanchizi, Liu was seriously wounded in his thigh in a storm of gunfire. With great difficulty the doctors saved his leg. As with Cheng Chunzheng, Liu's school refused to pay his medical bills, leaving him stuck in the hospital for ten months. He, too, was expelled from his school soon afterward.

19. Qi Zhiyong, male, 33, originally a sixth-level expert oil lubrication worker at the Beijing Urban Construction Sixth Company; later quit to become an independent entrepreneur

At 1:20 a.m. on the morning of June 4, Qi ran into the slaughter in Xirongxian Hutong in the Xidan District. He was shot in both legs. His left leg was amputated and he became handicapped, only able to move on crutches. Because he was willing to stand up and give interviews to Western journalists and accuse the Communist Party of murder, the police repeatedly detained him and put him under house arrest.

20. Unwilling to disclose name, male, 12, elementary school pupil, Beijing resident

Around three p.m. on the afternoon of June 6, after getting out of school, this boy encountered gunfire while passing by the entrance to the Muxidi subway station. He dropped to the ground as soon as he heard the gunfire but was hit in the lower abdomen and left arm. The troops yelled and ordered the crowd not to go near him. He lay there for half an hour, bleeding profusely. When the tank finally left, people rushed him to Fuxing Hospital, and he lived as a result. His spleen and kidney were removed and a rib was damaged, leaving him handicapped.

21. Unwilling to disclose name and age, male, physician from Yanbian City in Jilin

Prior to June 4, this doctor came to Beijing for an internship at the Beijing Obstetrics Gynecology Hospital. Because he had participated in patriotic street demonstrations, he was confined to Zhongshan Park for more than twenty days. He was beaten several times, leaving him disabled in his right arm and no longer able to work as a physician. He later returned to his hometown. His current circumstances are not known.

22. Unwilling to disclose name, male, 20, university student from Jinhua in Zhejiang.

After June 4 this student was arrested and confined for several months in Qincheng Prison in Beijing. He suffered from an acute mental illness.

23. Unwilling to disclose name, male, 20, employee, Beijing resident
During the night of June 6, this man went out with several people, including Wang Zhengsheng and An Ji (see entries nos. 25 and 26 on p. 267), when he suddenly encountered the slaughter. He was shot but managed to survive. He had two operations during his six-month hospital stay. That day still haunts him.

24. Unwilling to disclose name and age, male, employee, Beijing resident
During the night of June 6, this man had gone out with several people, including Wang Zhengsheng and An Ji (see entries nos. 25 and 26 on p. 267), when he ran into the carnage. Although shot in the abdomen, he managed to survive.

25. Unwilling to disclose name, female, 18, student at a vocational school
During the night of June 3, while in Wukesong, this student encountered the gunfire. She was hit in the right arm by a dumdum bullet. The street was sprayed with her flesh and blood. She received emergency treatment at Military Hospital 304 and was left handicapped, preventing her from being able to get a job after graduation.

26. Unwilling to disclose name, male, over 20, individual entrepreneur, Beijing resident
At an unknown location early on the morning of June 4, this man was hit in the thigh by a random bullet. After an operation, he seemed healed, but five years later the old wound troubled him again. He couldn't afford medical care, so he just muddled along one day at a time.

27. Unwilling to disclose name, male, over 20, university student, resident of Wuhan
This student was shot in the calf at an unknown location early in the morning on June 4. He had two operations, but still didn't recover. At the end of 1993, he had another major operation, but he still can't do heavy work.

28. Unwilling to disclose name, male, 32, laboratory technician, Beijing resident
Near Xidan, early on June 4, this man was shot with a dumdum bullet. His right leg was broken and his sciatic nerve was shattered. Emergency treatment saved his life, but he developed osteomyelitis. He was treated for several years at many hospitals, but his condition was never cured. After six operations, a steel reinforcing support was put into his leg, but walking is still difficult for him.

29. Unwilling to disclose name, male, around 20, university student and resident of Fuzhou

During daylight on June 5, as this student was strolling near the main gate of Beijing Broadcasting School, hysterical fire from a martial law tank crew hit him in the buttocks. He recovered but remains disabled.

30. Unwilling to disclose name and age, male, employee, Beijing resident

Early on June 4, about a third of a mile north of Muxidi Bridge, this man was shot in the right ankle. After treatment, he recovered completely.

31. Unwilling to disclose name, male, 34, sales manager, Beijing resident

This man encountered the slaughter near the Liubukou intersection early on the morning of June 4. Many people were shot and killed. While he was helping one of the injured, he was shot in the thigh, resulting in a comminuted fracture. After surgery, osteomyelitis developed. He consulted many physicians and spent two years in the hospital. Now he wears a steel brace on his leg. Moving requires strenuous effort.

32. Unwilling to disclose name, male, 28, company driver, Beijing resident

At two a.m. on June 4, near Xidan, a bullet passed through this man's back, near his vertebrae, injuring his liver and lungs. He was treated at Xuanwu Hospital for two weeks. After he was released, he developed a secondary infection and had to be readmitted. His work unit refused to pay his medical expenses and the large bill nearly bankrupted his family.

33. Unwilling to disclose name, male, 45, individual entrepreneur, Beijing resident

Early on June 4 at Fuchengmen, this man encountered the slaughter. He was struck by two bullets, one in each leg. One bullet shattered his right kneecap, leaving him handicapped for life. As he was rushed to Xuanwu Hospital, dying beside him in the ambulance was a twenty-year-old young man hit in the chest by a bullet.

34. Unwilling to disclose name and age, female, university student

The explosion of a smoke shell injured this student's right leg early on the morning of June 4 and she was sent to Xuanwu Hospital. She received extensive treatment, but her leg did not heal.

35. Unwilling to disclose name, male, 32, employee, Beijing resident

On the night of June 3, this man was attacked by martial law troops near Liubukou. He was following the tide of retreating demonstrators into a small alley, when he was hit by a bullet on the top right of his head, instantly fracturing his skull. He was sent to Peking University Third Hospital, where he remained for more than half a year. He underwent several major operations and survived, paralyzed in half his body. He could not lift his left arm and he could only move his left leg with great difficulty.

36. Unwilling to disclose name, male, 39, journalist, Beijing resident

At about eleven p.m. on the night of June 3, near the Military Museum of the People's Revolution, this journalist ran into the slaughter. He was hit in the lower abdomen by dumdum bullets, severing his intestines and damaging his liver. Some people took him to Fuxing Hospital for emergency treatment. The hospital was in chaos and medical personnel, seeing his mess of blood and torn flesh, thought that he was already dead and tossed him directly into the pile of corpses. Later, someone walking by heard him moaning, so they dug him out. After three major operations, he was able to leave the hospital, but he became the object of repeated police interrogations and investigations after his release.

37. Unwilling to disclose name, male, 27, unemployed

During the early morning hours of June 4, this man was shot in the pelvis at an unknown location. Emergency treatment at the Xuanwu Hospital saved his life. The bullet was never removed from his body.

38. Male, unwilling to disclose any personal information

On June 4, he was shot at an unknown location. The details are not known.

39. Unwilling to disclose name and age, male, deputy editor in chief, Beijing resident

Early on June 4, this man was shot at an unknown location. He was treated for a long time but his wounds did not heal completely. His work unit investigated him. Although he was not dismissed, he has never been given any position of responsibility.

40. Unwilling to disclose name, male, over 20, employee, Beijing resident

During the early morning of June 4, he was injured at an unknown location. His right arm was amputated, handicapping him for life.

41. Unwilling to disclose name, male, over 20, university student, Beijing resident
This student retreated from Tiananmen along with other students early on the morning of June 4. When passing by Liubukou, he was run over by a tank. He had fractures in his chest but survived in the emergency room.

42. Unwilling to disclose name, male, over 20, university student, Beijing resident
This man also retreated from Tiananmen with the other students during the early morning of June 4. While he was passing by Liubukou, he was seriously injured after being run over by a tank. He survived after emergency treatment.

43. Unwilling to disclose name, male, over 20, university student, Beijing resident
Near Tiananmen during the early morning hours of June 4, this student was shot in the abdomen but survived after emergency treatment.

44. Unwilling to disclose name and age, male, university student, Beijing resident
This student retreated from Tiananmen along with the student demonstrators in the early morning hours of June 4. When he was passing by Liubukou, he was run over by a tank but survived after emergency treatment.

45. Unwilling to disclose name, male, 18, technician, Beijing resident
This man was shot in the leg early on June 4 at an unknown location. His wounds did not completely heal despite extended treatment. No further details are available.

46. Unwilling to disclose name and age, male, Tianjin resident
This man was beaten at an unknown location early on June 4 and one of his legs was broken. No further details are available.

47. Unwilling to disclose name, male, 15, middle school student, Beijing resident
This student was shot in the leg at an unknown location early on June 4. Despite lengthy treatment, his wound was not cured. No further details are available.

48. Unwilling to disclose name, male, 21, worker, Beijing resident
Early on June 4, this man ran into a massacre on the road south of the reviewing stand to the west of Tiananmen. As he followed the fleeing crowd, he was hit by a bullet that entered at the front of his right shoulder blade and exited through

his upper right arm, resulting in a comminuted and open fracture. He was sent to a big van in the center of the square for emergency treatment, where there were more than forty injured people, including some already dead and others barely breathing. All had been shot in Tiananmen Square.

The driver of the van started heading east but ran into fierce strafing fire. He was forced to wave a white shirt, yelling, "This vehicle is transporting injured people! Please hold your fire!"

The bullet-riddled ambulance finally reached Peking Medical College School Hospital. Most of the wounded were already dead, but this man miraculously survived. He spent over a month in the hospital and underwent several operations. He made a complete recovery and again saw the light of day.

49. Unwilling to disclose name, male, 30, worker

Early on June 4, this man ran into a massacre unfolding near the Kentucky Fried Chicken in Qianmen. He was shot, leaving several bullet holes in his left leg.